PENGUIN BOOKS

WHEN CHARACTER WAS KING

Peggy Noonan was a special assistant to President Ronald Reagan from 1984 to 1986, then left Washington, D.C., for her native New York, where she completed her first book, the bestselling *What I Saw at the Revolution*. Since that time, her articles and essays have appeared in *Time*, *Newsweek*, *The New York Times*, *The Washington Post*, *Forbes*, and many other publications. She is also the author of the *New York Times* bestseller *The Case Against Hillary Clinton*, and a columnist and contributing editor at *The Wall Street Journal*. She lives in Brooklyn, New York.

Also by Peggy Noonan:

The Case Against Hillary Clinton

On Speaking Well:
How to Give a Speech with Style, Substance, and Clarity

Life, Liberty and the Pursuit of Happiness

What I Saw at the Revolution: A Political Life in the Reagan Era

When Character Was King

PEGGY NOONAN

A Story of Ronald Reagan

Penguin Books

PENGUIN BOOKS
Published by the Penguin Group
Penguin Putnam Inc., 375 Hudson Street, New York, New York 10014, U.S.A.
Penguin Books Ltd, 80 Strand, London WC2R 0RL, England
Penguin Books Australia Ltd, 250 Camberwell Road, Camberwell, Victoria 3124, Australia
Penguin Books Canada Ltd, 10 Alcorn Avenue, Toronto, Ontario, Canada M4V 3B2
Penguin Books India (P) Ltd, 11 Community Centre,
Panchsheel Park, New Delhi – 110 017, India
Penguin Books (N.Z.) Ltd, Cnr Rosedale and Airborne Roads,
Albany, Auckland, New Zealand
Penguin Books (South Africa) (Pty) Ltd, 24 Sturdee Avenue,
Rosebank, Johannesburg 2196, South Africa

Penguin Books Ltd, Registered Offices:
Harmondsworth, Middlesex, England

First published in the United States of America by Viking Penguin,
a member of Penguin Putnam Inc. 2001
Published in Penguin Books 2002

1 3 5 7 9 10 8 6 4 2

THE LIBRARY OF CONGRESS HAS CATALOGED THE HARDCOVER EDITION AS FOLLOWS:
Noonan, Peggy, 1950–
When character was king / Peggy Noonan.
p. cm.
Includes bibliographical references and index.
ISBN 0-670-88235-6 (hc.)
ISBN 0 14 20.0168 6 (pbk.)
1. Reagan, Ronald—Anecdotes. 2. Presidents—United States—Biography—Anecdotes.
3. Character—Political aspects—United States—Anecdotes. 4. Reagan, Ronald—Friends and associates—Anecdotes. 5. Noonan, Peggy, 1950—Anecdotes. I. Title
E877.2.N66 2001b
973.927—dc21 2001046824

Printed in the United States of America
Set in Bembo
Designed by Jaye Zimet

To the men and women
of the USS
Ronald Reagan, CVN 76

Acknowledgments

I am in the debt of those who in the spring and summer of 2001 shared with me their memories of Ronald Reagan. I thank Patti Davis, Nancy Reagan, Jim Pinkerton, Natan Sharansky, Bob Feller, Rush Limbaugh, former President George H. W. Bush, President George W. Bush, Matt Drudge, Ann Blackman, Jean Smith, Dan Rostenkowski, Bill Bennett, Ken Duberstein, Grover Norquist, Michael Deaver, John Fund, John Barletta, Congressman Ed Royce, David Fischer, David Frum, Anne Higgins, Michael Putzel, Douglas MacKinnon, Tom Williams, Jerry Parr, Dennis Le Blanc, Ron Robinson, Judge William Clark, Charles and Mary Jane Wick, Marion Jorgensen, Martin Anderson, A. C. Lyles, Robert Higdon.

Charles Wick provided me with a private videotape of President Reagan remembering his parents and childhood. His generosity is greatly appreciated.

I am in the debt also of the gifted and sturdy Pam Dorman and Susan Petersen Kennedy of Viking Penguin, and of Joni Evans of the William Morris Agency, who were among the friends and professionals who pulled into being this book. Gratitude goes also to Misty Church, who helped research names and dates, find quotes, and provide resources that proved invaluable.

I thank the staff of the Reagan Library, and the members of the Young America's Foundation, who made available to me the Reagan Ranch. I am grateful to Captain John William Goodwin and Ensign Daniel "Kirk" Nichols, Airman Bryant Hernandez, Airman Jessica Teston, Petty Officer Travis Little and Petty Officer Joseph Aguilar of the USS *Ronald Reagan*.

Final thanks to my patient and encouraging friends and family: Will Rahn, Richard Rahn, Ransom and Stephanie Wilson, Perry and Allie Wilson, Lisa Schwarzbaum, Dorian, Ed, Mike, Michelle and

Eddie MacPhee, Joan Ganz Cooney, Pete Peterson, Diane Sawyer, Linda Casey Poepsel, Joel Rosenberg, Lesley Stahl, Marie Brenner, Ernest Pomerantz, Bill Sykes, Andrew Breitbart, Susan and Vincent Woodbury, Jim Karas, Slade Gorton, George Osborne, Philip Delves Broughton, Peggy Byrne, James Higgins, Wendy Martin, Ben Elliott, Jim Pinkerton, Norma Ailes, James Taranto, Max Boot, and Adair Levinson.

Anything that is good in this book is here because all of these people made sure it would be.

The characteristic of heroism is its persistency. All men have wandering impulses, fits and starts of generosity. But when you have chosen your part, abide by it, and do not weakly try to reconcile yourself with the world. The heroic cannot be the common, nor the common heroic. Yet we have the weakness to expect the sympathy of people in those actions whose excellence is that they outrun sympathy and appeal to a tardy justice. If you would serve your brother because it is fit for you to serve him, do not take back your words when you find that prudent people do not commend you.

—*Ralph Waldo Emerson*

Contents

When Character Was King

"I Remember You"

It was like the last gathering of the clans, the reunion of five hundred friends, cabinet secretaries, aides, staffers, clique, tong and cabal members and appointees of Ronald Wilson Reagan, fortieth president of the United States, in Williamsburg, Virginia, on March 3, 2001. It was the biggest coming together of the Reagan hands since the day he left office, in January of 1989.

The big room in the Kingsmill Resort rocked with greeting. "I don't *beleeeve* it," "Great to *seeeee* you," "Where you hangin' your hat, where you causin' trouble?"

People with young eyes, lifted eyes, crinkled eyes from being in the sun; people with strollers, with walkers . . .

That guy over there—that young kid from what, OMB? I used to see him in the tall cool halls of the Old Executive Office Building. Now he's married, with a baby who, from the look of things, is teething, in full red-gummed wail. I get some ice chips for the baby to suck on, return and say hello to the parents. Yes, it was OMB, the young father says, yes, down the hall and up a flight. "Those were great days." He smiles.

Across the room I see a once-young advance man who now walks with a cane. And Tom Dawson, one of the famous Mice, the young aides to Don Regan whom we always saw as nibbling away at good work. He looked exactly like Tom Dawson, with all of his hair, only now what was black is gray. He looks like a photo negative of Tom Dawson.

I turn and see Don Regan himself, the Chief, the controversial former chief of staff. He still looks like George Raft, he is still in a sharp gray suit, and at the sight of him I laugh. He sees me and does the same.

"I'm an artist!" he booms as we hug.

"Did you know I paint?" he demands. "I have pictures in museums! Started after I left. They didn't teach me to paint in the marines or at Merrill Lynch or in the White House, I can tell you that!"

There's Ed Meese, with his soft pink face and soft white hair. George Shultz once said he reminded him of a jolly St. Patrick, and that is how Meese looks to me now, chuckling and patting people's arms. He was under bad pressure once, the focus of charges, but now it's almost twenty years since those days and he looks like he's found what everyone wants: happiness. He looks happy.

I stand and survey the room. Carl Anderson, who worked on domestic policy, now head of the Knights of Columbus of America, is talking to Becky Norton Dunlop, formerly of presidential personnel. I used to hide from her. I had come into the White House without having been politically vetted, was not a registered Republican, had no party background—only conservative beliefs. They snuck me in and hid me from her. By the time we met I'd been there awhile. We became colleagues, then allies, then friends.

There's Kathy Osborne, Ronald Reagan's personal secretary, and Elaine Crispin, who worked for Nancy. She's slim, bubbly, unchanged save in one respect—"Elaine Crispin *Sawyer,*" she says. "He changed my name!" The gray-haired man beside her beams.

Over there Judge William Clark is nodding at someone who's looking up at him and making a point. And Peter Robinson of the speechwriting staff, who was there to fight for the words "Mr. Gorbachev, tear down this wall." The State Department had scorned the demand as provocative, and Peter had waged a battle. Ronald Reagan fired the final shot: *Of course I will say it, I mean to provoke.*

"This is the inaugural party," someone in a cluster says. The gathering of the clans we would have had a few weeks ago if we'd all been in Washington when the eldest son of the man Ronald Reagan picked as his vice president was sworn in as the forty-third president of the United States. We forget how crucial that decision was, not only for immediate political prospects in 1980 but also for the generation that would follow. The new Bush would not be here if it had not been for the old one, who would not have been there if he hadn't been chosen in 1980 when the nominee was tired and the talks with Gerald Ford had collapsed and there was no other obvious choice. Reagan had not held Bush in the highest regard in those days, thought him weak from the famous "I'm paying for this microphone!" fracas in New Hampshire. But Reagan came to like him, to respect him. Now Bush's son was president and acting in a way that suggested that for a dozen years he'd watched both Reagan and his father up close in that old house, and had learned from the former what to do and from the latter what not. Well, not exactly, but close. At any rate, the old Reaganites viewed the new Bush with hopeful regard: good man, seems tough enough, but let's watch him on tax rates. In public they are respectful of Dubya, in private merrily irreverent. They send each other e-mails. "What was Bush's answer to the question 'How do you feel about *Roe* v. *Wade*?' 'Ah think it was the most important decision George Washington made when he crossed the Delaware.' "

Here is Jim Brady, in a wheelchair with an assistant, a nurse, a young Filipino woman who stands behind his chair holding the handles.

He is surrounded by well-wishers and poses for pictures. I say hello, introduce myself when he doesn't know me. He says, "Of course," and tells me ever since he was shot he suffers from CRS.

"What is that, Jim?"

"Can't Remember Shit."

We laugh, and I tell him there's a lot of that going around.

People kneel in front of him and look up at his face, or bend down to pat his arm. They feel an awkward tenderness. The thick lines of scar tissue are visible on his head and will be for the rest of his life, as they have been since the day twenty years before when the young man with the gun left him lying on the pavement, a thick scarlet stain pooling under his head.

"How is Sarah?" I ask.

"Not well," he says, and his eyes fill with tears. He began to weep and I stood there with my hand on his arm, his attendant staring straight ahead, as if she has seen this scene before. A few weeks later I was watching TV when Sarah Brady came on Larry King to tell of her struggle with lung cancer.

Nancy Reagan moves through the room, the center of a dense moving cluster. She's smiling the public smile that has become her private smile, shaking hands, kissing, greeting children, saying, "Of course I remember you." Still so small, size two, five feet two inches. In a pretty bright dress and black pumps. She is the same but older, of course, eighty now and frail, delicate as bird bones.

She has not always enjoyed big gatherings of her husband's supporters but she does this night. Later she would tell me, with the excitement of a girl, "I saw Rex Scouten! He's such a lovely man."

Rex Scouten, the head usher of the White House in the days of Reagan, whom she hadn't seen since the day she left, and who had been standing with her in the solarium in the residence the day the head of her Secret Service detail came and told her shots had been fired at the president.

She saw Don Regan too. He, of course, had bitterly left his chief-of-staff position in the White House after Nancy, and others, had moved against him in the wake of Iran-contra. He took revenge in a best-seller that charged she'd driven him mad with her belief in astrology and her insistence on delaying presidential trips until the moon was in the seventh house and Jupiter aligned with Mars. I'd never known of any of that back then, when I was a speechwriter for the president, but I believed it when I read it. The assassination attempt had turned a fretful nature fearful; she'd worried constantly about her husband's safety, and if the advice of astrologers offered solace she would have listened.

But you know what Nancy Reagan did when she saw Don Regan? She laughed and hugged him, and he laughed and hugged her back. "I'm an artist!" he told her too, and she asked him what he painted.

"I paint oils, landscapes!" (He's eighty-two years old and he still talks like Willy Loman's brother in *Death of a Salesman: Africa! Diamonds big as stars!*)

Nancy said she'd love to see them, spoke to Ann, his wife, wheelchair bound, observing life now from the middle of people and always looking up.

Later Nancy would muse to a friend, "I never would have associated Don with painting!" They laughed, but with pleasure. Isn't life full of surprises?

It was all so warm, and everyone seemed generous and kind. It was just like the old days, except that's not how the old days were.

The new captain of the *Ronald Reagan,* Captain Bill Goodwin, stands at a little stage on the side of the room and speaks of the reason for our coming together. We are gathered to go, en masse, tomorrow, to the Newport News Shipyards to witness and celebrate the christening of the aircraft carrier *Ronald Reagan,* CVN 76, Nimitz class. Nancy Reagan will swing the bottle to the bow.

The skipper tells us it is the honor of his twenty-five-year career to be the first commanding officer of the *Reagan,* that the ship is coming to life, 60 percent finished. "A ship with a crew is a living, breathing thing," he says. "Tomorrow if you see our sailors, they are the lifeblood. The average age of a sailor on our flight deck is nineteen years old. . . . If you see them tomorrow, shake their hands."

Nineteen years old. If the old Reagan was here, the one who isn't sick, he'd think: "They were born in 1982, when we were trying to rebuild the national defense, when we were going for the six-hundred-ship navy. They were babies, and now look. Isn't that something?"

The ship's logo, the captain tells us, has four stars for the "four pillars of freedom—liberty, opportunity, global democracy and national pride." Below the stars the ship will bear a motto. "It's one some of you will recognize," he says. "It says, Peace Through Strength."

This is greeted, as you might expect, with hearty cheers. Reagan's foreign policy, boiled down to three words.

Later the captain tells me that he was on the Indian Ocean, a flight instructor on the USS *Eisenhower* the day Ronald Reagan walked into the White House. "We were waiting for the [Iranian] hostages to come home." Those were bad days for the military, he says, and his plan was to get his golden wings and then go fly for Delta. But when Reagan came in, things got better, and he decided to make a career of the navy. "I'm a product of the Reagan administration," he said.

The evening ends with a small dinner. At just after eight, in a pretty room with a big stone fireplace at the Kingsmill, a fork hit a crystal glass and a throat was cleared.

This was a smaller group of the old friends and heirs and widows of the original kitchen cabinet, the small group of millionaires, businessmen and freelance philosophers that had come together in the early sixties and knocked on Ronald Reagan's door. You must run for office, they had told him.

Mrs. Earle Jorgensen is here—Marion Jorgensen, ninety-three years old, powdered like a sweet cake, in a flowered dress. "She had the most beautiful jewels of any woman in America," a friend breathes as we stand together on the side. "She was a beautiful woman," says another. Her late husband had been key in helping to support Reagan's early political career. And here is Bob Tuttle, son of Holmes, who had also been one of the founding group.

Everyone looks handsome, elegant in the candlelight. Most of them, not all, are old. They were there at the beginning. They were in history with him, and helped him be what he was.

Nancy had retired early but Betsy Bloomingdale is anchoring a table. A friend of the Reagans for almost forty years, she still sees Nancy almost every week. Imperial, saucy, with champagne-colored hair, she stands chuckling with a friend. Carol and Paul Laxalt are there, Paul the former governor of Nevada who became the close friend of Governor Reagan of California, and who then went to the Senate, where he supported his friend who was then president. Charles and Mary Jane Wick, again kitchen cabineters, both close and longtime Reagan friends.

And some nonpioneers, Buffy and Bill Cafritz for instance, down from Washington. They are a good and needed thing in our capital, bipartisanly friendly and implicitly supportive of whoever is president and first lady. You might call this fiercely practical, and it is. But it's also true that not everyone could do it, and there is a benefit to what they do not only for Washington but also, in a way, for the republic itself. For when a new president, some fellow from a peanut farm in Plains or a state house in Little Rock or the rarefied but still parochial palisades of the Pacific, lands in Washington, he needs an establishment to meet him and invite him in, to greet him and say we hope you have a good time here. Whoever comes to power, Buffy, Bill and a handful of others—Kay Graham was one—bring to them the welcoming (though not uncritical and not unobservant) embrace of The Permanent Washington, as if there were such a place. But in a way there is, and if you're from Plains or Sacramento or Hot Springs or wherever, you're sure there is.

Robert Higdon, a Washington figure and close friend of the Reagans, and our host, raises his glass with a toast. "To the great class of 1989," he says, referring to the year Reagan left the presidency. "And a toast to our friend Ronald Reagan, who will always be our president."

Oatsie Charles, formidable and witty, a voice of the old Washington and friend of the great, formerly great and never will be great but what the heck, stands.

"I just want you to know I'm absolutely enchanted—"

"Louder," yells a man.

"Shut up," she replies, to laughter.

"—enchanted to be here tonight, the only Democrat."

Everyone applauds.

"Curiously enough, the first moment I ever saw Nancy Reagan, whom I refer to as Beauty because I feel she is just as beautiful outside as she is inside, from the first moment I always felt immediately at home." She said that is how she feels tonight. She added that while you want to be friends with the Democrats, you want to party with the Republicans, which made everyone applaud.

The next morning half a dozen buses stood outside the hotel to take us to the shipyards, and as we stood in line to board I found myself standing next to Charlie Wick, head of the United States Information Agency in both Reagan administrations. I had thought of him once, when I first saw him almost twenty years ago, as fierce and glowering. But I don't know that's what he was, and it's not what he seems now. Maybe I was wrong; maybe he's changed. It seems to me age can make people softer inside just as it makes your skin softer—as if the soft pliant skin on the outside is a physical expression of a new give inside, in the personality. You get to a certain age and get dressed for the party and you really just want to laugh and be good to people, be nice to them. The urgencies of yesterday have fallen away, the demand for this or that concrete objective evaporates, and what is left is the most patient and well-meaning you.

Charlie and I make some stupid joke and then for no reason I can remember I begin to sing an old song, softly. He joins in, and we are standing in the lobby crooning, "I Remember You." *You're the one who made my dreams come true/Yes you did, many years ago . . .*

Forty minutes later we were at the shipyards and suddenly there she was, berthed on the James River, built by ten thousand hands. Massive and elegant, a great beauty jutting into the air, a big flat-topped ship painted the color of a hazy day at sea. More than a thousand feet long, with a displacement of almost a hundred thousand tons. And arching overhead, a huge thousand-ton crane that read NEWPORT NEWS SHIPBUILDING.

One after another we'd stop and stare as we walked to our seats. Big ships have such a dense presence and a massive silence.

There was bunting on the port bow, a string of American flags trailing down from the bull nose to a sign that said RONALD REAGAN, CVN 76. It seemed appropriate and yet cheesy, like sale day at Kresge's.

The U.S. Navy Atlantic Fleet Band was playing the Sousa-like music you only hear at events like this and patriotic parades.

The day was sodden, freezing, overcast. We sat in steady rain in a field of folding chairs on a makeshift plywood platform, shivering in our boots in the early March cold. We wore little soggy ponchos that had been left on our seats, and it was so unrelentingly awful that there was a kind of delight in it. No one could look nice and so no one tried, and no one, therefore, was dignified.

There was some oratory, but not too much.

Virginia's new senator, George Allen, quoted Reagan: " 'History comes and history goes, but principles endure, and ensure future generations will defend liberty not as a gift from government but as a blessing from our Creator. . . .' " Admiral Vern Clark said the United States has named a number of aircraft carriers after former presidents—the *George Washington,* the *Abraham Lincoln,* the *Theodore Roosevelt,* the *Harry S. Truman,* the *Dwight D. Eisenhower,* the *John F. Kennedy.* "Ronald Reagan's name stands for freedom," he said. "As it has been with his name, so also will it be with this ship."

Senator John Warner of Virginia called the ship "an island of democracy sailing the seas," and said it was fitting that the most recently commissioned aircraft carrier before this was the *Harry S. Tru-*

man. "For these two presidents, Truman and Reagan, will always be remembered for standing firm against the spread of communism."

The new secretary of defense, Donald Rumsfeld, quoted Reagan's farewell speech when he left the presidency. "(A)s he reflected on his years in the White House, he recalled an incident from the 1980s when the aircraft carrier *Midway* was patrolling in the South China Sea. It came across a leaky little boat crammed with refugees from Indochina. And as the refugees made their way through the choppy seas one spied a sailor way up on the deck of the carrier. And he called out, 'Hello American sailor. Hello Freedom Man.' What President Reagan called that 'small moment with a big meaning' captured what America symbolized. . . . And today we stand in the shadow of another big ship, to reaffirm that shining spirit."

It was all fine, all appropriate, but everyone was waiting for the new president, George W. Bush, to speak. In the holding room just before the speeches the Bushes had met Mrs. Reagan and been solicitous. They don't know each other well, had really only been people who stood together at great occasions in years past. It was the first time they'd seen each other since Ron Reagan, Nancy's son, had said in an interview during the election that Mr. Bush's only accomplishment in life had been that he'd stopped being a drunk. Nancy had been mortified, and had called Barbara Bush to apologize. Mrs. Bush had laughed and said, "Oh Nancy, don't give it a thought, we can't control our children."

President Bush asked how the former president was, and how Nancy was holding up. It is a struggle to live with those who suffer from Alzheimer's, an added struggle if you are old yourself and have them at home. "It's hard," Mrs. Reagan said. "Thank you for asking, it's hard." And then she changed the subject.

"Please tell me," she said to Laura Bush, "that all those modern sculptures are gone." The recently departed president and first lady had placed some modern sculptures in the gardens and throughout the house; Nancy Reagan had thought them heavy, discordant. "You have to play to the architecture of the House," she had worried to a friend.

"They're gone," said Laura Bush softly, smiling.

"And in the first lady's garden?"

"They're gone," Mrs. Bush assured her.

Mrs. Reagan smiled. She was relieved. She loved the old mansion, had been alarmed at the inclusion of art that seemed at odds with its spirit.

There was enthusiastic applause as the president now stood and walked to the podium. He was still new at these things, awkward and full of shrugs, but friendly and unpretentious. He wore a dark overcoat and had come in holding the hand of his wife, whose pleasant, inexpressive smile seemed today, as always, to mask more than it reveals.

When the applause died down Bush said he was proud to attend the christening of "the newest ship of the greatest navy in the world." He said that it is certain the *Reagan* "will sail tall and strong, like the man we have known. . . . We live in a world shaped in so many ways by his will and heart. As president, Ronald Reagan believed without question that tyranny is temporary, and the hope of freedom is universal and permanent; that our nation has unique goodness, and must remain uniquely strong; that God takes the side of justice, because all our rights are His own gifts. . . . Some achievements fade with the years. Ronald Reagan's achievements grow larger with the passing of time.

"What he wanted, what he fought for, was a stronger nation in a more peaceful world. . . . The values that Ronald Reagan brought to America's conduct in the world will not change.

"So as we dedicate this ship, I want to rededicate American policy to Ronald Reagan's vision of optimism, modesty and results. Ronald Reagan's optimism defined his character, and it defined his presidency. More than a habit of mind, this optimism sprang from deep confidence in the power and the future of American ideals. Great democracies, he believed, are built on a strong foundation of consent. . . . Any government built on oppression is built on sand. . . .

"We will stand by those nations moving toward freedom—we will stand up to those nations who deny freedom . . . and we will assert emphatically that the future will belong to the free. . . ."

Bush said that twenty years ago Ronald Reagan had visited the USS *Constellation* and told the sailors there that America was grateful to them. In two years, Bush said, the *Reagan* would actually replace the *Constellation*. But the *Reagan* is a very different ship.

"The island on the *Reagan*'s main deck is almost the same height as that of its predecessors, but it has one less level. The empty space will be filled with cables that will tie the ship into a vast network that connects information and weapons in new ways. This will revolutionize the navy's ability to project American power over land and sea . . . wherever our vital interests are threatened. . . ."

The new president said the revolution in technology will change the face of war itself. "Today the *Ronald Reagan* begins its journey into the bright and peaceful dawn that President Reagan helped to bring. All of us here wish the ship *Ronald Reagan* Godspeed, as we wish Ronald Reagan God's blessings."

He had used the ceremony to take Reagan's stands on military strength and reclaim them, as he had during the campaign, as his own. He used the day not to assert military impregnability but to call for a continued commitment of resources.

It occurred to me that Mr. Bush always seems to laud Reagan from a certain height. Maybe that's inevitable; it's how today praises yesterday. But I thought as he spoke: Every time he praises Reagan, who was different in so many ways from his father, I bet he wonders if his listeners are thinking *Yes, Reagan was the man your old man wasn't.* I wonder if little slivers of frustration or resentment shoot through his blood. I thought: I bet there will be another aircraft carrier commissioned before his presidency is over, and I bet it will be named the USS *George H.W. Bush,* and I bet George W. Bush will speak then not from a superior position but as a son speaks of a loved and wounded father, not praising him so much as raising him up.

Now President Bush joined Mrs. Reagan, who was seated to his left on the stand, and the two of them went hand in hand to the bow of the ship.

The band played "The Sailor's Hornpipe." An officer put a bottle of Virginia sparkling wine in Mrs. Reagan's white gloved hands. The bottle had been specially made to break, so that what happened to Bess Truman when she christened a ship—the bottle refused to break in a dozen tries—would not happen here.

Nancy held the bottle the way a child holds a blow-up baseball bat. She said, crisply, "I christen thee the United States Ship the *Ronald Reagan,*" and as she reared back someone in the crowd called out, "Break one for the Gipper!"

She swung, smacked the bottle on the break bar.

It burst—and then came the lonely whale sound of the shipyard whistle filling the air.

The crowd erupted in cheers, the band went into "Anchors Aweigh" and the new president and the former first lady laughed and shook the wine from their hands.

And we all went home in the rain.

It was a good day. There were a lot of hugs, a lot of long goodbyes—"And this is my e-address, this is my cell." It all felt affectionate and appropriate and—and what?

Like it didn't quite capture the thing that hasn't been captured, the thing we're all trying to say.

Five hundred came to the christening but it easily could have been a thousand or two, or five. There were at least a thousand standing outside the gates in the unrelenting rain, waving flags and applauding. They were people we'd all known and worked with who somehow hadn't gotten on the haphazard invitation list, and who had come anyway, in caravans from Virginia and Maryland and New York, who'd brought their children and gone home without rancor, happy to have been there.

Whether inside or outside the gates that day, there is something that's grown among us, something you could really see that weekend. We were like veterans. We were like people who'd been through something together. That's why we threw ourselves into each other's arms when we used to not speak. We felt like people who'd fought for something side by side, who'd been crowded together in a foxhole in our youth and had given each other a hard time: "You talk too much," "You always think you're boss," "You act like you don't care if the Huns win!" But we had ducked some incoming together, had been in some cold rain. And now, having gone on to other wars and seen our country in other struggles, having lived more years, known more life and seen more things, having come to understand what the meaning of those old days was . . . well, old resentments and rivalries fell away, disappeared, and what was left was: *us.* And the meaning of what we'd shared.

We'd been in a war, and we had a leader.

There is, I think, a growing national consensus that Ronald Reagan was great. In February of 2001, a CNN/*USA Today*/Gallup poll asked

Americans to name the one man they consider to have been America's greatest president, and the winner was Ronald Reagan, with 18 percent. (Next was John F. Kennedy with 16 percent, and after him Abe Lincoln with 14 percent.) But there is no real consensus on why he was great. Liberals say he made us proud again, made us feel good. Conservatives are sometimes impatient with this: He was a man who laid down a path whose sense and destination the country supported; it was the progress made when the country was allowed to follow it that made people proud again. It was as if we still had the power to turn things around.

And there's this. Reagan started as "the first" and wound up "the last." He was the first California governor, first actor, first divorcé, first modern conservative of serious principle to become president. And he became the last—the last, for now, to have moved so many so profoundly, the last, for now, of the great ones, the last to have the massive presence of a ship. The last to lead in a way that the majority of America's grunts and grandees—the working striving heroes of "flyover"—instinctively trusted because they knew he would try to do right. Imagine Ronald Reagan reading a poll to tell him what to think.

There was a sense, the day of the christening of the *Reagan,* that we may not see his like again, which is a very un-Reagan-like thought, quite pessimistic. But it may explain some of what happens to people who loved him when they hear again something he said, or did. A kind of wave comes upon them unawares, surprising them with its fullness. A young man in Los Angeles watches a tape of Reagan talking to his friends about his youth, and when he turns away he has tears in his eyes.

Dave Fischer, a businessman now and for years Reagan's personal aide, tells me at lunch at a hotel in Washington that he thought his memories of the old man would fade, that he'd think of those days less and less. But they haven't receded in his mind; they've grown. He tells me of the time he said good-bye to Reagan in the Oval Office and his eyes fill with tears and we sit there, the tape recorder silently turning.

"You loved him," I say, and he nods and smiles as if to say, *Yes, and I didn't know how much.*

There is something about that old man, something beyond the specific actions or triumphs you can point to, something that brings tears to their eyes, all of those who knew him. They see an end coming and they look back and think: *He was a giant.* He was our giant, a giant of history, we know that now, and we wish we could put our arms around him and rock him to sleep.

But it is what the young think that counts, because what they think is what the future knows. The young men and women on the *Reagan,* the ones the captain said were nineteen and twenty, who were just born when Reagan became president—what do they think, how do they see him?

The one thing they all know about Reagan is that he was a movie star. The thing they've picked up since coming on the ship is that he was a friend to the armed forces.

Airman Bryant Hernandez, nineteen years old, born April 9, 1982, grew up in the South Bronx. He is enjoying seeing a carrier "built from the bottom up." He told me he remembered Reagan leaving office and the first George Bush coming in. Then he laughed and said he had been paying more attention to Ninja Turtles and Thundercats in those days. I asked what he knew of Reagan. That he was an actor, he said, and that he became president. "And he cared about the military."

Airman Jessica Teston of Jacksonville, Florida, was born December 10, 1980, a few weeks after Reagan was elected president. She's "striking to be an AE," to work on the electronic parts of the aircraft. She remembers "seeing things on TV about Reagan." She has a recording of him talking. Her sense of him is that "he was a good person." And "I think it's wonderful that he came from being an actor to being president."

Some of the older crew naturally remember more. Petty Officer Joseph Aguilar, thirty years old, was ten and in public school in Miami when he first heard of Reagan. He remembered the invasion of Grenada, and remembered Reagan talking about "the Star Wars project." The future sailor thought it might be like the movie and maybe he could become part of it. He studied electronics, and now here he is. "I remember the wall coming down," he told me. "I saw a movie about East Germany at the time, and Reagan was trying to influence that, get it overridden. I saw on CNN the wall coming down in pieces."

And Petty Officer Travis Little, thirty-four, from Robersonville, North Carolina, population twelve hundred, said he remembered Reagan running for the presidency. "I remember the articles, the movie star becomes president." He said he didn't know much about him when he was young but now every day he learns more, and he's started to admire him. I asked if the crew had a nickname for the ship. Yes ma'am, he said, "We call her the Gipper."

They all wondered how Reagan was, and some of them asked me what he was like.

He's a sick old man now and he lives in a house on St. Cloud Road in leafy Bel Air, in Los Angeles, in his beloved California. There are people who feed him and see to his safety and make sure he isn't awake and about without their knowledge; there's a mat on the floor next to his bed that is rigged to let them know if he gets up. He doesn't speak much anymore, can't converse, isn't really there.

And still with all that he's so hardwired for courtesy, for a regard for others, that when he accidentally bumps the arm of the woman who is feeding him he will say, with perfect enunciation, "Oh, I beg your pardon." And whoever is with him will be startled because it's as if he's there, and taking part.

Which in a way of course he is.

Nancy is with him every day, keeps him at home, lets no one see him but his children and those who help him. It's good to remember him as he was when he had all his powers, she says. Let everyone remember him as he was.

So this is my attempt to show him as he was—a retelling of his life and a look at its meaning, a look at who he was as a man. It is commonplace now to see him as an ordinary man who did extraordinary things, and that's the way I saw him, for many years. But the more I think and listen and read and remember, the more I think he wasn't ordinary at all. He wasn't like other people. There was some huge kind of destiny playing out within him.

So let me tell you about him.

Let me try to say what hasn't quite been said.

Let me tell you about the old man of St. Cloud Road.

All Presidents Come from Something

Presidents tend to come from something. When you look at the books that carry their stories you see that they've usually been born to people who have things, to mill owners or ministers or millionaires. They enter the world heirs to some kind of stability or standing, which gives them advantages both obvious and not. Obvious: They have physical comfort, and are objects of local inherited respect. Less obvious are the intangibles that can in certain lives make all the difference. When you come from people who have achieved in life you will tend to absorb the habit of achievement: You think it natural to go on and excel, think it realistic to dream big dreams. And presidents' parents have often lived lives their children can be proud of, and can experience as part of their own virtue. John Adams, who knew virtually every great man of his age, thought the greatest man he'd ever met was his father. That he knew he had his father's blood must at hard moments have comforted and lifted him.

This hasn't been true of all presidents, of course, and was not true most famously of Lincoln and Jackson, who came from real distress.

And there are other stories of presidents who were born with little. But when you read of them you see that they were usually disadvantaged in comparison with others who became president, and not with ordinary people in their time and place.

Ronald Reagan's beginnings were the most modest and lacking of any president of the past hundred years. And the odd thing about that is it never quite gets said. But Reagan is unique in that his family had no status or standing, was neither of the local gentry nor the middle class, had no profession to claim such as nurse or doctor and owned nothing, no humble farm or small store.

Richard Nixon's father had a lemon farm and then a gas station;

Harry Truman's, a family farm; Bill Clinton's grandparents owned the local general store and minded him while his mother got a nursing degree. The only president who comes close to Reagan in terms of lack is Dwight Eisenhower, who grew up in a clapboard house, one of seven children, the son of a railroad worker. But President Eisenhower's father worked steadily, and his family was respected locally.

For the Reagans it was all more problematic because the facts of their lives were built around an embarrassment that was also a shame.

He was born in Illinois, in a town called Tampico, in a one-bedroom rental over a bank building. It was a hard delivery. The day he was born, February 6, 1911, his father ran up the stairs, took a look and said he looked like a fat little Dutchman. His mother named him Ronald and called him that but he never liked it, and when he was a boy he started asking people to call him what his father called him, Dutch. (For the rest of his life, in the great crowds that accompanied his adulthood, whenever someone called out "Dutch!" he'd stop and turn eagerly because he knew it must be someone from town. But it was usually just someone who'd read somewhere that he'd had a nickname as a kid.) Maybe he was inspired by his brother, Neil, two years older, who decided along the way that he preferred being called Moon.

Jack Reagan was not yet twenty-eight years old when his son the future president was born. He was tall, just a shade under six feet, broad shouldered and handsome, with thick dark hair. He was Irish Catholic, a natural salesman, a chain-smoking raconteur. "No one I ever met could tell a story better than he could," his second son said. He was street smart and had dreams. In another day he might have become something other than what he was and stayed, which was a shoe salesman.

Jack had a dark side. He tended to be cynical, and his cynicism pained his son, who flinched at the sourness of it. The boy wanted a father who was idealistic, in part because it would have made it easier for him to be what he was, which was hopeful. Once, during the Great Depression, Dutch hitchhiked to Chicago to look for a job and didn't even tell his father because he knew what he would have said: Don't bother, no one is going to hire you. (He was right, for a while.)

Ronald Reagan never developed an affinity for pessimists, and the defeats they seemed to summon.

Jack somehow always let you know he didn't expect the best from people, didn't think the right thing would happen. And while he was humorous and funny when he was in the mood, and had a gift for accents and mimicry, he could also be sarcastic, and surly, especially when he drank. Which was, as we know, often.

For most of his life when Ronald Reagan spoke about his parents he tended not to say much about his father. He did not hide that he was an alcoholic but referred to it as his mother had taught him to do—as a disease from which his father suffered. Only once is he known to have been blunt, to his young friend the producer A. C. Lyles, when they were young men new to Hollywood. "My father was a drunk," he told him.

With everyone else, delicacy. A few years ago Jack's granddaughter Patti Davis, who'd never met him but knew of him from family stories, told me, "Jack was a binge drinker. He didn't drink all the time but when he drank he got drunk, he went on binges." She used to ask her father if Jack had been violent, and Ronald Reagan would answer that alcoholism was a disease, it's no one's fault. Patti would say, Yes, I know, but was he abusive, did he break things? Ronald Reagan would say no, but she didn't believe it. "I mean," she asked me, "did you ever know a quiet, peaceful Irish drunk?"

In fact she was onto something. In his second and final memoir Ronald Reagan wrote of what had seemed for many years a "mysterious source of friction" between his parents, of arguments, slammed doors and sudden separations.

Jack's affliction had a twist that made it particularly hard on his family. He was usually able to suffer through hard times and boredom but when things were looking up, when progress seemed possible, when the family was gathering to have a good time, a binge would begin, and three days later Jack would emerge, wreckage around him. The future president, never much given to complaint, would say that in his childhood he never knew whether to look forward to Christmas like other kids or dread it, because it meant Dad would start drinking and the fights would come.

So that was Jack. His people were potato famine Irish from Tipperary. His parents had died of tuberculosis before he was six years old.

He was raised by an elderly aunt. His life had been hard and had hardened him.

The future president's mother, on the other hand, was a little tornado of goodness named Nelle Wilson Reagan. She's the one who saved him. She was a Christian of the evangelical school and pretty much her whole life was bringing the good news to people who hadn't heard it or maybe hadn't listened hard enough. She did good works. Ronald Reagan later said in conversation, "My brother and I, we were truly influenced by our mother, who was truly religious but also a great kindness she had. We were a rather poor family, and yet my mother was always finding people worse off than we were that she could bring help to."

She was of Scots-English ancestry, met Jack in a small farm town on the Illinois prairie and married him on November 8, 1904. She'd been brought up in want too.

Nelle was solid, reliable and small—she looks in pictures to have been about a size two, about five feet two inches. She was busy and bustling and she believed completely in what was known as, in the title of a popular book of the era, *The Christian's Secret of a Happy Life*. This was the secret: Jesus is with you, is aware of your life and fully engaged in it; God is in everything; He will let little befall you that will not be to the ultimate benefit of your soul. Sometimes He steps aside for trouble coming your way but only if it will refine you or prepare you to be with Him someday in heaven, where you'll know a happiness beyond all human understanding. So there is no cause then for sadness, only for joy. "Do not be afraid."

She filled the family air with her belief, with her sureness about the meaning of it all. Young Dutch breathed it in and it helped shape his temperament, which was trusting and placid.

Of Jack's religious observance, Ronald would say, when he was an old man, "My father was Catholic, but my mother was the one. I think sometimes—this is unkind of me but I think sometimes that my father gave up going to church for Lent! Because it was my mother who was Sunday morning church. My brother and I started small, at an early age, going to Sunday school."

———

This is what they say, those who knew the family and knew Reagan best, and they include his closest friends, his wife and his children. They say Ronald Reagan was just like his mother, and Moon took after Jack. When they say this they're not quite complimenting Moon and not quite explaining Dutch.

In some way or in some degree that is lost to history the Reagan boys were brought up to be unusually independent. Early on they absorbed the information that they were responsible for amusing themselves and getting along in the world. Sometimes when their mother was out visiting people in jail or doing good and the father was out and about, the boys were left alone, and sometimes it frightened them. They didn't call their parents Mom and Dad but Nelle and Jack. (It is interesting that Reagan nicknamed the woman with whom he had his longest and most successful adult relationship, his second wife, Mommy.) While the boys looked to their parents for guidance you get the impression they were maybe four people occupying the same galaxy but not always orbiting each other closely. This is true of many families, maybe most, but is interesting in this one because it yielded a great man.

This is the big thing Jack Reagan gave his sons besides his presence and his love: Jack felt he had been discriminated against in the old "No Dogs or Irish Need Apply" days and ways, and it made him despise prejudice with a committed and consistent passion. He established the idea of equality as part of the family conversation, part of the way the family understood itself. They were people who stood for tolerance.

As an old man, shortly before his final illness hit him with full ferocity, Ronald Reagan said, "I'll tell you, I am so happy that my father and mother—if ever we started, my brother and I, started downing somebody because of their difference in religion or race or anything else—that was the biggest sin to my father and mother. They would take care of us and—*wham!*"

He shot his left arm out as if to show a kid being whacked by a parent.

"And I don't think my brother and I have ever lost it."

He continued, "My father and mother, her Protestant and him Catholic, the biggest sin in their eyes was racial or religious preference.

This would go not only between black and white but if you started picking on Jews or anything. Any kind of bigotry, they'd really lay into you."

Jack believed—really believed, didn't just say it—that all men are created equal. He believed racial and religious bias were cruel and un-American and he actually fought them in his life, an unusual thing in a white working-class turn-of-the-century Midwesterner. Once Jack, on a shoe-selling trip, went to check into a hotel and was told by the clerk that he'd be comfortable here, no Jews allowed. Jack got mad and told him off and spent the night in his car in a blizzard. (Ronald Reagan thought it led to his father's first heart attack.)

Jack also believed in the rights of the working man, and was ever wary of their infringement. He was, Ronald Reagan later wrote, "suspicious of established authority, especially the Republican politicians who ran the Illinois state government, which he considered as corrupt as Tammany Hall."

These are the things he taught his boys, or at least the things he meant to teach them. They became Democrats just like him, but more important they knew the reasons they were Democrats, and they were good reasons.

Even more important, Jack established in the household this value: We care about things outside of us. We don't just talk about our wants and our ambitions in this family, we talk about what's wanted in the world.

Jack's lessons, that is, were broadening, not narrowing. It gave the boys the sense that they were responsible for putting good things into the world.

Nelle held the same views on prejudice but not because she'd been discriminated against. Nelle thought everyone was a child of God—literally His baby, literally made by Him. So by definition no one was better than anyone else and no one was worse.

The boys got a double dose of this and, as children do, internalized it and acted it out. Moon's best friend was black, and when they went to the movies the boys sat together in the segregated balcony.

And there was what happened with Burghie, Dutch's football teammate a few years later at Eureka College. The team had an away game and had to travel by bus and when they got to a hotel the owner told the coach the two black players, including Burghie, couldn't stay there. The coach was upset, and Reagan overheard and took him aside. "My parents live a half hour from here, I'll take the guys home with me." He couldn't call to tell his parents they were coming because they didn't have a phone, but he knew if he showed up all of a sudden with two black strangers his parents would say: Great to see you, come on in. Which is what they said.

Reagan and the coach didn't tell the excluded teammates what had happened, they told them the hotel was just full up. But they probably knew. And one of the players, Burghie, drew close to Reagan, and they stayed in touch for the rest of their lives. Burghie became Dr. William Franklin Burghardt, and in 1980 he told *The Washington Post* that he and Reagan just had "a natural respect" for each other. "I don't think he was conscious of race at all," Burghie said, meaning Reagan didn't see any difference.

Burghie never had it easy. He played center on Reagan's team, and when both teams were lined up there would often be a player on the opposing team who'd try to distract him by hurling racial epithets. Reagan later said, "I remember one game, the center opposite Burghie . . . just was vicious and talking to him and calling him 'nigger' and all of this. And they'd collide (as they played). And in the get-togethers in the field there (the huddle) some of us would say 'Burghie, I'm gonna kill that guy, I'm gonna—' And he'd say 'This is my do'; he said, 'I'll take care of this.'

"Now Burghie didn't do anything dirty but he was a hell of a football player. And he—when he had to block and that sort of thing he did it, and he did it great. And he never said a word in reply to all this conversation from the white center, the [one] talking to him.

"And then there was one day that this went on and on and finally they had to take the [white] center out, because Burghie had just played him off his feet. And he was almost limping when he started to leave the field. And he only got part way, and we saw him turn around and he started back. Now, the two teams are just kind of standing there waiting for him to be off it and waiting for it to be time to play football again. He came elbowing his way through the two teams, and there were tears here [in his eyes.] And he stuck out his hand to Burghie and he said, 'I just want you to know you're the whitest man I've ever met.'

"And with that handshake he turned and he went off the field crying.

"So—Burghie done pretty well."

Ronald Reagan told that story to his friends more than sixty years after the events he recounted had taken place. It's from a privately made videotape by Charles Wick. It is almost painful to hear with modern ears the center's compliment—"the whitest man I ever met." It makes you wince. Reagan told the story, however, with no embarrassment. He was speaking the language of his youth, a language in which the white center was understood to be telling Burghie, "You're like me—only better."

Burghie died in 1981 and the last phone call he got before he went into the operating room was from his friend the president.

But I've jumped ahead.

"When I was a child we moved a lot." Those are laconic words, the kind Reagan tended to use when referring to major facts of his life that he didn't want to dwell on. Jack's big dream in life was to own a shoe store and he kept thinking that if he kept moving, sooner or later the opportunity would come. Or at least that was the official story in the family. Another way to look at it was that after Jack had gone on a binge he'd come back to work and suddenly the boss wasn't so charmed by him anymore. Anyway, they moved a lot.

Tampico, Dixon, Chicago, Galesburg, Monmouth, Tampico again, Dixon again.

Sometimes they lived in rentals where the whole apartment was lit by a single gas jet that came on if you put a quarter in a slot down the hall. Nelle learned to make a soup bone last a week. She'd tell the butcher she needed liver for the family cat and then use it for Sunday dinner. They ate oatmeal hamburgers. In the last days of his presidency he told me about them. They weren't made with meat but with oatmeal, and he didn't know they ate them because they didn't have any money, he thought they ate them because they were good. (Let me tell you how he looked seventy years later, when he talked about them and the gravy his mother would make: He looked hungry.)

I should note here that Ronald Reagan was not some Andy Hardy nostalgist for the good old days. He was not nostalgic for the past, and didn't hanker for it. His childhood was not something he looked back on in a golden glow. He thought he came from tough times, wanted to leave them, and did. He wanted to get out of the flat dry Midwest and his father's busted dreams, and he was glad he did and never wanted to go back.

He was nostalgic about how far he'd come, not where he'd started. He thought most Americans were like this.

World War I came to America when he was six. He saw the flags, heard the songs, and sometimes Doughboys came through town on troop trains heading east. The windows would be open and the soldiers would wave at everyone who came to the depot to cheer. His mother took him once, held him up and put a penny in his hand. Dutch leaned toward a khaki-clad soldier and gave it to him and said, "Good luck." He never forgot it.

All the moving had compensations and implications. Dutch couldn't really keep friends so he learned not to need them too much. He turned somewhat inward, became a reader and a boy who spent hours drawing. Another compensation involved new experiences. Once when they'd moved into an old house he found that previous tenant had left his collection of bird's eggs and butterflies in the attic. He'd go up there and study them for hours, touching them, seeing all the delicacy. He thought: God made all this intricacy and color and weave and beauty. It gave him a feeling of reverence, and in later years when he tried to speak of his religious feeling he'd talk about what he'd seen in the attic.

But the implications went as deep as the compensations.

This is the famous story:

Ronald Reagan came home one night, aged eleven, from the YMCA. His mother was out doing a sewing job. His father was passed out on the steps that led to the door. He'd come back from a speakeasy and he reeked of whiskey, and everyone, the whole neighborhood, could see him lying in the snow, arms outstretched, flat on his back.

His son wanted to step right over him and get into the house. Instead he got the door open, dragged his father in, put him to bed and never told his mother.

He wrote about it in his first memoir, *Where's the Rest of Me?,* thirty-six years ago. It was in parts a frank book, especially for one written to tell the public more about his life just as his political career was beginning. But the most interesting thing about the story is not that he dragged his father in but that he made it clear he had to struggle with himself to do it. That's how embarrassed he was by the old man.

None of the marks left by his father's illness ever left him.

Jump to 1987. There was a young man, twenty-nine years old, in President Reagan's correspondence office in the White House. He wrote presidential messages and video greetings and his name was Doug MacKinnon. He'd done some good work that caught the president's eye, and Reagan called him one day to thank him. He invited him to stop by the Oval Office and chat. A week later Doug walked into the Oval Office for the first time and found himself talking with the president. And he said something he hadn't planned on. The president was so friendly and natural that Doug found himself saying, "Mr. President, my father has the same thing your father had."

Doug didn't have to explain what he meant; Reagan knew. His eyes lit up and he leaned in. Doug told him that his family had been chaotic, there'd been bad problems with money, they had moved around a lot, thirty-four times by the time he was seventeen, that it had been embarrassing and painful to always be the new boy in school.

"All the things you've just mentioned happened to me," said the president. "Everything you have said one way or another applies to me."

He talked about his father and how tough it had been for Jack to have that sickness, and for the rest. As for school, yes, "Children can be cruel."

"He was really warm and he seemed to want to reach me," MacKinnon later told me. "He wanted to reach out and help someone who was going through what he had gone through. It was just a short visit but it told me everything I needed to know about Ronald Reagan—that he had an enormous heart, that he could empathize with people and that he wanted to make sure you knew he understood and felt for you. . . .

"To have him spend time out of an incredibly busy schedule to talk about an issue that was still so big for me, so burdensome—it meant the world to me. That he could persevere and become what he became—to be the son or daughter of an alcoholic is a tough lifestyle to make it out of and many people don't, but he did. I was able to move on and it was because of one man's kindness."

When Reagan was nine they lived in Dixon, and that was the place he came to think of as home. It was small but it had a main street and businesses and families, and beyond that was farmland, and everyone was close. If a family had a crisis the neighbors brought them dinner, if a barn burned down friends pitched in and raised a new one. The town was like a family that functioned well, a place that was peaceful, ordered, reliably affectionate—*there.*

So many of the big decisions we make in life we make in childhood, and we don't even know we're making them. But somewhere along the way Ronald Reagan decided he was a Protestant and not a Catholic (Moon would choose the reverse). Somewhere along the way he decided he was an American and a Midwesterner, not an Irishman who was displaced.

Would he drink or be sober, tell stories or be quiet, be a cynic or an idealist, go to meeting like his mother or refrain like his father? He would be sober, tell stories, be an idealist, often go to meeting. He would do these things and be these things pretty much all his life.

And he would be something else, a romantic drawn to the movement of history, to the importance of doing what you think is right, to the idea that it is good to become part of some big thing that moved for good.

But when you read about his life and talk to people who were close to him, you get the impression other decisions were made.

Sometimes when your life starts out as painful you come to experience your emotions not as something to feel or revel in but as something to defend against. You come to see your emotions not as feelings you can enjoy and experience but as feelings you have to fight. Otherwise you might be overwhelmed.

Children often make decisions to protect themselves without knowing it. They don't say to themselves, "I think I'll do this to survive," they just start taking unconscious actions to dull the stimuli. They look away, or don't notice or interpret things in a highly individualistic or idiosyncratic manner.

I think Reagan did some of this. I think embarrassment at his father's status in a Midwest that, after the Bible, believed most in striving and success; I think the tension of fights and silences between his parents; the moving, the moodiness, the financial worries—I think they all took their toll.

So maybe without quite deciding to, Ronald Reagan decided to avoid his emotions by distracting his mind with other things. Like novels, like tales of adventure, like stories of heroism.

The point is so many of our defenses are not deliberate, and if you asked the adult Reagan why he seemed more involved in the things in his head than he was by the gatherings of people around him, he would have been surprised. But he was more involved by the things in his head.

And to make it all just a little more interesting, a little tougher, he couldn't see. Literally couldn't see. Or rather he couldn't see well. But no one knew it—or at least nobody noticed. He didn't know either. Children with weak eyesight think the world sees the way they do, cloudy and unclear. (Just as children who are color blind think everyone is, and when asked if they can see red say yes. They can see their version of red, which might be brown or deep gray.)

Every summer the big store in Dixon filled one of its windows with mannequins dressed in the football uniforms of the local high school team. He'd walk in front of the window and think: I'll wear that uniform someday.

But he was no good at sports. He wasn't badly coordinated or poorly motivated but for some reason he'd miss every catch, even the easy ones. Once when he was in the eighth grade he was playing second base when a ball was hit straight toward him. He could feel everyone looking at him and he wondered why. Then he heard a sound. It was the ball falling to the ground just behind him. And the whole crowd went, "Oh no!"

It was awful, another embarrassment. It gave him the beginning of a real inferiority complex, or as he put it, "a deficiency of confidence."

Then a wonderful thing happened to him, and it was all an accident.

He wrote of it in his memoirs. When he was thirteen or fourteen years old his father took the family for a ride in the country. Nelle and Jack were in front, Dutch and Moon in the backseat. Nelle had left her eyeglasses in the backseat and as the car rolled along Ronald Reagan absentmindedly put them on.

He made such a sharp and urgent sound his father almost ran off the road. He couldn't contain himself. Something amazing had happened. He could see. He saw a world he hadn't known existed.

He thought everyone had seen things as he did, in a big blur. Trees on the side of the road were green blobs, billboards were a fuzzy haze. That's how he thought humans saw life. But now he could see branches on trees and leaves on branches. There were words on billboards.

"Look!" he shouted as he pointed at a herd of dairy cows.

He was astounded. So were his parents. They took him for glasses the next week and he wore them all the time, kind of clunky heavy things. They called him Four Eyes but he didn't care.

Now he knew he was bad at sports because he couldn't see the ball. He'd always sat in the front of the room at school so he could see the blackboard, but now he knew the kids in the back could see it too.

His coordination seemed to improve with his eyesight. He went out for the football team and they let him suit up but he was benched until junior year. Finally he got to play first string right guard, taking the place of a guy in a slump. Reagan never let the guy get his position back. By senior year he was a starter from the first game.

And he began to act in school plays. He began reading original essays out in class and getting laughs, and the laughter was like music. And so he began writing them to entertain the class.

He fell in love with a pretty girl, a pastor's daughter, and they were a couple for six years and thought they would marry. Once they almost broke up over Jack—her family had heard about his drinking and disapproved—making Reagan angry with his father. His mother counseled him: Remember, it's a sickness, and remember that he's good to us when he's well.

And he became a lifeguard. Fifteen and then twenty dollars a week, good money, and in seven years he saved seventy-seven lives at Lowell Park on the Rock River. (It was the last job he remembered having when he was old and sick.)

Senior year he was elected student body president.

And suddenly he wasn't so insecure anymore.

He read a lot of novels—the Rover Boys, Tarzan, Frank Merriwell at Yale, *Brown of Harvard*. He started to draw cartoons and caricatures, and he thought he might become an artist.

The novels made Reagan want to be a college student. He wanted to go to an Ivy League school and wear a raccoon coat and a porkpie hat and wave a pennant from the window of a Tin Lizzie. He wanted to be glamorous and all-American, and know the scions of rich old Eastern families and catch the pass that won the game. He was as romantic about all this as Scott Fitzgerald, half a continent away and a generation older, writing his stories of diamonds as big as the Ritz.

Reagan's ambition was not, strictly speaking, realistic. Only 10 percent of the public school students in those days graduated from high school and only 7 percent of those went on to graduate from college.

But Reagan had come to see himself as a person who would. And he passionately wanted to go, wanted to study and learn and rise and play ball in an arena. Also, his girl was going.

So those were his beginnings, modest and obscure. He and his family were American nobodies, like most everyone else. They were imperfect and hoped for better and worked for it. They thought they could and should be idealists, and believe in things. They hoped to rise, and did. Moon wound up an advertising executive in radio and TV; Nelle wound up tooling around the Hollywood Hills in a little car Dutch bought her, and the car was always full of neighbors needing a lift to the hospital or a cleaning woman who needed a ride to visit a cousin in jail. Dutch, of course, became a movie star. And maybe what happened with Jack was even more amazing.

Movie Star

Eureka College was a small school in a small town in northern Illinois, a midlevel school with 250 students. It cost almost four hundred dollars a year for tuition, room and board and Reagan couldn't afford it even if they'd accept him. But when he drove his girlfriend there he was bowled over—Georgian-style buildings covered in ivy, acres of rolling lawn surrounded by trees.

He had to stay. So he walked into the office of the president of the school and then the football coach's and convinced them he was a terrific football player, a lifeguard and no doubt a future winner of swimming trophies. And they actually let him in, with a needy-student scholarship and a job that would pay for meals and books. He had some savings from his lifeguard days that would pay the rest, at least for a while.

At Eureka, Reagan knew sustained success for the first time. He played football and went in for campus politics. He became the leader of a student revolt against deep and sudden campus cutbacks; he was chosen as speaker for the cause and when he rallied the other students, he felt his words hold an audience for the first time in his life. When he called for a strike vote, everyone rose to their feet and passed it by acclamation. Even teachers joined in. By the time it was over the president of the school stepped down, his cutbacks rescinded. Reagan was becoming a campus force.

He runs out of money, gets a job washing dishes in the girls' dorm, plays football first string. He had two years in the student senate, two as features editor of the yearbook, was a cheerleader, president of the boosters club and by senior year he was president of the student body. He started to smoke a pipe, thinking it made him look debonair and sophisticated. One night he got drunk on illegal liquor with his friends and was so sick the next day he decided he had no future with demon rum.

And he wrote. You sit in the reading room of the Reagan Library, in Simi Valley, California, where they used to make westerns in the brown scrubby hills, where bandits shot it out with the sheriff's posse. It is a modern library, spacious and airy, built on huge rollers to take heavy earthquakes. A few floors below the glass-cased Reaganania—his football sweater, the gear he wore as George Gipp, the reproduction of his small childhood living room, the family Bible with his mother's words scrawled in the margins—is the reading room. And that is where you find young Ronald Reagan.

As you sit, another scholar is making dry writing sounds. It's so quiet you can hear the pencil on the paper. They give you the young Reagan papers. You hold them in your hand, delicate old papers once white but now beige with age. Unlined paper, lined paper, the rough paper of old public schools.

He wrote in pencil, in the black ink of a fountain pen. In green ink he wrote a story called "Hallowe'en," in blue ink a story called "Yale Comes Through."

Here he doodled a man's head in the margins; here he wrote his name in letters a half inch high, as if practicing his autograph.

As a teenager and a young man of twenty he wrote of men and war. There's a kind of faux terseness, hard-bitten and war weary, in which it is possible to hear the influence of Hemingway, whose *The Sun Also Rises* had been published in 1926, when Reagan was fifteen, and whose *A Farewell to Arms* had been published in 1929.

Reagan wrote of the theater sometimes, of local theatricals and of football.

But always blasted men come home from war, dispirited, embittered by what they'd seen. His young heroes are bruised, burdened by flashbacks to the trenches.

The handwriting is small, beginning to lose its rightward slant.

But what is most remarkable in his stories is the enormous fluidity. He has a broad vocabulary, an ease; he rarely corrects what appear to be first drafts; his work is not blotched up with corrections as he spins out a young man's romantic tales.

Here is a story he wrote called "Killed in Action":

James Edward dropped the evening paper in his lap and stared thoughtfully into the blazing fire.

"David Bering," he said softly, "David Bering of the AEF suicide club."

Slowly the book lined walls receded. His comfortable arm chair was the yellow slime of a shellhole as he crouched, shivering from the damp chill that "issue blankets" and army ponchos would not keep from eating into the very bones of a man. Ten feet away his companion loosened the top on an ammunition box, prying it up with a trench knife. Edwards rose wearily and pulled a torn canvas over the machine gun to protect it against the drizzling rain.

There was a [stepping?] noise from behind them and Sergeant Riley slid from the communications trench into the shell hole. "Cozy place you got here boys," he grinned through a weeks growth of beard. "Sure the waters fine", growled Edwards. "How's the ammo holding out," asked Riley. The bent figure over the box straightened up. "Fine, we got plenty," he said, "but we can't eat the d—n stuff, the lead gets in our teeth." "Out of grub eh? Well the brass hats must think we left our bellys back in training camp. There isn't a kitchen within ten miles of the front," answered Riley. . . .

Riley tosses him some mouldy rye bread, tells them to have a banquet with it. He tells them *"[T]he 'Jerrys' are coming over at noon, it's 8:10 now, so tighten your belts and hang on til then."*

Bering is a good looking youngster about twenty-two years old, a veteran of two years in the army and one in the trenches. He muses aloud that Riley is a *"cheerful devil."*

"Why not be cheerful," demanded Edwards with a bitter laugh, "this is nobel work we are doing, you know. Making the world safe for democracy."

Bering is amused. *"Poor old Jim . . . after a whole year of glorious combat you're still a cynic."*

"That's just it," says Edwards, who explains, "this whole mess is a mistake". "Why what in God's name have any of us got against those Heinies? Not a thing. We're heros now, but when we get it in the neck and the fracas is all over we'll be tramps."

No, says Bering, when it's all over it will have been worth fighting for. He says he knows he has a future. *"Well I'll have one more year to go at Harvard and then the city and a job. There's a girl in my home town and—well we've planned things together from then on."*

Edwards is older than Bering, *"his thirty years had robbed him of some of Bering's optimism, his idealism and youth. A lump came to his throat as he listened to the boy talk of sacrifice and glory and heroism and he cursed mentally at a world so ordered that once every generation it must be bathed in the blood of youth like this one."*

The two are silent, prepare for battle. A half hour earlier than expected *"the fireworks started."*

"The Boche laid down a certain barrage behind our front line and then proceeded to flatten the trenches." For thirty minutes *"the very heavens seemed shaken by the blasts."*

"A whistle rising to a shrill scream, then an earsplitting crash rocked the earth."

The Germans advance, *"A gray wave . . . crawling slowly across the mud a scant hundred yards away."*

Allied artillery come into the fight but the Germans press on. Bering is crouched over a machine gun *"as it spouted a stream of death."* Under that fire the Germans retreat.

Edwards straightens up and then crumples forward. Bering drags him down to the bottom of the trench, rolls him over, loosens his tunic, sees he's wounded, an ugly wound in his left shoulder, he is losing blood fast. Bering bandages him, rigs a sling from his belt.

Hours later Riley comes up with a relief crew. Riley and Bering carry Edwards back to a base hospital.

Edwards survives, is released from the hospital after Armistice is signed. He searches for Bering, cannot find him, learns only that he was gassed a week before Armistice and sent home.

It was all thirteen years ago. Now Edwards picks up the newspaper again and glances at an obscure news item.

"A tramp, David Bering, met his death today beneath the wheels of a fast Santa Fe freight." Bering, an ex-serviceman who had been gassed in the war, was *"bumming his way"* to a veterans hospital for treatment.

"He attempted to board the moving train and lost his footing. He was thrown under the wheels when he fell.

"Notices have been broadcasted but no relatives of friends have claimed the body. He will be buried in the potters field."

Another short story of the Great War has a remarkable few words near the end. A veteran is returning home from the war. *"He walks fast anxious to see everyone. 'Lord it was great to be back. Never knew I missed so much.'"* He muses that his girl would be home now, reading, and he will walk in on her. *"No, he should call first. He'd wait until she said hello and then he would say, 'This is the President.'*

He walks through town, sees a *"big brick house softened and covered with ivy."* He is surprised to find himself ready to weep.

Up the steps, the cool hall, voices coming from the library. He drops his bag. *"What the heck? Isn't anyone going to greet an old soldier?"* The voices stop, they gather toward him.

Another story is about a local theatrical company, the cast scurrying home from a nighttime rehearsal *"to revel in Barrymore dreams until alarm clocks call them to grocery counters & chores."*

Another begins as a ghost story: It is a rainy night, raw and nasty, when a man stops by at his local club and joins a group already gathered. Someone advances the statement that *"anytime three or more men get together the conversation will eventually turn to either Women or Religion."* But this night talk turns to the supernatural. One man speaks of werewolves. Then he remembers *". . . experiences of the war: of the famous Marne battle where Allied troops followed a vision of an Angel of the famous Green archers of Agincourt who appeared before demoralized Canadians and inspired them to turn sure defeat into victory."*

A local doctor argues that everything has a natural and physical explanation, that superstition, psychology and hypnotism are the true reasons for visions.

And here is "Yale Comes Through," which he wrote when he was sixteen, in high school.

> Two men are overhead planning *"a gigantic robbery."* It appears they plan to move on *"the United States Treasury building at Washington."* They will pump gas into the building's ventilation system and *"a hired murderer clothed in a specially constructed gas mask would empty hundreds of canisters of gas into the ventilating tubes."* Everyone—clerks, bookkeepers and marines guarding the vaults—will be killed. Then the thieves will plunder at will.
>
> But wait—two handsome young Ivy Leaguers overhear the plan. And after the robbers leave they see that they have left a piece of paper behind—a map of the U.S. Treasury building!
>
> Can *"two mere undergraduates of Yale"* stand between the robbers and the deed?
>
> Yes. These two members of the *"much discussed, and oft times cursed"* younger generation go to the police. They tell what they've heard. The police take them to find the men.
>
> The robbers, however, are *"rocked by gales of laughter."* It turns out they are escaped prison inmates. The honor of Old Eli is upheld.

I read the future president's adolescent imaginings and wonder: More than half a century after he wrote it, when he was president, when I worked for him and walked the halls of his White House and saw what we called the Harvardheads—did those men of Yale and Harvard whom Reagan hired have an inkling of his adolescent desire to be where they'd been and live as they had?

And here, I think, is his most touching and moving piece of writing, "The Stadium," which Ronald Reagan wrote a few weeks after his twentieth birthday. It's a kind of prose poem about a sports stadium in the silence of a day in deep winter. It has "two tiered walls" with "their great hanging balconies" rising "massive and empty above the drifted snow." The "windows of the press box gleam black and empty."

The stadium is a "temple of the great goddess youth."

> Here the worshippers rise in frenzied victory or go down in bitter defeat. The clear sky receives their chants of acclaim, their disapproving cries, their anthems of loyalty.

> On the level sward between these temple walls boys tear their hearts out for an ideal. They toil, strain and sweat, batter and battered, snarling with primitive savagery at the opponent whose hand they will soon clasp in friendly congratulation. In short, they live life. Life with its triumphs and defeats, its jeers and praise. All the mingled brutality and kindliness of an adult society is met in this short season by these young gladiators.

As I read that paragraph I thought, This is the Reagan of the White House—the rhythm I remember from his rewriting on drafts.

His handwriting deteriorates as he becomes more excited.

> In "the brooding loneliness of the stadium" the eager goddess sees the stands filled with a roaring crowd. And now "a graceful figure breaks from the tangle and skirts around & down the field." He is "twisting and dodging toward the goal." Now the crowd "rises to its feet and a great roar swells forth. Up in the press box, typewriters bang, a radio announcer barks into the microphone—'He's loose, loose—five—ten—twenty and—he is over.' "
>
> And now the narrator realizes the stadium is never empty, "for the ghosts of past heros play great games over and over for the Goddess who holds sway for them as well as she does over the living crowds."

When you read Reagan's youthful writings you get a sense that he is not only betraying his preoccupations but suggesting his future. He is not writing about life as he knows it but life as he imagines it—if he were a hero, if he were a gentleman in the wood-lined walls of a gentleman's club taking brandy near the fire, if he had been born to go to Yale, to be a pennant-waving son of the American aristocracy.

In his writings you can see the style and assumptions of his time, but also a yearning, a wistfulness. And you can see, and not only in the half-inch-high autograph, a nascent ambition so natural to him, so smooth as silk, that he seems not to have noticed it, and seems never in those days to have declared it to others. No one remembers him saying that he would someday be a star, a leader, a great man in the world. And yet when he surprises his girlfriend as he comes home from the war he tells her who is calling: *This is the president.* An ambition so well hidden he kept it from himself.

Ambition for its own sake was tatty; ambition for the things of this world was out of keeping with his mother's teachings. So he took his mother's assumptions—we must do good—and added them to his own ambitions. And together they made him: *him.*

Something that is not fully understood about Reagan, something that he might not have fully understood himself, is this: Ronald Reagan did not so much have the natural talents and cast of mind of a businessman or economist or political figure, he had the natural talents and cast of mind of an artist. It is what he thought he would become, his first arguably serious ambition. As an adolescent he had thought he might become a cartoonist. And indeed he went through all his life drawing faces, caricatures and cartoons, designing leather crafts and memorizing poetry.

But he wasn't primarily a natural businessman or politician, he was primarily by nature an artist. His daughter Patti seemed to touch on this once when she told me that he was a gifted father when she was young because he had a creative mind.

"I think my father was a brilliant father for young children," she said. "He was a brilliant father because he could talk about magic, and heaven and paint pictures. . . . He could carry us on his back in the swimming pool when we were children, and I pretended a corner of the pool, the shadowy corner of the pool was the Amazon. So he'd go to the Amazon and I'd ride on his back. I'd go out into the ocean with him and he'd tell me about the waves, and everything was really simple and lovely and he could pull me into any imagery or fantasy that he chose." He liked to describe heaven to her. He liked to talk about what Jesus might have been like.

It is Reagan the writer that I find so interesting though. We have learned of the extent of his writings throughout his life from Martin and Annelise Anderson and Kiron Skinner, and their book *Reagan in His Own Hand.* The documents they quote at length—old radio scripts, old speeches and stories—had long been available but not all who wrote about him had seen them, and some saw but paid them little mind. Reagan wrote at home at his desk, in the office, sometimes on planes going from speech to speech in the years between the end of his governorship and the beginning of his presidency.

If you have seen this book you've seen the scripts, marked still by the calm fluidity. He is never overwhelmed by his material, takes it on himself to define liberty, to define the founders' intents, to assert the meaning of this part of the Constitution. I always think of his style as having a roundness—his prose never jerks, stops short, surprises. It has the smoothness of a simple stream.

But I never knew any of this when I worked for him. Amazingly, no one who worked in the White House when I was there, in what might be called the heyday of Reaganism, 1984–86, knew what we later learned in the Anderson and Skinner book. Jim Baker didn't know and Dick Darman and all the other important people didn't know; if Mike Deaver knew he never said it. And Reagan himself didn't talk about his experiences as a writer, or of his writings, or at least not that I heard or remember.

It had all been lost to time; there were few people in the Reagan White House by the time I got there who'd been with him decades past and knew all the facts about him. And those who knew were onto other things and didn't talk about it. I had followed him closely and yet still knew him mostly from *Time* and *Newsweek* and magazine and TV profiles. And years later I felt some shame, when I read what he had written. Because he was a good writer, had in fact made his political career based on the speeches he had written and rewritten—on cards, famously shuffled to keep things fresh. And I hadn't known any of it.

And I also realized why he had not become a writer. It was because he had turned his talent for writing into a talent for political communication. He had turned his art to the service of his beliefs.

The Great Depression hit when he was eighteen. Jack lost another job and Nelle got work as a seamstress. They moved again, this time to a place that didn't have bedrooms for the boys. Jack was laid off from a new job on Christmas Eve, and became a traveling salesman. Nelle borrowed money from Dutch for food. By 1932, the year he graduated from college, unemployment in America was over 26 percent. All his life Reagan remembered the radio crackling with word of plant closings and layoffs. He remembered rural families in Illinois losing their land, and men gathering on street corners near boarded-up shops.

Just after graduation he hitchhiked to Chicago on a job-hunting trip. This was the trip he didn't tell his father about because he knew he'd just discourage him. Reagan didn't find a job and hitchhiked home by himself in the rain.

He heard Montgomery Ward was going to open a big store in Dixon. They wanted a local sports star to run the sports department, and they'd pay $12.50 a week. Well, he was a sports star, and he could support his family on that money. He'd also be joining a big company where with time and effort he could work his way to the top. He was hopeful, but another local sports star got the job and Reagan was crushed. His mother told him again that all things are part of God's plan, even the most disheartening setbacks. If something went wrong you didn't get down, you kept going. Later on, she said, something good would happen and you'd find yourself thinking, "If I hadn't had that problem back then, then this better thing wouldn't have happened to me."

He believed it, every word.

At Eureka he'd gone out for plays. The school had wangled an invitation to an acting competition at Northwestern University, and Reagan got the part of a shepherd who is killed at the end of Edna St. Vincent Millay's antiwar play, *Aria da Capo.* He loved dying on stage, and played it to the hammy hilt. He was up against boys from all the big schools, from Princeton and Yale, but he came in second in the competition. And he was one of three students singled out for a special award. Northwestern's esteemed drama coach took him aside and told him: You should go into acting.

He enjoyed acting, loved the pictures, actually wanted to be an actor, a movie star but was embarrassed to say it.

How to start? Broadway and Hollywood were far away but Chicago wasn't and Chicago had broadcasting. Radio. Which he also loved. When he was a kid at the movies and the most popular radio shows came on they'd turn off the projector, put up the lights, put a radio on the stage and let the audience listen to their favorite shows. Then when it was over they'd put out the lights and start the movie again.

Radio had created a brand-new profession: sports announcer. Which in a way Reagan already knew how to do. When he was sitting around his fraternity house he'd grab a broom, make believe it was a microphone and imitate play-by-play and do mock interviews for laughs.

He'd also seen movies in which sports announcers got to play themselves on film. So he thought: That's how to get in the movies.

He told a local businessman that he wanted to be a sports announcer on the radio. The businessman told him to go knock on doors and tell them, "I believe in the future of broadcasting and I'll take any job."

And he got any job. He took a car and traveled west. They needed a sports announcer at WOC—World of Chiropractic—in Davenport, Iowa. He got the job, did college football games, lost the job, got it back, was laid off, got it back again and then went on to WHO in Des Moines—an NBC station, 50,000-watt clear channel.

He was twenty-two years old and his life was completely coming together. He was making seventy-five dollars a week, a lot of money—a heck of a lot more than Montgomery Ward would have paid him—and throughout the Midwest they were starting to know his name. And all of this happened just when his father began to have heart trouble and could no longer work.

When you think of Ronald Reagan's love for America you have to factor all of this in. He loved America not only because he'd been taught to by his family and by the culture of his day to love it, and not solely because he believed completely in the startling trueness and worth of the assertions of its founding documents. There was also the concrete and personal fact that he loved America because the freedom it offered (anyone can open a radio station, even some nutty chiropractor) gave him opportunity (anyone can be on the radio, even a know-nothing nobody from Nothingtown) not only to enter adulthood on a firm footing but also to rescue his family during the Great Depression. It wasn't all abstract to him. And in later years he thought that he, without having tried to be, was living proof of the American dream. He didn't think it was a perfect dream, didn't think everyone got an even shot, he thought life was hard and fate full of injustice. But he thought that as human systems go America's was wonderful, and ripe with achievable promise.

One of Reagan's listeners in those days was a teenager named Bob Feller, who would make his name as one of the great baseball stars of the century. Feller loved what he heard. "Every time he did a game I listened," he told me. "I was in the American Legion baseball team in Des Moines. He'd give you the facts and not all the details, and he'd let you know it was a game, it wasn't a war. He'd sort of keep you calm, you know. He'd tap the mike with a pencil to do the sound of a hit. He didn't make the fans nervous but calm. He was like that because he respected people, and he got respect himself because of it."

Reagan's high school and college girlfriend broke up with him because she'd found somebody else, and the way he wrote about it in his first memoir you can tell it hurt, but it didn't seem to slow him down. He continued to do his work and have some interesting experiences, some of which he often referred to in old age.

Once when he was a sports announcer the flamboyant evangelist Aimee Semple McPherson came to town, and someone at the station decided Reagan should interview her. On the air he asked her a few serious questions and she gave him some answers. She then launched into a fervent plea to the audience to support her ministry and come to her meetings. And then she said good night.

But there were about four minutes to go. Reagan furiously signaled to a sleepy engineer to play some music. Then he ad-libbed, "Ladies and gentlemen, we conclude this broadcast by the noted evangelist Aimee Semple McPherson with a brief interlude of music." The engineer nodded and Reagan sat back waiting to hear "Ave Maria." Instead what he heard was the first record the engineer grabbed, the Mills Brothers' "Minnie the Moocher's Wedding Day."

He covered the Chicago Cubs, and volunteered to follow them to spring training camp in California. He hoped this would look dedicated but he later said he just wanted to get away from the cold Iowa winter, and have some fun. What he didn't say, oddly enough, is that he wanted to go there because that's where the movies were and maybe something would happen. Which is surprising because it seems pretty obvious that's what he was thinking. But Reagan didn't always share with people his particular ambitions, or their scope. Which is odd because he was very ambitious: Wherever he went, from school to college to radio he managed to compete, win and rise. But somehow he doesn't seem to have liked the picture of himself as someone who wanted a lot.

He arrived in Los Angeles and took a trolley to Republic studios to see a local Midwestern band play in a Gene Autry cowboy movie. He stayed at the Biltmore Hotel and looked up a girl he knew who sang in the hotel's show. They had dinner and he told her about what he'd seen at Republic that day, the actors and cameras and lights.

Then he told her of his longing. She'd gone to California to be a movie star herself, and was pretty savvy. She told him to take off his glasses. She took a close look at him and said she'd send him to an agent, Bill Meiklejohn. Reagan walked into his office the next day. He wasn't wearing his glasses so he looked better but he couldn't see Meiklejohn's expression. He later said it was a nice conversation if you don't mind talking to a skin-colored blur.

Meiklejohn called the casting director at Warner Bros., Max Arnow, and announced grandly, "Max, I have another Robert Taylor sitting in my office."

"God made only one Robert Taylor," Max Arnow said.

Reagan still couldn't see a thing, but he gathered things were going well. Arnow agreed to meet with him and Reagan went to his office. Arnow wasn't wild about Reagan's looks but he liked his voice. He gave him a screen test and Reagan did a scene from *The Philadelphia Story.* Then he went back to Des Moines. He got a telegram offering a seven-year contract at two hundred dollars a week and sent Meiklejohn a wire: "Sign before they change their minds."

He bought a car, a Nash convertible, and drove to California, and what he remembered was the way the sun shone on his head the whole way. (Let me tell you something that is both too corny to believe and true. Those who were there the overcast day he was sworn in as governor of California swear that as he took the oath the sun peeked out of the clouds and shone on him. And those who were there the cloudy day he was inaugurated as president in 1980 say the sun spilled out of the clouds as he put up his hand to take the oath. I know it doesn't sound true, but it is.)

Ronald Reagan got to Hollywood in 1937. That's the same year they made the original version of the movie classic *A Star Is Born* with Janet Gaynor and Fredric March. Gaynor is Esther Blodgett, midwestern innocent, who comes to Hollywood to break into the movies. They hired her because they liked her looks, so the first thing they did before giving her a role was change her looks.

Something like that happened to Reagan.

The studio stylist looked at his haircut and sniffed that it looked like it had been cut with bowl number seven. They changed his part from the middle, gave him a new hair style, told him his head was too small and his clothes were all wrong and his neck was too short. They got Jimmy Cagney's shirtmaker—Cagney had a short neck too—to make Reagan some dress shirts with his special collar, short in the back of the neck and long in the front.

They came up with new names for Esther Blodgett and they tried to do the same with Reagan. But once again Ronald Reagan, aka Dutch, was sensitive about what he was called and pointed out he had a lot of name recognition back in the Midwest. It would be a shame to lose it.

They said, We can't call you Dutch Reagan on a marquee.

He said, Okay, how about Ronald?

They thought that wasn't too bad.

He was twenty-six years old and rubbing elbows with Errol Flynn and Olivia de Havilland. He'd never been east of Chicago, north of Minneapolis or south of the Ozarks and now he was breezing through the lot with Warner Bros. stars.

His first role was in a B movie called *Love Is on the Air.* He played a radio announcer. He had the worst stage fright of his life. Then they slapped makeup on him and the director yelled "Camera . . . Action!" and his fears disappeared, dropping away like the skin of an old self. (When he was old and one of his early movies would appear on TV, he'd watch and later remark that it was like watching a son you didn't know you'd had.)

Other parts followed—male ingenue, cadet, newspaperman, teacher, cavalryman. The *Hollywood Reporter* called him fresh faced and natural, and Warner Bros. renewed his contract and gave him a raise.

He fit his times, or rather the style of his era. He entered Hollywood in the great days of Stars Are Nice. It was considered important for your career in those days to show you were a nice person. Happy stars like Jack Carson and Mickey Rooney and Ann Sheridan posed for magazines smiling merrily, playfully. Manly stars like Clark Gable and Gary Cooper smiled for the cameras too. Sultry stars like young Jean Harlow had press agents to alert the papers that they entertained orphans at dinner and helped at the old peoples' home.

A later generation—maybe it started with Robert Mitchum, or Marlon Brando or James Dean—knew how deeply uncool it was to be a grinning idiot in a movie poster. The 1950s were called, by W. H. Auden, the age of anxiety, and its stars reflected this mood in the surly look, the mumbled dialogue, the slouch—all of which seemed proof of authenticity, which was more important than niceness, and certainly hipper.

Reagan's generation of stars never understood the new generation any more than the new generation understood them. Among the things that startled and displeased the classically trained Raymond Massey about the young James Dean when they starred together in *East of Eden* was not only his raw emotionalism and his wiggy-seeming artistic improvisation, but also his posture. He couldn't even stand up straight!

Raymond Massey understood James Dean about as well as Ronald Reagan understood Patti, his daughter. Which is to say, not much.

Reagan sent for his parents. They came to California and he bought them the first house they'd ever owned. But he didn't want to injure his father's pride so he came up with a plan. He told his father he had so much fan mail he felt overwhelmed, couldn't handle it on his own, could his parents help? Sure they could. His father became head of the Ronald Reagan fan club, and took care of the mail and other demands of young stardom.

He was doing well but he hadn't hit the top. That changed with the part of George Gipp, the Gipper, in *Knute Rockne, All American.* Reagan had actually arrived in Hollywood with an idea for a screenplay about Gipp, and had talked to people about what a wonderful movie it would make. But by the time they were making it Reagan got none of the credit, and he had to fight for the part. The studio executives didn't see him as a football player, so he brought in his pictures of being suited up in college.

He played Custer in *Santa Fe Trail* and Drake in *Kings Row,* a bestselling novel and then movie of the time. In *Desperate Journey* he costarred with the great Errol Flynn—they were RAF pilots together.

He learned the ropes, learned his lines, was clearly ambitious but never struck people as driven or hungry. He was not without guile though. His friend from those days, the producer A. C. Lyles, remembers the sand story. "I never saw Ronnie in any scene try to take something away from another actor. He was always helping other actors, really. But in this scene the director set up a shot, and Ronnie had the second lead, and someone was obstructing Ronnie, getting in his way in the shot. They were on location, as I remember, and there was sand around them on the ground. And before the scene began, while they were all talking—and this is the only time I've ever known Ronnie to do this—before the camera started he very gently moved together some dirt with his boot. And he moved more and more, and soon he had a little mound of dirt. And just before the camera started he very gently put himself on the mound, which elevated him a couple inches and put him in a much better spot for the cameras! But the thing that's interesting is Ronnie told that story on himself—that's why people knew it, he laughed at the humor of it and how he tried to protect himself."

He fell in love with an actress who was playing a part that he could understand. They met on the set of a comedy, a good one that still stands up, *Brother Rat.* He was a cadet at the Virginia Military Institute (VMI), she a secretary. It was a hit for both of them and they fell in love, which seems to have surprised nobody.

"Janie Wyman was adorable," A. C. Lyles told me. Lyles is eighty-three now, still goes to work on the Paramount lot every day. When he and Reagan met, Reagan was new in town, and Lyles was a young publicist. They hit it off and got to know each other well over the years. Lyles knew Wyman well too, and still does.

"Janie Wyman started out in little bit parts," he tells me in the commissary at Paramount in the spring of 2001. "Janie Wyman got to be an important star. Jane Wyman won an Academy Award, she had great respect in the industry as an actress and great respect as a person. And she had an acute sense of humor, a wonderful sense of humor. And she really, like Ronnie, came up the hard way, with small parts. Louella Parsons took a particular interest in Jane before they were married, and used to publicize Jane and Ronnie a lot. . . . You have to admire Jane because she never took advantage of being Ronnie's first wife, she never talked about it. And every now and then I'd see her and we'd talk and I'd just insert, 'Ronnie's fine, he's in good health.' She'd nod but never picked up on it. She's a class lady. She's a devout Catholic. Down in Palm Springs she was very close to Loretta Young, who was also a very good Catholic. I think she went to mass every morning at nine o'clock." With Irene Dunne, he tells me. "They used to call them the Vatican Set."

"I finally met her," Patti Davis told me.

In the difficult winter of 2000, when Ronald Reagan was on one floor of a hospital with a broken hip and his daughter Maureen, recovering from cancer surgery, was on another, Patti went to visit them. "We were never allowed to talk about her, and I never met her. And when Maureen was in the hospital and I went to see her, Jane Wyman came in. And Michael [the adopted son of Ronald Reagan and Jane Wyman] was there. And I said to her, 'Hi, it's so nice to finally meet you.' And Michael said to me, 'You've never met her before?' And I said, 'Michael, when would I?'

"She's in her eighties, she's quite thin, dyes her hair brown, she's pretty, her makeup is very well done. It was around Christmastime and she was dressed in one of those kind of Christmas sweaters. Black pants. But she was in a wheelchair because she has terrible arthritis. Very thin. I looked at her looking at Maureen and the sadness in her eyes—it hurt my heart. . . . She and Maureen seemed very loving."

When Janie and Ronnie married, on January 16, 1940, in Beverly Hills, he knew it was for life. He felt his life had really come together, that he was part of something and that it worked. She was a wonderful actress and just as ambitious as he and when they became a couple it enhanced them both. She was six years younger than he, but had been married before, twice. She had had a hard life: abandoned by her father when a child and later abandoned by her mother with neighbors, who brought her up. She had gone to Hollywood in her teens, had worked her way up, had learned to be wary. But from the moment she met Ronald Reagan she knew she could trust him, knew he was decent. He made her feel safe.

They built a house on Cordell Drive in Los Angeles, and they brought home money and he didn't drink and they rose in the world and soon they had a daughter, Maureen, and then adopted a son, Michael.

Ronald Reagan made thirteen movies in his first year and a half in Hollywood, and he was told he had to join the union. He balked—why did actors need unions? Actors were artists, artists don't have unions. But then he learned that while the big stars could negotiate their own contracts, the marginal players and walk-ons and others didn't have that power, and were often abused by studio heads. Then he found out some of them had been blacklisted for trying to start a union to protect themselves.

Reagan got mad. Maybe he heard the sound of Jack Reagan talking about the rights of the working man ringing in his ears. He eagerly joined the Screen Actors Guild, and soon he was put on the board to represent the younger players.

And this was when his father changed. After living in California a few years something happened to him. He was approaching sixty years of age, and he had seen his son become a great success. He had seen life turn sweet, and he wondered if it couldn't have been sweeter long ago. He told his wife he'd been thinking their life would have been much better if he'd never drunk, or if he'd stopped drinking ten or twenty years before. He told her that he would never drink again.

Nelle sighed, "You've said that before."

He said, "But I've never done this before." And he got a jug of wine he'd hidden from her in a cupboard, and poured it down the sink.

And he didn't drink again.

Just before that he'd had the greatest moment of his life. Jack went to Notre Dame, the great Irish Catholic college of America, for the premier of *Knute Rockne.* He was transported by what he'd seen on the screen—little Dutch, the Dutchman, and his speech at the end—"Win one for the Gipper."

He told his wife what it had meant to him. "I was there when our son became a star."

He died at fifty-eight, of heart disease.

Nelle lived on another twenty years, the last ones hard because she was sick. She had a disease that was then known as hardening of the arteries or senility but later came to be called Alzheimer's.

In August of 1942, Ronald Reagan wrote an essay for *Photoplay,* the fan magazine, called "How to Make Yourself Important." You can hear in it the MGM-approved aw-shucks tone of the 1930s movie star, but you can also hear the happy ego, the real if slightly forced humility.

It sounds too like dialogue from a war movie with all the guys in the company sitting around talking about life. He'd be the young farm boy, not quite a hick but not quite sophisticated.

Here is his hearty proletarian voice:

> *A fine and fancy storyteller holds his punch for the story's end, I'm sure. But as I'm a plain guy with a set of homespun features and no frills, I may as well write accordingly. . . . I hold that all of this business about making yourself important by means of externals is no good. Clothes, being seen in the Right Places, show, swank—No! . . . Nor do I believe that you have to be a standout from your fellow men in order to make your mark in the world. Average will do it. Certainly if I am to serve as my own guinea pig for this little homily, it will have to do it. For I'm not Flynn or Boyer, and well I know it. . . .*
>
> *I like to swim, hike and sleep (eight hours a night). I'm fairly good at every sport except tennis, which I just don't like. My favorite menu is steaks smothered with onions and strawberry shortcake. I play bridge adequately, collect guns, always carry a penny as a good-luck charm and*

knock wood when I make a boast or express a wish. I have a so-so convertible coupe which I drive myself. I'm interested in politics and governmental problems. My favorite books are Turnabout *by Thorne Smith,* Babbitt, The Adventures of Tom Sawyer, *and the works of Pearl Buck, H. G. Wells, Damon Runyon and Erich Remarque. . . .*

Lots of kids write and ask my advice about how to make their mark in an indifferent world. . . . So what I'd like to tell 'em is this: Look, you must love what you are doing. You must think what you are doing is important because if it's important to you, you can bet your last ducat that other people will think so, too. It may take time, but they'll get around to it. And one thing more, one really important thing: If, when you get a job, you don't believe you can get to the top in it, it's the wrong job. . . .

For me, one job in the world I want to do is acting. Offer me ten times the money for something else, and I wouldn't do it. And right from the start, down there in "B" pictures where I began, through four years of "bit" parts (the "Poor Man's Errol Flynn" they called me), I was sure that I was in the right business for me, I knew I'd get to the top, if I went on working and learning. That's not brash self-confidence, either. Put me in any other job and I'd eat humble pies by the dozen. I'd lack self-confidence because I'd be in the wrong job. . . .

Thanks to some good advice from a guy named Pat O'Brien, I played those "B's" as if they were "A's." You see, the boss only goes by results. If I do a part carelessly because I doubt its importance, no one is going to write a subtitle explaining that Ronald Reagan didn't feel the part was important, therefore he didn't give it very much. . . .

Quite a few times, before Knute Rockne, *parts came up in pictures that I thought I'd like to play. In* Dark Victory *with Bette Davis, for example, they handed me a bit part. I stewed around a bit, wishing I'd got the part Bogart played in that picture. Then I realized I couldn't top Bogey in that. It was his dish, not mine. In* Kings Row, *Parris was not for me, but Drake, I think, was. In* Desperate Journey, *Flynn's spot is his, not mine.*

But I knew that I could deliver the Gipp. I knew it because when I was a kid, George Gipp was my hero, Rockne was my candidate for A Man. There was that love of what I was doing figuring in again. In addition, I knew I could play football and they wouldn't have to use a double for me. . . .

That part opened a door for me. A few people on the lot knew me by name. . . .

I've just been told, here at the studio, of two very important parts that were to be mine. They are in pretty big pictures, so I guess I can say my rules work. But I won't be doing those pictures. Uncle Sam has called me, a Reserve Officer in the Cavalry, and I'm going off to war, still true to my precepts: (a) to love what you are doing with all your heart and soul and (b) to believe what you are doing is important. I love the Cavalry. . . . (A)nd along with a few million other guys I feel pretty strong about my country. As for believing what you are doing is important—well, if fighting to preserve the United States and her Allies isn't important, you name it.

And who knows—maybe when I get back again, "when the world is free," there will be other good parts waiting for me and for my buddies.

So long!

You couldn't be more cornball, you couldn't be more the happy young man on the way up, believing in the possibilities provided by America and believing in its war. It is the sound Tennessee Williams affectionately nailed when he created the Gentleman Caller in *The Glass Menagerie.* Which is who Reagan reminded me of forty years later when I worked for him in the White House.

When Ronald Reagan was thirty years old the Second World War began. He was an officer in the U.S. Cavalry Reserves, and three months after Pearl Harbor he was called to active duty at Fort Mason, outside San Francisco. They made him a liaison officer loading convoys with troops. He had to take a new physical and he failed it because of his eyes. One doctor said, "If we send you overseas you'll shoot a general." A second doctor said, "Yes, and you'd miss him." Reagan was confined to noncombat service and transferred to army air force intelligence back in LA. There he worked under General Hap Arnold making air force training films and documentaries.

He was a second lieutenant, and he helped develop a new method for briefing pilots and bombardiers before their bombing missions.

No more officer with a pointer and a map pointing out targets—now they'd put a replica of Tokyo and the Japanese coast on a soundstage, and with a camera on a derrick they'd make a movie of what the crew would see. The film was airlifted to bomber bases in the Pacific.

The unit also received and prepared classified films to be shown to the general staff in Washington. There were things in those films that other people didn't know. That's how Reagan saw the death camps, and he never got over what he saw.

He remembered one especially. "It showed the interior of a huge building," he said. "Our troops had just taken over a camp and had entered the building. It was cavernous, like a warehouse. And the floor was covered with bodies. Then, as we watched in horror, one of the bodies rose up on an elbow and a hand reached up—a hand rising out of a sea of bodies, as if it were pleading for help." That was Reagan writing about it almost fifty years later.

He kept a copy of the film for a very serious and sophisticated reason. He remembered that after World War I there had been charges that America had been manipulated into the war with phony propaganda about "Bleeding Belgium." He wanted to keep proof of who Hitler was and what Nazism stood for and had done. In later years, when anyone voiced doubt about the Holocaust, he showed the film to them. He showed it to his sons when they became teenagers. His daughter Patti told me that he'd shown the film to her too, that her father had wanted his children to know what the war was about. It had been upsetting for them. It gave her nightmares.

When he was president, the fact that he had seen those films before almost anyone else in the country would become the basis for an embarrassment. And I think I know how it happened. Visitors to his White House had spoken to him pleadingly of the villainy of the Nazis and the horror of the camps, and he had replied that he knew, he'd been there, he'd seen it. Meaning: He was there when the films came in, he'd seen them in their rawest, most immediate form. His visitors thought he was saying he'd been at Auschwitz. "You were there?" they said. "Yes!" said a half-deaf and wholly confident Reagan, who thought he was being asked if he'd been present when the first films came in. His visitors, unhappy with him, told the press that poor Reagan is such a fantasist or so senile now that he thinks he was in the concentration camps.

But Reagan never thought he was in the camps. He wasn't a liar by nature, and it would have been extraordinary if he'd started lying about this when he was president after he'd told the truth about it all his life. He had written extensively of his experience in the war—and of his experience receiving the death camp films, and what they meant to him—in his first memoir, and in many speeches, and in interviews over the years. And he wasn't senile. But he was half deaf.

When the war was over he became a movie actor again, but he'd missed four years. So had Jimmy Stewart and Clark Gable but they were bigger, more important stars than he, and their return was big news. They fit right in and picked up pretty much where they'd left off. Reagan didn't. It was harder for him now. He didn't get a lot of the big parts that he was hoping for, and now they were putting him in movies like *Stallion Road* with Zachary Scott. His wife, meanwhile, was becoming a very big star indeed, starring in *The Yearling* and soon receiving an Academy Award as Best Actress for her role as a deaf mute in *Johnny Belinda*.

It was a tough time for Reagan. And what was ahead for him was tougher still.

And Here He Becomes the Man He Was

What he returned to when he went back to his career was strife of all kinds, personal, professional and political. Up to now his life had been marked by challenge met by effort which yielded reward: "Ask and it shall be given you; seek, and ye shall find." He'd sought and asked, worked hard, dreamed big and wound up doing work he loved that gave him wealth, satisfaction and respect.

His life had been guided by an internal logic. But now, in his midthirties, effort would no longer achieve what it had and faith would sometimes seem foolish. Things turned murky, mysterious even. Ronald Reagan was forced back on his resources, and forced to develop new ones. New parts of his character would emerge and come to dominate.

More than ever he was preoccupied by talk of politics and public policy, and now he gave more time to them in after-dinner speeches to groups that wanted to have a say in the roiling post–World War II world. The studio hadn't found work for him and speaking made him feel part of things, as if he were still a voice in the community. His standard speech included support of New Deal programs, of fair breaks for the veteran, of the rightness of collective bargaining and justice for unions. He spoke in support of Americanism and against neofascism, by which he meant the rise of groups that promoted discrimination based on race or religion. He wanted, he later said, to save the world, and joined every group that said it knew how, from the United World Federalists to the American Veterans Committee.

And it was on the local speakers' circuit that he began to see that something new was going on. Once, after a speech at the Hollywood Beverly Christian Church, the pastor approached him to say he agreed with everything Reagan said about neofascism, but he might consider adding a warning about communism too.

Reagan had always felt that people who worried about "the Russians" were "paranoid," blind to other, bigger issues. Russia had been our ally in the war, had been brutalized by Hitler. Reagan thought "the nearest Communists were fighting in Stalingrad." And he was a Democrat; anticommunism seemed a preoccupation of reactionaries and Republicans.

He told the pastor he had never given much thought to denouncing Communists, but sure, if they ever seemed a threat to freedom he would oppose them. In the next speech he made he repeated what he'd said at the Beverly Christian Church, and was interrupted by applause, as he remembered it, twenty times. Then he added on a new ending. He said that though there is a continuing threat of fascism in the new world following the war, there is "another ism." It is communism, and "if I ever find evidence that communism represents a threat to all that we believe in and stand for, I'll speak out just as harshly against communism as I have fascism."

He walked off the stage to something he wasn't used to hearing: silence. He remembered it as shattering, an actual shock.

A few days later he got a letter from a woman in the audience. She said she'd been disturbed for some time about something sinister going on within the organization he'd spoken to. "I'm sure you noticed the reaction to your last paragraph when you mentioned communism. I hope you recognize what that means. I think the group is becoming a front for Communists. I just wanted you to know that that settled it for me. I resigned from the organization the next day."

This, Reagan later said, is how he began to "wake up" to the fact that something new and disturbing might be happening in the motion picture industry. And the key to what disturbed him is a phrase the woman used—"front for Communists." Reagan loved argument, loved freedom and thought everyone should join the fray—anarchists, Wobblies, monarchists, whatever. But if a political group refused to come forward publicly and put forth its programs in the democratic daylight; if it chose to pursue power secretly, by guile and deception, silently taking over institutions and moving for power through force—well, that was what the Nazis did in Germany. That's what Fascists and the supporters of dictators do. That wasn't the American style at all.

Union strikes had largely been suspended during the war, but when it ended, they broke out with a vengeance. There were more than forty professional and crafts unions in the movie industry with different brotherhoods, conferences, histories and jurisdictions. A number of them had had to resist mob influence in the 1930s, and now, as Reagan and his friends came to see it, they were struggling with an even greater challenge.

From the remove of more than half a century the words "Communist infiltration" sound archaic, paranoid and intellectually embarrassing. It's the kind of phrase the bad guys use in movies about the victims of the Hollywood blacklist. There was no Communist infiltration, these movies seem to say, it was all the result of hysteria and bigotry, and those who warned against communism in Hollywood were liars, bullies and cynics. This is a compelling, dramatic and emotionally inspiring vision of events, and it may well endure, or—at least through our lifetimes—be accepted as the essential or at least poetic truth.

But the hard facts of those days continue to war with the easy myths.

A strike was called involving a number of industry unions. Should the actors cross the picket lines? Meetings were held, fact-finding initiatives launched.

Reagan, as a member of the Screen Actors Guild, was part of a group asked to come up with findings. They concluded that the strikes weren't over wages and working conditions but over jurisdictional disputes—who got to do what work. Reagan recommended that, in keeping with Guild bylaws, the strikes not be honored. Guild leadership agreed.

The entire Guild would meet at a Hollywood stadium to discuss the issue, and Reagan was to present the Guild's findings to the membership. A few days before the meeting he got a call on the set of a movie he was working on. An unidentified man warned him that if he showed up and made the speech, "Your face will never be in pictures again."

The Burbank police came to the studio and hung a .32 Smith & Wesson and a holster under his arm. He had to wear it for the next seven months. He was put under twenty-four-hour guard. He later found out there was a plan to throw acid in his face so he would never work again.

Reagan made his speech and Guild membership backed his view—2,748 to 509—but the strikes continued, and the gates of the studios became a battleground. Actors and studio workers started traveling together to the studios in caravans. Cars were firebombed, people beaten, arms broken.

Strike talks were called and continued every day. For months Reagan and SAG tried to make progress, but just when a settlement seemed within reach there would be new demands, new walkouts.

Later, the reason would become clear. Members of the Communist Party who had been involved in the unrest went public and admitted Moscow had directed much of the action. When the California Senate Fact Finding Committee on Un-American Activities held an inquiry they concluded the strike was part of a Soviet effort to gain control over Hollywood and the content of its films. Outside Los Angeles, the national leaders of the unions involved charged that the principal local leader of the strike was "willfully and knowingly associated with groups subservient to the Communist Party." Reagan did not know this at the time, and neither did almost anyone else who was trying to take an honest stand. But he had inklings, and soon enough, convictions.

As Reagan struggled to understand the labor unrest he felt secure, at least, in this: His allies in the fight to oppose Communist influence were many of Hollywood's most respected New Deal liberals who were battling in Hollywood what Eleanor Roosevelt and others were at the same time battling back east, in New York and Washington: the rise of a radical left within their party that accepted or supported communism. (One of the best books on that struggle is Arthur Schlesinger's recent memoir, *A Life in the Twentieth Century.*)

As Reagan learned more about communism, he spoke about it more often, and withdrew his membership from groups he later learned were Communist fronts. One night the FBI came to his house and told him that anyone as hated by the Communists as he was must know some things that could be helpful. Reagan protested that he wasn't a red baiter and the agents said fine, but if there is ever anything you can tell us that would help us, we'd appreciate it. Reagan asked how they'd heard about his anticommunism. They said his name had come up during a meeting of the party in downtown LA, that a member had stood and said, "What are we going to do about that son-of-a-bitching bastard Reagan?" The agents said anyone who was that despised should know about it.

What Reagan seemed to have gathered from their visit was that they seemed well meaning, and, obviously, they were also monitoring Hollywood citizens.

He joined a group called the Hollywood Independent Citizens Committee of the Arts, Sciences and Professions, HICCASP. It was a Democratic Party group formed to support New Deal and Democratic Party programs. He was asked to join the board, was flattered, went to his first meeting and wound up confused. The room was full of stars, actors, writers and others in the industry, about seventy in all. But a number of them were known by Reagan to be on the hard left. And everyone there, it turned out, was a board member.

Reagan sat down next to the head of MGM, the respected and powerful Dore Schary. Reagan whispered to him that there were people there he was surprised to see. Schary looked at him strangely and said, "Stick around."

The meeting went smoothly until James Roosevelt, the son of Franklin D. Roosevelt, rose to his feet and said that some members of HICCASP were concerned about rumors that the group had become a Communist front. He asked that they reassure the public by issuing a declaration of principles that repudiated communism.

Reagan was heartened; Jimmy Roosevelt, son of his hero, was seeing things the same way he was. But the reaction to Roosevelt's request astonished him.

As Reagan later wrote in his memoir *Where's the Rest of Me?*, "A well known musician sprang to his feet. He offered to recite the USSR Constitution from memory, yelling that it was a lot more democratic than that of the United States. A prominent movie writer leaped upward. He said that if there was ever a war between the United States and Russia, he would volunteer for Russia . . . "

Reagan took to his feet, defending Jimmy Roosevelt and endorsing his proposal. Now he found himself "waist high in epithets such as 'Fascist' and 'capitalist scum' and 'enemy of the proletariat' and 'witch hunter' and 'red baiter . . .' "

Reagan was shocked. A group he held in high regard had broken out in a brawl over "a simple statement which I thought any American would be proud to subscribe to."

The meeting broke up. But on the way out Dore Schary whispered, "Come up to Olivia de Havilland's apartment."

Reagan did. He found a dozen people in a festive mood. They had deliberately asked Jimmy Roosevelt to make his request in order to smoke out who would oppose such an innocuous statement. They had become convinced that local Communists were trying to take over the organization. (Olivia de Havilland had become suspicious when a speech she was supposed to make as a member of HICCASP, and which was obligingly written by the gifted screenwriter Dalton Trumbo, had been full of left-wing propaganda. It had given her pause.) What they hadn't apparently expected was Reagan's speech in support of Roosevelt.

Hearing all this, Reagan started to smile at de Havilland. She asked why. "I thought you were one," he said, meaning a Communist or a sympathizer. She smiled back. "I thought *you* were one," she said.

The de Havilland group drafted a statement of policy, with Reagan scribbling—"me and Lincoln"—on the back of an envelope. The new statement was bland right up until the final phrase. "We reaffirm our belief in free enterprise and the democratic system and repudiate communism as desirable for the United States."

A few nights later there was a joint committee meeting at Jimmy Roosevelt's home. The statement was read. Again a verbal brawl ensued, with screenwriter John Howard Lawson shouting that HICCASP would never endorse free enterprise and repudiate communism. "And, for your information," Reagan later quoted him, "I may add that a two-party system is in no way necessary or even desirable for democracy!"

Reagan said the draft statement was too important to be decided only by the board. He suggested it be decided by the entire membership, and by secret ballot.

Lawson said the membership wasn't "sophisticated enough" to make a decision. The phrase struck Reagan as telling, and elitist. Ultimately the draft statement was voted on—and defeated—in special executive committee. Olivia de Havilland phoned her friends later to report she was the only yes vote.

Reagan resigned, as did a number of others, and soon HICCASP disbanded. In 1948, a California State Senate investigation said HICCASP had been a Communist front group whose depredations included a "callous . . . betrayal of Jewish victims of Nazi persecution during the Hitler-Stalin pact."

Hollywood in those days, at that time, was a hard place in which to be an honest man or woman. Reagan was trying to remain a liberal at a moment when it seemed to him that liberals had gone blind. They had understood in the thirties and forties who the Nazis were, and led the fight against them. But now, as evidence of Communist efforts within the film industry grew, they seemed not only unwilling to oppose them but a number of them seemed to support them.

Throughout these days, Reagan had gone from surprised to perplexed to indignant to coolly angry. It was his great education, the time when he went from naïve and trusting to knowing and tough. He said, "I was to discover that a lot of 'liberals' just couldn't accept the notion that Moscow had bad intentions or wanted to take over Hollywood and many other American industries through subversion, or that Stalin was a murderous gangster."

Reagan received a phone call one day from his close friend the actor William Holden. It was right after the big HICCASP fight. There would be a meeting at Ida Lupino's house that night, Holden said, and the now-usual cast of characters would be there. Reagan, he said, should go with him. Reagan protested, "Ida isn't one of *them*."

Holden said he knew that, that a handful of innocents, big names including Lupino, had been invited to hear about the industry strike situation. Ida was just lending her patio.

Reagan and Holden talked more, agreed it looked like an attempt at "a brainwash job" by the hard left, and decided to go.

Ida Lupino greeted them warmly, but when Holden and Reagan got out to the patio the air thickened. It was a big group, and Reagan and Holden quietly took seats in the corner and listened as the meeting began. A speaker gave an explanation for all of the strike activity, but Reagan could see that it was not honest, was in fact extremely biased. He immediately wanted to speak.

But Holden held him back, kept telling him to wait. Finally, after all the others had had their say, Holden told Reagan, "Now!"

Reagan stood. It was a hostile audience. Reagan told them the real history of the strikes. He spoke for almost forty minutes, praising them for their interest and telling them what the SAG investigations had learned. He was telling them things they had never heard, and when he was done he was pounded with questions, many of them hostile. There were boos and some name-calling. At one point the actor John Garfield spoke up for Reagan. "Why don't you listen to him? He does have information you don't have."

This was a surprise: Garfield had long been close with those on the left in the industry.

Reagan continued to speak, and as he did, he saw something he would never forget. As he stood in front of the group he saw, over the heads of the audience facing him, one of the most poignant moments in that terrible time.

Again, Reagan: "I saw a well-known character actor take John [Garfield] to the back of the garden. . . . I could see him back John up against a tree and, with one hand holding him by the shirt front, he read an angry riot act, punctuated by a jabbing finger. While I could hear nothing of what was said, I was so fascinated by the tableau I almost forgot to parry the hostile shots coming my own way. John stayed back there, leaning against the tree, hands deep in his pockets, after the actor left him, and finally he edged his way to a back gate and left."

Later Reagan told Holden what he'd seen, and they talked about calling Garfield to discuss it over a few drinks. But they didn't, and for the rest of his life Reagan regretted it.

When Garfield died of a heart attack a few years later, "like a voice from the grave, the press carried the story of his last forty-eight hours. He had gone to the FBI and the House committee and poured out a story of fourteen years in which the Communist Party had turned him on and off like a hot water faucet." Garfield had told them he had tried to break away once, but they had talked him back into line.

Reagan thought he knew exactly when that happened: that night in the garden at Ida Lupino's.

And yet—paradox within paradox, complexity within complexity

—Reagan saw that as the Hollywood wars heated up, Washington politicians were demagoguing the issue, drawn by the lights. They held congressional hearings, issued subpoenas, accused people of being Communists or being part of intentions to subvert and politicize the industry. Reagan felt they were focusing on Hollywood in part to advance themselves: going after the famous would make them famous, and going after libertine Hollywood would appeal to lingering puritan prejudices against entertainers, artists and show folk.

Reagan also resented the feds zeroing in on artists who, in his view, were often more passionate than informed, more idealistic than sophisticated; they were actors and artists for goodness' sake, not academic interpreters of the Marxist dialectic.

Reagan understood that for so many people in those days it was a time when you could be honestly confused about where to stand to be a decent person, because who—what group, what individual—was decent wasn't always clear. You had to pick your way through a lot of broken glass to get to the patch that was clean and safe. Reagan picked his way through and tried to help others do the same thing. Ultimately he came to feel that what he was doing was this: He was trying to remain a liberal when liberals were blind.

These days were the crucible, the central experience of his adulthood, the great educator, the time that formed him and that he referred back to all of his life. "Back when we were fighting over the Communists and the unions and so forth . . ." When you worked with him it wasn't really his youth he talked about, or his young stardom that he referred to. More than broadcasting, more than acting, more than succeeding, this is what shaped the Reagan we came to know years later.

And it was not only the reality of communism, and the malign intent of Communists that pushed him to step forward. It was also the fact that Communists were fighting for control of Hollywood, his professional town, the great maker of the stories that explain America to Americans. (If you are middle aged and from the East and have a picture in your mind of the American West, what it looked like, its vast silence, you got it from the director John Ford; if you know what middle-class and suburban teenage life looked and sounded like in the 1950s, it was Nicholas Ray; if you can see Porkchop Hill or Anzio Beach or the office of a San Francisco private eye in the 1930s, it was a host of other producers, directors, writers and actors who gave it to you. To this day they show America to Americans, and the world.)

And precisely what stiffened Reagan's resolve was what might have weakened another person's, and that was the reaction of so many Hollywood stars and leaders with whom he'd stood at previous barricades, with whom he'd fought the war, with whom he shared a love of Franklin Roosevelt and the Democratic Party and the New Deal. A lot of them ducked. A lot of them argued that Communists were just messy or dramatic or vulgar or confused liberals.

In putting his name and livelihood on the line in a murky and charged era in Hollywood and American history, he was becoming a person of heroic fairness. His new enemies—the kind of people who yelled at him at big meetings and told him to sit down—were committed. His new friends—the kind of people who yelled back—were besieged.

Because of the integrity and moderation he showed in this atmosphere, and because of the leadership he showed, he was nominated to become president of the Screen Actors Guild. He accepted and was resoundingly elected.

Now he was a union chief, and now he faced issues beyond strikes and communism and congressional investigations. There were other complicated and demanding questions, from the development of contract-negotiating positions to fighting international treaties under which actors and entertainers were forced to pay double income tax if they worked overseas. There were battles between SAG and studio chiefs such as Jack Warner over the right of the chiefs to fire Communists; Reagan and SAG opposed any blacklists, and spoke against blacklisting publicly. There were continued jurisdictional disputes between other unions and within SAG itself. On top of it all, there were censorship disputes, including one in which the Hays Office, to Reagan's dismay, cut dialogue that might have become unforgettable. Reagan later wrote of a scene in Howard Hughes's movie *The Outlaw*:

"In the improbable plot," Reagan wrote in *Where's the Rest of Me?*, "the sheriff had found Billy the Kid with his girl. 'O.K.,' said Billy, as the mammacious figure of Jane Russell stood sideways between them. 'You stole my horse, I stole your girl.' The sheriff nodded. 'Sure,' he replied. 'Tit for tat.' "

Reagan said, "It was kind of a shame to lose such dialogue. A scene like that could become as immortal as Shakespeare's 'Alas, poor Yorick.' "

He also spent time negotiating SAG contracts between actors and studio heads, exhausting work on its own.

His experience leading the Screen Actors Guild would have great impact on his future. A. C. Lyles told me, "Being the president of SAG gave him a lot of self-confidence in governing a body. It also was great experience for him in that he had a lot of opposition in the Screen Actors Guild because they were a very liberal group. And being president of SAG is not easy because you're dealing with people who make tons of money and have a lot of adulation, as they should be because they're talented people. . . . And when he was head of the Guild, the contracts and facing the heads of the studios. And he could work with the opposition and work things out. His sense of humor was so great and so wonderful, and I never knew him to be in a situation that was so unpleasant that he couldn't use his sense of humor to come out of it. And it was just a natural sense of humor! He was so quick."

The Hollywood Communist wars of the late forties and early fifties continued, intensified by the attention of Washington. By the end, there were victims of injustice on both sides. A number of innocent political activists, Reagan later wrote, "were accused wrongly of being Communists simply because they were liberals." Reagan accused Washington of being drawn by the glamour and lights of the movies. "I was all for kicking Communists out of Hollywood, but some members of the House Un-American Activities Committee, ignoring standards of truth and fair play, ganged up on innocent people and tried to blacklist them." Among them, his close friend Jimmy Cagney, his admired colleague Humphrey Bogart "and other good Americans" were falsely accused.

Reagan went before HUAC to declare under oath that Hollywood was taking care of its problems, and didn't need or welcome the federal government's intrusion, or its investigations and subpoenas. "Ninety-nine percent of us are pretty well aware of what is going on, and I think we have done a pretty good job in our business of keeping those people's activities curtailed. I do not believe the Communists have ever at any time been able to use the motion picture screen as a sounding board for their philosophy or ideology."

Reagan, Olivia de Havilland and others with whom he had become close were determined to protect the innocent. And so they joined together again, forming an industry council to reach out to people who were being threatened with blacklisting and help them clear themselves. Reagan also pushed for the council to protect actors who were the focus of rumors and innuendos regarding their politics.

Near the end of the Hollywood Communist battles, Ronald Reagan received the greatest review of his life. The actor Sterling Hayden, a hero of World War II who had won a Bronze Star for fighting behind the lines in Yugoslavia, had come home to America and joined the Communist Party, in part as an act of loyalty and support to those anti-Nazi Communists he had fought alongside. But soon he renounced the party. He was later asked why the Communists had not succeeded in winning control of the movie industry. Hayden said they ran into "a one-man battalion of opposition" named Ronald Reagan.

"In the end, we stopped the Communists cold," Reagan later said. It was a brag, but few those days would have argued with his right to it.

And I would add, simply, that it was in this drama that Reagan's character was fully revealed. In a time of malice he was not malicious; in a time of lies he did not falsify; in a time of great pressure he didn't bend or break; in a time of disingenuousness he was clear and candid about where he stood and why. And in a time when people just gave up after a while and changed the subject, he remained on the field through all the long haul.

In January of 1998, to mark the fifty-year point since the blacklist battles began, the magazine of the Screen Actors Guild ran a special edition. It took the stand, unsurprisingly, that the Hollywood Communist wars were simply a matter of right-wing paranoia against mildly leftist artists.

But even in this history they could make no charge against Reagan except one, and the one they chose was, on the face of it, absurd. They suggested that Reagan, as he rose within SAG, became conservative because he knew "which ways the political winds were blowing." That is, he was a cynic operating for personal gain.

A cynic is absolutely the last thing Ronald Reagan was. He had grown sophisticated and with age would show skepticism, but Ronald Reagan was an idealist, and his lifelong struggle in whatever context he found himself was to determine what was right and then stand for it no matter what. And as for "which ways the political winds were blowing," they weren't blowing toward conservatism in the 1950s and 60s and 70s and 80s in Hollywood; they were blowing toward liberalism.

But even in the special SAG blacklist issue, when an interviewer tried to get one of those who had been blacklisted, the talented actress Marsha Hunt, to speak of Reagan's SAG leadership, she could make no criticism of him.

She said she knew him at the time. "He was a boring liberal. He would buttonhole you at a party and talk liberalism at you." Hunt then giggled, and suggested that whenever Reagan started talking about the New Deal she wanted to escape.

In the late forties there was a national backlash against Hollywood. Reagan was no longer a contract player; he'd been let go by Warner Bros. in a studio cost-cutting move, and was now a freelancer. Hollywood was becoming a popular target for politicians who considered it "a hotbed of reds and immoral conduct." And so now Reagan began to speak out in defense of the industry, telling conventions of theater owners how the citizens of Hollywood had responded on their own to the threats that had faced them. He was giving a couple of speeches a week, and soon he was speaking outside the industry and even the community, going to Rotary Clubs and Chambers of Commerce.

By 1950 his political transformation was in full swing. He still believed in the power of government—and the responsibility of government—to help people. He held to his father's convictions about helping the working man. But he was also seeing that the government, which had grown and taken new powers to itself to fight and win the war, was continuing to grow. Now it seemed to be promising what Reagan called "womb-to-tomb utopian benevolence." His own marginal tax rate was at 94 percent. He went to England and concluded that its now entrenched welfare state was sapping the will of a great country. Moreover, his brother, Moon, had left the Democratic Party. Ronald Reagan had argued with him and they'd shared joking debates, but in time he started to agree with Moon.

It is often said of Ronald Reagan that he became a conservative largely under the influence of his future father-in-law, Dr. Loyal Davis. He was a well-known neurosurgeon and the stepfather of Reagan's future wife, Nancy. I asked Mrs. Reagan about this, thinking that Dr. Davis must have made some kind of impact on Ronald Reagan. Mrs. Reagan said that it's an old story but not true. "My mother was a free spirit, and Loyal wasn't," she said. "But you know, if someone was operating on my brain I wouldn't want a free spirit! I'd want someone strict." She told me that Loyal Davis had a reputation as a very conservative man in part because of a sense of propriety. Once, in the sixties, he was doing rounds in the hospital at which he worked. It was late in his career, and one of the young doctors had long hair and love beads. Dr. Davis asked who he was and what he wanted. The young doctor said, "I'm here to go on rounds with you."

"No, you're not," said Davis.

"Yes, I am," said the young doctor.

"Oh no, you're not." Loyal Davis thought a doctor should, in the words of Nancy Reagan, "not be dressed in a long-hair, love-bead kind of way." The young doctor threatened to sue him.

So that was crusty old Loyal Davis. But when I asked Mrs. Reagan if Dr. Davis's conservatism hadn't affected her husband she said, "No, no, that's incorrect . . . Loyal didn't care that much about politics. He was conservative, but politics wasn't on his mind a lot as it was on Ronnie's mind. He didn't contribute to Ronnie's philosophy, Ronnie contributed to Loyal's interest in politics."

America owes a lot to the people who tried to do what was right in those days. But it should be pointed out that America owes a lot too to the old buccaneers who invented Hollywood and who came to head the studios—Jack Warner, Sam Goldwyn and others.

As president of the Screen Actors Guild, Ronald Reagan learned how to negotiate from these men. He learned how to play tough and be tough, how to feint, stall and vamp for time, how to wait them out, how to hold 'em and how to fold 'em; he learned how to smoke out the real reason for an impasse, or the one person who was standing in the way of agreement and why. He learned it's not personal, it's business, and sometimes it's not personal, it's politics.

The absorbing of these skills was the making of him. He would use them all the rest of his life, in every crisis of his life—knowing when to challenge a sitting president of the United States, when to quit, how to play it in the party afterward. He also used the skills he learned in Hollywood in every negotiation of his presidency, including at Reykjavik, where he came to the brink of a breathtaking historic legacy guaranteeing arms control . . . and left it on the table because he was convinced it would not be in America's long-term interests. The deal hinged on SDI, the system he hoped to create that would make America safe from incoming nuclear missiles. Soviet premier Gorbachev promised Reagan huge arms cuts if he would abandon SDI. But that convinced Reagan more than ever to hang tough: If the Soviets hate SDI that much, then SDI must be as promising, and as potentially reality changing, as Reagan thought it was.

Reagan learned how to think like that, and how to leave a good deal on the table, from Jack Warner and Sam Goldwyn and Louis B. Mayer. They taught him everything he knew by pulling every trick in the book on him. He never resented it, and always filed it away. And so America is greatly in the debt of those rough old pioneers.

A final note on how Reagan experienced his SAG leadership—the long meetings and arguments, the inevitable stresses. One of the reasons he enjoyed it so much was that he got to deal with show folk—with entertainers, with artists, with people whose first interest wasn't politics or collective bargaining but moving people, one way or another, from a stage or screen. They weren't stuffy or pretentious. Reagan painted a tender little moment when he wrote of those days.

It was the middle of the strikes, just before an important board meeting, when a handful of influential members were waiting for an elevator to take them up to the meeting room. The "dignified" Paul Harvey, "who played so many bankers and senators"; the song and dance man George Murphy; and the great dancer Gene Kelly talked, as they waited, about a serious matter that they would soon have to decide. Suddenly a door that led to a drugstore off the lobby opened, and a jukebox tune filled the air. Gene Kelly began to tap his foot and then execute a dance step; George Murphy began a tap routine; Paul Harvey went into a time step. "The elevator door opened and they stepped in, and none of them had changed expression or paused for a second in their heated discussion."

The years 1947–1950 were full of movement and action for Reagan, but they were also the worst years of his life, or at least the worst since the worst of his childhood. He almost died, his career almost died, and his marriage died.

"When sorrows come, they come not single spies/But in battalions." That's what happened to him as the century reached its midway point.

Reagan's career almost died for a number of reasons, including a movie called *That Hagen Girl.* It was Shirley Temple's first adult starring role after a life as the country's favorite prewar childhood star. Reagan didn't want to do the movie but had been pressured by the studio, and he couldn't fight back because he'd just been through a battle in which he'd resisted another role. The director-writer John Huston had, in Reagan's words, "dangled a role in his now-classic picture, *The Treasure of the Sierra Madre,* under my hammy nose." Huston didn't give him the part, and now Jack Warner made him do the Shirley Temple movie.

She played a high school girl who falls in love with a teacher, Reagan, who was in real life old enough to be her father.

Reagan could see trouble coming, kept pushing for rewrites in which Shirley would fall for a high school boy. He told the director, Peter Godfrey, "You know, all sorts of people sort of frown on men marrying girls young enough to be their daughters." Godfrey gave him a look and said, "I'm old enough to be my wife's father."

When the picture was almost complete there was a sneak preview. At the moment when Reagan's character says "I love you" to Shirley Temple the entire audience, Reagan later said, cried "Oh no." It must have been like the time he was a kid playing baseball, and the ball was hit straight to him, and he couldn't see it and let it fall.

He slunk down in his chair, then walked quickly from the theater.

Shortly before the screening he had become sick enough to be hospitalized. He had been rushed to Cedars of Lebanon Hospital with viral pneumonia. His temperature spiked, he was delirious; days and nights, he said, "went by in a hazy montage in which I alternately shivered with chills or burned with fever." He did not know it but on one of those nights, across town in another hospital, his wife Jane Wyman was suffering a miscarriage.

Reagan came near death. His behavior regressed, and he insisted on being wrapped in blankets and fed hot tea through a glass tube, which is what his mother had done when he was sick as a child. One night in his delirium he seemed to see a street lamp and a lonely patch of sidewalk. On it was Humphrey Bogart. Reagan saw them playing a scene over and over in which they would exchange trenchcoats, while saying lines to each other. Reagan could feel that they were surrounded by a feeling of danger.

He later said he did not know the meaning of "this Freudian delirium," but that night, the Bogart night, he almost died. He was so exhausted by the effort to breathe that some part of his brain decided it would be better not to. He told a nurse he was too tired to breathe anymore. She stayed with him, took his hand, coaxed him: *Take a breath, she'd say, now let it out. Good, now breathe in again. Okay, now out.*

She saved his life. He said she was so nice and persistent that he felt he had to do what she wanted.

Weeks later he was released, almost twenty pounds lighter and he couldn't get enough of looking out the windows of the ambulance because the world was so beautiful. He felt to a most extraordinary degree the sweetness of life, saw that it was full of fragrant gifts—lilies and flowers and freshly mowed lawns, hedges, beautiful houses, children walking by. It was the first time he remembered feeling that way, but not the last. He would feel it again thirty years later.

He was weak for months, even slight effort bringing on breathlessness and perspiration. Before he was fully recovered he had to report back to the set where they were finishing *That Hagen Girl*. As luck would have it, in his next big scene he had to run through driving rain and then plunge into a tank of ice-cold water to rescue Shirley. The only thing that kept him afloat was the knowledge that if he folded before the scene was over, he'd always be known as the guy Shirley Temple saved from drowning.

He then went into protracted union negotiations over a new complex and comprehensive SAG agreement with the studios. Then to Washington to testify on communism in Hollywood.

He got home to be told by Jane Wyman that their marriage was over.

From his first memoir: "I suppose there had been warning signs, if only I hadn't been so busy, but small-town boys grow up thinking only other people got divorced. The plain truth was that such a thing was so far from even being imagined by me that I had no resources to call upon."

The gossip, which hardened into a cliché, was that Jane Wyman could no longer endure her husband's unceasing interest in and talk of union and political matters. This was no doubt true, at least to some degree. She had married a young star on the way up, like her. She had married an actor, an artist who loved politics. She had wound up with a political leader who loved acting. It is easy to imagine that one morning she woke up, got some coffee, sat down at the kitchen table, heard her husband launch into a series of observations on the latest HICCASP infighting . . . then looked out the window, saw the light blue sky and the free birds and thought: *I would rather set my hair on fire than listen to another word from this man.*

Jane Wyman's career was more intense and satisfying than it had ever been, or would ever be again. Everyone in Hollywood wanted her to be in his movie; not so many in Hollywood wanted Reagan. She'd won an Academy Award as best actress.

There were no doubt many reasons and causes for the divorce, maybe most of them lost to time. It was half a century ago. They are both old, unwell and never speak of it. As for their friends, some remember the dynamic of the marriage differently. A. C. Lyles remembers both Ronnie and Janie as happy, thought they were well matched, remembered them as always in love. Reagan's friend the baseball player Bob Feller would remember it differently. He told me Jane Wyman was "a tough broad," that they'd all gone to Ciro's one night and he'd seen Jane snap at Ron, belittle him. "She was short with him. She was a big star and he wasn't."

In the divorce papers, Wyman alleged mental cruelty. And that was the last time she's spoken publicly of what passed between them. She routinely turns down requests for interviews. She has never denigrated Reagan in public, never criticized him, never helped his political friends or foes.

As for Ronald and Nancy Reagan, they didn't speak of her over the years unless they had to, and when they did they called her Wyman.

Jane Wyman would keep their children Maureen and Michael and the house, Ronnie would get an apartment. He was shocked and sad. He was also full of shame, like a person who'd not only failed at the most important thing in life, but failed publicly. The divorce was, for months, fodder for Hedda and Louella and the other gossip columnists.

Reagan did a lot of crying on a lot of shoulders; he did a lot of talking, shared his heart with friends. It is hard not to wonder if that time in his life, that openly heartbroken time, didn't ultimately prompt or lead to the more taciturn part, the famous detachment that those who loved him and worked for him years later always spoke of.

There's an old cliché about Ronald Reagan that I always believed because it's what my eyes saw. But sometimes your eyes miss things.

The cliché is that Ronald Reagan didn't really have any close friends. He had a lot of acquaintances and a lot of people with whom he was friendly; he would act the part of a friend, calling if someone was sick or some reversal of fortune had occurred. But he had no intimate friends, no man with whom he really revealed himself, no woman he'd known years ago at Warner Bros. with whom he'd pour out his heart, remember the old days.

Friends who visited the Reagans when they were in the White House were mostly Nancy's friends and their husbands. Those who were the president's friends were the kind who had to be scheduled in by schedulers; they called when they were in town to ask if they could come over, but the president didn't call them, and everyone who worked around him thought: He doesn't need them. Dave Fischer and Mike Deaver have each told me of an evening at Blair House, shortly before Ronald Reagan was sworn in as president for the first time. The president-elect called in his friends and supporters, the kitchen cabinet, and thanked them for all they had done to make this day possible. But what was surprising, jarring even, was that he talked to them as if they were good people whom he respected and who deserved a briefing. He talked to them as if they were important Republicans. He didn't talk to them as if they were his friends. Because he didn't see them, or anyone else to my knowledge, as close friends.

But there's another truth that I think has been lost to history. Ronald Reagan once had deep friendships and close friends. He had men who knew all about him, but by the time he'd reached the presidency they were dead. He'd outlived them.

The men who were his friends had been his peers in Hollywood and he loved them. They were men like Robert Taylor and William Holden and Dick Powell. They were close, and the key is that they were his equals; they were professionals, they were his age and they knew Ronnie and Janie and then Ron and Nancy.

When Robert Taylor died in June of 1969, Reagan, who in later years didn't always go to funerals, gave the eulogy for his best friend, and something happened in that little speech that I'd never heard of happening before with Reagan. He began to weep, and he had to struggle to continue. The *Los Angeles Times* reported "his voice shaking with emotion," when Reagan spoke of Taylor's history and struggles, of his gifts. He ended with, "Some day I'll see him on the late show, resplendent in white tie and tails . . . and I'll smile because I will see him in blue jeans and boots, squinting through the campfire." He loved Robert Taylor. He loved Bill Holden too, who was like him—an outdoorsman, a cutup, a genuinely funny and nice man, and in the great Hollywood wars of the late forties and fifties, a philosophical and political confederate.

But when Reagan went into politics, in the mid-1960s, and rose to great heights by 1980, he wasn't surrounded by peers anymore. He was surrounded by staff. He was the boss and they worked for him—Mike Deaver and Ed Meese and Judge William Clark and Marty Anderson and James Baker. He liked them, felt varying degrees of affection for them, but they weren't his age and they weren't his peers so they weren't his intimate friends. The same was true of his friendships with men such as Charlie Wick and Earle Jorgensen and Henry Salvatori—members of his political kitchen cabinet. He liked them, had fun with them, but he was the candidate and they were his supporters.

Why didn't Reagan replace the friendships of his young and middle adulthood? Why didn't he find another Bill Holden or Bob Taylor? It is true that with time his life became more dense with action and responsibilities, and that marriage and a family and earning a living took up his time. But I think another element of the story is that the old close friends had seen firsthand and close up all the wild sadness and pain of the end of his marriage to Jane Wyman. He had not only opened up to them, he had cried on their shoulders until their shoulder pads were damp. When things got better and calmed down, and as the years passed, one senses that some part of Ronald Reagan decided, consciously or not: *That was a little embarrassing. I'm not going to let that happen again, I'm not going to let that tiger out of the cage. I'm going to take my heart off my sleeve and put it back in my chest, forever.*

Reagan went to England to star in *The Hasty Heart* with Patricia Neal. He was sad, had the blues. He wrote, "My loneliness was not from being unloved, but rather from not loving. Looking back, because at the time I wouldn't admit it to myself, I wanted to care for someone—yet I was building a sizable resistance to doing that very thing."

That sounds poignant, and touching. But he was building up his sizable resistance by dating every star and starlet in town. His future aide Marty Anderson once explained to me Reagan's high degree of confidence by reminding me, "Peggy—Ronald Reagan had nothing to prove to anyone. Ronald Reagan dated Lana Turner."

Reagan came back from England, lost out on a part he hungered for because of the bad box office reaction to *That Hagen Girl,* got another movie, this time with his friend Ida Lupino. But three days before shooting began, he played in a benefit baseball game for the City of Hope Hospital. At the end of the first inning he dashed for first base, got tagged, hit the dirt and broke his right thighbone in six pieces. Months of traction followed; he wore a steel and leather brace, used crutches, then canes, and underwent a year of physical therapy.

While he was in the hospital, he wrote a long letter to his friend Bob Feller. It had been years since he'd seen the baseball great, and he reintroduced himself. Feller thought it extremely modest the way he did it—Reagan was a famous man. He was writing about a little boy in the hospital with him.

Feller told me in the spring of 2001, "The boy's father had killed himself, the boy was mentally troubled, or hurt. It was a long letter, handwritten, and Reagan told me about the boy, asked me to write to him and send him a ball." Feller did, and it sparked a half century of letter writing between the actor and the sportsman. Feller, eighty-two years old and living in Cincinnati, still has the letters. I asked him why he kept the first one, the one about the boy, written by an actor who was well known but down on his luck. He told me that Ronald Reagan too had asked him that question years later. "I told him 'I thought you might make something out of yourself sometime.' "

He met a girl who said she had a problem. Her name was Nancy Davis and she was a young actress in town, a contract player. She feared her career might be in jeopardy because there was another actress named Nancy Davis who was on lists of groups known to have Communist leanings and involvement.

Nancy Davis was afraid she'd be confused with the other actress and blacklisted. Or at least that's what she always said, that's the official story.

She went to her friend the producer Mervyn LeRoy, who heard her out and told her not to worry; he'd call Ronnie Reagan at SAG. Reagan checked into it and reported back there would be no problem, tell the girl not to worry.

But Nancy Davis was worried. Half a century later, at her regular table in the outside garden area of the Bel-Air Hotel, she told me what she was worried about.

LeRoy had said, "Nancy, don't worry about it, I spoke to Ron Reagan, he says there's no problem." I asked her what she had said to that. She laughed and then spoke with a straight face. "I said, 'Oh no, I'm really, *really* worried about it and I really think I have to meet him.' "

I said, "Something tells me he was attractive, single and you had to get to know him, right?" And she laughed and said, "Absolutely." She had seen him in movies and heard things about him—that he was a great guy and a person of respect. He was handsome too, and single and maybe looking.

LeRoy seems to have understood. He called Reagan again, and Reagan protested: The girl has no problem. LeRoy said, "But the poor kid's so worried; take her to dinner and reassure her." Reagan knew now what LeRoy was doing. He reluctantly called Nancy, introduced himself, asked her to go to dinner and told her it would have to be brief, he had an early call the next morning.

He was lying.

She said fine, she had an early call on the set herself.

She was lying too.

She told me, "It was a blind date for him but not for me. I had seen him in pictures, of course, and I'd heard about him."

They went to a restaurant on the Sunset Strip and they hit it off and talked and joked, or rather he joked and she laughed. He thought she had pretty eyes. And she liked to listen. He admitted he'd lied about the early call and she laughed and said she'd lied too. Then they went to Ciro's to see Sophie Tucker, and then they stayed for the second show, and went home at three in the morning.

"Oh, I thought he was wonderful from the minute I met him," she told me. "He didn't talk about himself the way actors do. He didn't talk about 'my last picture' and 'my next picture.' He had a great sense of humor. He was a Civil War buff. He was interested in things. He was attractive. And we were both putting our best foot forward."

"We saw each other the next day. We saw a lot of each other after that. I saw other people for a while and he did too."

She knew what she wanted from the beginning but he did not. "He didn't want to make a mistake," she told me. "He'd been brought up to believe you only marry once, so it took time for him . . ."

She had been in town for a few years, she was ready to marry, she knew she wasn't going to be a big star and doesn't seem to have had the hunger to be one. She told me once, five years ago at a dinner in New York, that before Ronnie she had gone out with some other interesting men, such as Clark Gable. This almost made me drop my fork, which seemed to delight her. Yes, she said. "I was living in New

York then." Clark was in California, coming East, and had asked his friend Spencer Tracy if he knew anyone in New York. Tracy, who had known Nancy's mother when they had both been young actors, said yes, Edie Luckett's daughter.

"Spence called my mother and said, 'Did I do the right thing?' She said sure, and called me. She said, 'If somebody calls you and says "I'm Clark Gable," don't say "Sure and I'm Greta Garbo" and hang up.' "

When they went out it was the first time she'd ever witnessed the presence of a security detail. The police would protect them when they went to the ballpark. "It's the first time I ever knew anything like that," she said. Gable didn't like to go to parties, he liked to go to his ranch, and when she was in California he would ask her to his ranch in Encino. Once he asked if she could see herself ever living on a ranch some day. She said she didn't know.

One night at a slow point in a SAG meeting, Reagan turned to Bill Holden and said he was going to marry Nancy Davis. Holden said it was about time. They married on March 4, 1952, at the Little Brown Church in the Valley. Bill Holden was best man, and his wife, Ardis, the matron of honor. Including the minister there were just the five of them.

Nancy Reagan stopped working, and their first child, Patti, was born seven months later. She worked now and then afterward but mostly not. "Oh, I wanted to give up my career," Nancy told me this spring. "It's the best decision I ever made. I'd seen too many marriages fail because both were in the business. Every day, you know, you're told how dear and darling you are in the studio, and you come home and you want to be treated that way at home and that's not the way it is. But Ronnie never asked me to give up my career, I wanted to give up my career."

Six years after Patti there was a son, Ronald Prescott Reagan.

Ronald Reagan's responsibilities were expanding just as his financial situation was tightening. He wasn't getting good parts, he didn't have a studio contract, he was getting older, and increasingly in Hollywood he was more associated with politics than acting. Studio heads were starting to see him not as a romantic lead but as the guy negotiating across the table for the actors' union. He had houses, mortgages, children and a wife.

He was out of style. He couldn't sing or dance, he wasn't a classically trained stage actor. He could speak, and loved to, but he often spoke for free, about politics and patriotism.

Then he got an offer. Would he emcee the floor show at the Last Frontier Hotel? The money was right and he had no other offers so he said yes.

Reagan played Vegas. He came out on the stage every night with a line of dancers and waved a white straw hat, did some jokes and introduced a singing group, the Continentals. He did it for two weeks, with Nancy in the audience every night.

He never did it again, and he didn't talk about it in later years unless someone brought it up. His friends noticed, and in time they almost never did.

"Honey, Roy Rogers Is Here"

He didn't want to go into television. It was a new medium in the 1950s and with some affectionately remembered exceptions—the comedy of Milton Berle, Sid Caesar and Imogene Coca, of Lucy and Desi and Jack Benny; the artistic ambitions of *Playhouse 90, Alcoa Presents*—TV was what Newton Minow later called it, "a vast wasteland." Bob Hope called it "a piece of furniture that stares back at you."

Much of the early fare of TV seemed geared toward children, consciously in the cases of *The Mickey Mouse Club* and *Sheena, Queen of the Jungle,* perhaps unconsciously in the case of so much else, entertainment that was so innocent but also so flat, shallow and unlayered it seemed to reflect life as it had been lived nowhere by any human being in the history of man.

But if TV's early fare was bland it also represented a placid ideal of life that may have been perfect for young fathers just home from Iwo Jima or Korea and young mothers fresh from the Depression and childhoods marked by want. They'd had enough excitement. Let's watch Danny Thomas. (Their children, who were not until late 2001 handed by history the same level of challenge, would demand that TV become more exciting.)

Two myths: One is that the 1950s were TV's golden age—we are living in its golden age right now. The second, that TV in its early days uniformly celebrated the middle class and shunned the ethnic. *Life of Riley* was a long-running hit about a guy who worked in a factory; *The Goldbergs* was about a working-class Jewish family; there was Nat King Cole's show and Julius LaRosa's; *The Honeymooners* was about a working-class and seemingly Irish American bus driver and his wife and friends. There were Ernie Kovacs and Phil Silvers, and, of course, Danny Thomas's Uncle Tanoose.

The fact is a lot creativity was just beginning in the early days of TV, largely, ironically enough, because Hollywood saw TV as competition and wouldn't allow its stars, contract players, directors and writers to work in it. This opened opportunities for newcomers like Paul Newman and Richard Kiley, who started out in TV dramas, and writers like Paddy Chayefsky, who started out writing teleplays.

Reagan, like others of his generation in Hollywood, saw television not only as a step down but as an admission of defeat. Movie theater owners had warned studios that people wouldn't pay to see an actor they could see for free at home, so if an actor accepted a TV offer, he wasn't only deciding to moonlight for a while, he was deciding to leave movies. Going to TV also meant, or seemed to mean, giving up certain creative ambitions. Movies were where the great talents still flourished; movies still had art in them.

TV wasn't art, not yet; it was barely craft.

But Reagan had to earn a living, and TV saved him. And once again in his fated life his bad fortune turned out to be good. The Hollywood Communist wars and the SAG presidency had left him politically astute and capable of leading other leaders, but that was the inside game of negotiation and influence. It was TV, or rather General Electric, that taught him the outside game—how to lead through reaching common citizens, not one by one but en masse.

In Reagan's case this didn't mean teaching him what he didn't know, but teaching him that what he knew had an audience far greater than he could have imagined.

In 1954, General Electric asked Reagan to host a weekly "dramatic anthology." He agreed. Thus was born *General Electric Theater,* nine o'clock on Sunday nights. It was a hit and ran for eight years, half of them as one of the top twenty rated shows.

That's when I first remember him. I remember being at my great-aunt Etta's, in her little house in the potato fields of Selden, Long Island, in the late fifties. On Sunday nights, after Ed Sullivan, we'd watch a handsome man in a gray suit and shiny hair stand and tell us about the story we were about to see. I liked him, though I didn't know why and don't remember thinking about it. I just remember him standing there and talking with a strong soft voice, like a good teacher. Like a teacher in a college. My great-aunts pronounced his name REE-ginn, hard G, Ronald Reeginn. They somehow communicated to me that he was Irish, as we were. I remember my father didn't like him and the reason seemed again to be the name: It was phony to call yourself Rayginn, Reagans are Reegins.

When Reagan signed with General Electric, his contract included traveling to each of their 139 plants in 39 states. He'd be GE's goodwill ambassador, telling Hollywood stories and forging a link between the home office and the plants.

The job supported the Reagans well, and GE fully stocked their house with its products, so that every appliance in the house was electric, even the can opener. But Reagan wasn't completely happy with his newfound security. He was an actor who wasn't acting anymore; moreover, he'd come all this way and now look: He was a traveling salesman, just as his father had been at the end of his work life. He was taking the *Super Chief* and going to Chicago and El Paso, or taking the car to San Francisco. He'd walk miles and miles of assembly lines in the huge plants, shaking hands, asking questions, making a speech and then moving on. He didn't know it at the time but he was spending his days as modern politicians do, as presidents often do.

He was often on the road and Nancy was often lonely. In the summers, when the children were at camp, she was often at loose ends. The Reagans' friend Marion Jorgensen remembers the night there was a fire in a house in the Reagans' neighborhood. Nancy called Marion, who sensed something. "I felt so sorry for her. I said 'Nancy, you want Earle and I to come get you? Why don't you come here and stay?' So we did. She came in and stayed for two nights. She was alone."

There were challenges to being married to Ronald Reagan that were significant, Mrs. Jorgensen added. I asked her if she thought he was aware of them. "Oh, I think so," she said. "He was aware of everything. Everything. He was very—without making a point of it or anything—I think he was very conscious of everything that went on around him. Very."

Patti Davis doesn't remember her father being away; she was young and says she just remembers "gaps when he wasn't there." She remembered the nightly phone call—her father would call and talk to her mother every night. And when he'd come back from his trips, Patti would jump on him and say,"What did you get me?" He always brought her a gift.

One day in the spring of 2001, I walked into the commissary at Paramount Studios in Burbank, California. I was with A. C. Lyles, after seventy years still a producer at the studio. He is a man viewed with such affection that there is a building named for him on the lot, and to walk into the commissary with him is a lucky thing, for everyone comes to say hello. A woman stood as we passed her table and said hello to A.C. We were introduced, and she asked what I was working on. I told her a book about Ronald Reagan, and she asked if she could tell me a story.

Her name was Mona Kantor, and she told me of meeting Reagan in his early traveling and speaking days. "I was a young woman, it was about 1951. I met him on the train, on the *Super Chief,* and we got talking. I was going to be a teacher of the deaf, and he told me about the anxiety Jane Wyman had when she was making *Johnny Belinda,* trying to get it right. And he was going to the Soap Box Derby in Ohio. We were talking and I told him it was my birthday that day and my first time away from home. The next thing I knew he had reserved the Turquoise Room on the *Super Chief,* and there were about six people whom he'd met and invited on the train. And when the train stopped in Albuquerque—he had ordered a cake, and when we got there the cake came on, and he gave me a party."

If you want to, you can bump into someone with a Reagan story just about anywhere you go. He has lived a long time, and he's led many lives. But what has surprised and even astonished me is that the stories are almost invariably about his graciousness, generosity, good humor. In all the years I have asked people about Ronald Reagan, in all the years they've volunteered stories, I have never heard a critical anecdote except once. I loved it because it was such a relief. It was a dozen years ago when I met a man who told me he had once worked in a hotel restaurant in the desert of the Southwest, and one night Reagan came in and said he had a reservation. He was alone. For some reason his name wasn't in the book, and the restaurant was full. But Reagan was a famous face and they nicely asked him to wait a few minutes. Reagan lost his temper, however, berated the man, was rude and impatient and left.

I was so delighted to hear this story: Reagan acts like a jerk, like an entitled star! I told the man the story seemed out of character for Reagan, and he said he knew that, but it happened. I asked if he'd ever seen Reagan again. He said, "Oh sure, the next morning when he came to apologize."

I am still searching for an anecdote about Reagan that truly reflects badly on him. When I talk to or read the works of people in politics, entertainment or journalism who didn't admire or agree with him, they will, if they get going, tell you Reagan was lazy, or naïve or a bore. But they never say he was low or unkind or dishonest or untrustworthy. I think his character is the least criticized of any great political leader of the century.

Reagan thought he had probably met, in all, a quarter million GE employees. In the first few years he gave speeches about the joys of giving and the blessings of democracy. But in time, as he grew more conservative, so did his speeches. He warned of the potential abuse that can come when a government is allowed to grow too big, too powerful, too demanding. He spoke of what he'd learned about the abuse of government in Hollywood—from HUAC to high taxes, from overregulation to the breakup of the studios after Washington had brought an antitrust suit that severed the studios from the theater chains they owned.

And he found that as the focus of his speeches changed, more people came up from the audience afterward to tell him their own experience of government waste or bullying. He remembered they'd say, "Hey, if you think things are bad in your business, let me tell you what is happening in mine."

What the people were telling him, he later said, was that the federal government was not only expanding but encroaching on liberties Americans had taken for granted. Reagan took notes on what he was told, did some research, and if a story could be verified, he'd include it in his next speech.

An example: He was told the government had six programs to help poultry growers increase egg production, and a seventh program that cost just as much to buy surplus eggs. He researched, it stood up, and it became a standard illustration of how a costly government is also often an incompetent one.

Soon there was less and less Hollywood in his speeches and more and more about government. Soon he was telling audiences that no government has ever voluntarily reduced itself in size, that history showed it usually had to be forced to do so.

And that became his theme. He'd say, "We, the people." He'd say our whole system was based on all of us together standing firm to put things right.

Naturally there were those who heard the speech who didn't like it, and complained to headquarters. Reagan was supposed to be selling toasters and Americanism—mostly toasters—but instead he was wading in with a call to action on the great issues of the day. To Reagan's surprise, GE didn't try to censor him, even though it was arguably in the company's interests to do just that—they had government contracts, after all. Reagan was grateful to GE for the freedom to speak his mind, and it gave him new insights into the nature of big business. All his life he'd shared his father's skepticism about big companies; he was skeptical of great power centers that had the ability to push people around and abuse workers. Now he was giving the workers of a big business a fairly controversial message and the big business was neither censoring him nor pressuring him to switch his emphasis.

He concluded from all this that opposition to big business should not be knee-jerk, should not reflect cultural conditioning. Some big businesses were pretty good, some not. It all depended on the integrity of the people who led them and staffed them.

So that was Reagan in the 1950s: becoming a leader in Hollywood but no longer being a movie star, becoming a television star but no longer being a liberal Democrat.

By 1960, by the time of the presidential election, he knew he had made the transition, was now a Republican and something even rarer in Hollywood: a conservative. A deeply committed philosophical and economic conservative.

One day he called A. C. Lyles at home and told him that a local registrar would soon show up at Lyles's house with papers that would change his political registration. "Really?" asked A.C. "What are we going to be now?"

"We're Republicans," Reagan told his friend.

"But I thought we were Democrats. Why are we changing?"

"We didn't change," said Reagan. "They changed."

And for the rest of his life, that is what he'd tell people both on and off the stump when he was asked why he left the Democratic Party. "I didn't leave the Democratic Party, the Democratic Party left me." He felt it had turned left—toward higher taxes and more government power, toward an antibusiness bias and a weaker foreign policy.

Reagan turned right at a moment that could hardly have been less advantageous to him. There was a new Democratic administration in Washington headed by John F. Kennedy. Liberalism was in the air, conservatism was yesterday.

As a Republican in a Democratic town, Hollywood, and as an increasingly high-profile Republican at the start of a new Democratic era, Reagan was vulnerable.

He was getting more invitations to speak than GE could handle, but something new was happening. Reagan found that even though the nature of his speech hadn't changed in years, he was now being labeled a "right-wing extremist." And all of a sudden every time he'd give a big speech, a member of the Kennedy cabinet was sent to speak too, in the same town. Reagan was being taken seriously now, but he was also becoming the focus of powerful resistance.

In 1962 there was a change of management at GE, and it led to the end of his relationship with the company. New management asked him to stay on *General Electric Theater,* but also to go on the road and pitch GE products. In other words, be a salesman. He said that after speaking for years about what he believed in he didn't want to go out and peddle can openers.

They insisted. He said no. They canceled *General Electric Theater.* He had a lot of time to make speeches about what he believed in now.

In 1964 he was making those speeches, receiving a strong reaction from audiences and getting ready to host another show, *Death Valley Days,* a TV western.

He was asked to become cochairman of Barry Goldwater's presidential campaign in California, and said yes. His decision was based in part on something big that had happened to him. He had read Goldwater's best-selling book, *The Conscience of a Conservative,* and it spoke to him. It reflected his belief that the proper stance of a patriot right now was against a bigger government and for a smaller one. Just about the only part of the government he wanted to see grow was the armed forces, because he felt America must have an unsurpassed and unsurpassable military arsenal in order to protect freedom in the world.

One night, late in the summer of 1964, he gave a speech to eight hundred people at the Coconut Grove, the nightclub of the Ambassador Hotel. He had rewritten it to endorse Goldwater.

After the dinner, half a dozen people came up to him and asked him to do the speech on television. They said they would try to raise the money to buy the airtime. Sure, he said, if you think it would do any good. He added that he thought it would be better if he gave the speech in front of an audience, as he had that night.

The group bought a half hour from NBC, and Ronald Reagan gave The Speech, which was taped at an NBC studio in Los Angeles, in front of an audience of invited Republicans.

It was to run a week before the election.

Then Barry Goldwater heard about it. He called Reagan and said he'd been told the speech was incendiary, and maybe they ought to run a Goldwater speech or Goldwater tape instead. Reagan was taken aback; he didn't think the speech was incendiary, and because he hadn't bought the airtime, he couldn't make the decision. Why didn't Barry watch the tape? Barry did. And called again to say go ahead.

But by this time Reagan and Nancy were worried. His confidence had been shaken. Maybe he should ask them to cancel it. Then he thought, no, he'd given that speech before and it had gotten a fine response. Besides, it was what he truly thought.

And so on the evening of October 27, 1964, Ronald Reagan took a huge and fateful step.

They watched it with friends, at home. The Reagans went to bed not knowing the reaction, if any; he worried that he might have let Goldwater down. At three o'clock in the morning Washington time, they got a call from Goldwater's headquarters. The campaign's switchboards had been lit up ever since the broadcast, thousands of people had called in pledging support. In the days before the election it was replayed on local stations across the country.

It was a milestone, both for Reagan and for the new conservative movement.

He stepped into national politics, became a presence in the nation's political life. He stepped into history.

He did it in part by making for Goldwater the case that Goldwater had never managed to make for himself. And in making the case for Goldwater, he made the case, in effect, for modern political conservatism. And no one, standing and speaking into a microphone on television, had ever quite done that.

To those of us who worked for him, and for all of those who followed, it came to be known as The Speech.

This is part of what he said:

> I have spent most of my life as a Democrat. I recently have seen fit to follow another course. . .
>
> I believe that the issues confronting us cross party lines. Now one side in this campaign has been telling us that the issues of this election are the maintenance of peace and prosperity. The line has been used, "We've never had it so good!" But I have an uncomfortable feeling that this prosperity isn't something upon which we can base our hopes for the future. No nation in history has ever survived a tax burden that reached a third of its national income. Today, thirty-seven cents out of every dollar earned in this country is the tax collector's share, and yet our government continues to spend seventeen million dollars a day more than the government takes in. . . .
>
> This idea that government is beholden to the people, that it has no other source of power except the sovereign people, is still the newest and most unique idea in all the long history of man's relation to man. This is the issue of this election: whether we believe in our capacity for self-government or whether we abandon the American Revolution and confess that a little intellectual elite in a far-distant capital can plan our lives for us better than we can plan them ourselves
>
> You and I are told increasingly that we have to choose between a left or a right. There is only an up or down: up to man's age-old dream—the ultimate in individual freedom

> consistent with law and order—or down to the ant heap of totalitarianism. And regardless of their sincerity, their humanitarian motives, those who would trade our freedom for security have embarked on this downward course. In this vote-harvesting time they use terms like the Great Society, or, as we were told a few days ago by the president, we must accept "a greater government activity in the affairs of the people." But they have been a little more explicit in the past and among themselves. . . .

He spoke of a "rendezvous with destiny" for those who would fight for our freedoms; he asserted that the most important words in the Constitution are the ones that begin it: "We, the people . . ."

Nancy Reagan and the kids were in the audience, including daughter Patti, then twelve years old and observant. She remembered that the people in the hall were wearing flags on straw hats, flags in their jacket pockets. "I remember so clearly sitting in that hall, the Goldwater speech, and being aware of three things. One being that Republicans are really dorky looking. Not him, of course, but all the other people in that hall were like really dorky looking." She laughs and says, "I thought I certainly shouldn't be there because I'm much too hip. I was already in my beatnik phase, with the hair over the eye.

"And the second was that he was an absolutely brilliant speaker—even though I didn't agree with what he was saying he was bringing me to tears. And the third was he was not going to be an actor very much longer."

She added, "That's why this whole thing about the shift into politics, that it happened suddenly—I never saw it as sudden, and I don't think my brother would have thought it was sudden." All they had talked about at home—at the kitchen table, on drives—was politics, for as long as she could remember.

Goldwater went down to defeat, crushed in the liberal landslide of Lyndon Johnson.

But Reagan rose from the ashes. Barry Goldwater hadn't been able to define conservatism except for what it wasn't—it wasn't for big government, it wasn't for socialism. Reagan could define it by what it was for: *for* greater individual authority and freedom, *for* the right to hold on to more of your own wages, *for* defending democracy against totalitarians.

The local businessmen who paid for The Speech went to Reagan and said: Run for governor of California. He laughed. He'd been asked years before to run for Congress as a Democratic candidate, and he did now what he did then, he laughed and said, "I'm an actor."

They came again.

I'm an actor, he said.

A. C. Lyles remembered it for me. "When we first started talking to Ronnie about running for office, there was Moon, of course, Ronnie's brother, and Holmes Tuttle was very important. And Ronnie used to say, 'You folks love me, of course you want me. But what about the people out there?' He didn't believe he'd have enough support. So we talked about it, and he decided to go door to door, talk to people, get a sample. He said, 'I'll show you.'

"And he walked up to a door in Los Angeles and a lady answered. And he said, 'I'm just in the neighborhood and thought I'd drop by. I'm sort of thinking about running for governor and—'

"And she says, 'If you're runnin' for governor, whatta you do for a living? How do you support yourself; what experience do you have?'

"He said, 'I'm an actor.' She said, 'Oh gosh, I know all you actors, I see movies and I read about you; you look familiar.' She said, 'My friends play a game with me, they just give me the initials, RM—that's Robert Mitchum—or JC—that's Joan Crawford. So we play the initial game and I know everybody.'

"So Reagan laughs and says, 'Okay, I'm RR.' She smiles, recognition on her face, she says, 'I know you. I recognize you. I've seen all your movies, you're wonderful.'

"She said, 'I'm gonna call my husband to the door, I want him to meet you!' Ronnie said, 'I'd love to meet your husband.' She says, 'Honey, come to the door, Roy Rogers is out here!' That's a true story."

They kept pressing him. *You're the only one who can bring the party together. You're the only guy all the Republicans like.*

To give himself time he told those who were pushing that he would not only volunteer to speak for the eventual Republican nominee but he'd also solicit names for potential candidates when he was out speaking.

The reason he held off, the reason he didn't want to run for office, was that he knew it would change his life, and he liked his life. He and Nancy had children and friends and a Hollywood life, they had a home and a ranch and a pool and privacy.

Nancy was forty-four years old, he was fifty-four. It seemed late in the day to change his career. He had all the speaking engagements he could handle. His father-in-law told him not to do it, politics was seamy, full of soul-killing compromise.

But the boys—Holmes Tuttle, Henry Salvatori, Earle Jorgensen, Justin Dart—kept pressing. Tuttle kept saying he was the only man who could bring the party together. Tuttle was a rich man who sold cars for a living, and he wouldn't take no for an answer.

Reagan started having trouble sleeping at night. They kept pounding away. He countered with an offer: Get me on the road in California for six months, you arrange it, and I'll speak all over the state—but not to Republican groups, just to regular citizens. And on the last day of 1965 I'll tell you whether you're right that I can beat Pat Brown.

Brown was the incumbent governor, and a popular man.

They agreed. Reagan was delighted. Because he knew he'd find someone else to run on the road.

And so he spoke to the Rotary and United Way and Chambers of Commerce from San Diego to the Oregon border, driving up and down, stopping and speaking, giving a speech like The Speech, like the GE speeches: against big government, for freedom, for lower taxes, against arrogant bureaucrats and officials who thought they could solve problems by throwing money at them.

And wherever he went there was the same response. People would come up to him and ask, "Why don't you run for governor?"

He thought they were plants, from Holmes and the boys.

He'd laugh and say, "I'm an actor, not a politician."

He'd ask for other names. They'd say, *you*.

It happened so often and in so many places he realized it wasn't a setup, these people were just citizens, they weren't plugged into any power structure, they were individuals.

Finally he came back from the road. And he told Nancy he didn't think he could avoid it, didn't think he could run away from it. She was not surprised. She could see it building outside him and inside him, and she remembered the moment when she knew everything was going to change. "Everything changed after the Goldwater speech. He'd been asked to run before, but after the Goldwater speech it was different. He still said no, he still said, 'I'm not gonna run for office.' But somehow we both just knew. Ron said, 'Let me think about it, let me go out and test the waters, let me see.' But there was this time, it was right after the Goldwater speech and we went to San Francisco. Ron was giving a speech, and there was a reception at a big hotel. Well, people were lined up from the ballroom into the lobby, down the hall, out to the street and down the block. We were in line saying hello on this reception line for four to five hours. The next day I couldn't move, my shoulders kind of locked. I'd never done anything like that before and I realized I must have tensed up."

And then she said, "Well, he had his answer."

He called the boys, the people pressing him, and said he would do it. It was January 4, 1966.

The day he announced his candidacy he thought he'd also ended his political career. After his statement reporters had questions. One asked if he would agree to appear on television with Pat Brown. Reagan thought of *Death Valley Days* and got the slightly blank look he sometimes got before he popped off a one-liner. He said, "Well, sure, our audience is accustomed to seeing both ends of the horse!"

The reporters laughed, but he immediately saw his career flash before his eyes. He was calling the incumbent a horse's ass, not the most politic thing to do when you're announcing your entry into the electoral fray. But to his astonishment no one used the quote the next day in the papers, and no one ever mentioned it in the campaign. He told me the story almost twenty years later in the White House. He had called to thank me for my work on a speech and somehow we got on the subject of speeches that don't work. He told me the story of his announcement, said no one knew it and to this day he didn't know why reporters didn't mention it. He laughed and told me to take it and use it sometime.

She sits in the gardenlike outside dining room of the Bel-Air. She is beautiful, slim; has the kind of posture you get only from discipline, from exercising and maybe horse riding; she is in a sunny yellow suit with earrings and bracelet and necklace of gold. Big sunglasses, the really big kind the old wear. She is ninety-three years old and she is Mrs. Marion Jorgensen, widow of Earle, of Jorgensen Steel, a self-made man who became rich in America and who was an early supporter of Ronald Reagan. He had died two years before, at the age of one hundred. "He had a great life," she said of her husband. "He really did."

She is a strong, soft-voiced woman.

I ask her when she first started to hear about Ronald Reagan from Earle, and she said it wasn't from Earle.

"First I heard about him was from a dinner party I was at, Earle and I. I was seated next to Holmes Tuttle, who spent the whole evening telling me how great Reagan was. Now we'd all heard the speech he gave for Goldwater, and that was the thing that did it. Holmes said to me, 'On Sunday are you going to be home?' I said, 'Yes, we're playing tennis in the morning, we're going to be home all day.' He said, 'I want to come and see Earle.' Well, I'm very curious. I knew he wanted something, Holmes always did. And I said, 'What do you want to talk to him about?' And he said, 'I want to talk about how I want twenty-five thousand dollars for Reagan.' I said, 'Oh, Earle will give you that.' On the way home in the car I told Earle. He said, 'Since when are you giving away my twenty-five thousand dollars?'

"I said, 'Since tonight.' He said he'd love to do that, and did. He was one of the first. He was one of the kitchen cabinet."

The campaign was easier than Reagan expected. Once he had made his decision ambivalence fell away, and he found himself competitive, wanting to win, as if he were back in Dixon and suiting up. Pat Brown, a good man, made himself easy to oppose. With sincerity and then desperation he embraced more spending and more government both as a philosophy and a practical way to win. He was an incumbent with a record Reagan could attack. And Brown made the mistake, until near the end, of fighting back like someone who thought he'd win in a walk. Reagan was a cream puff, a movie star in makeup, a novice who wouldn't know the moves.

Brown ran a commercial in which he reminded a group of schoolchildren that it was an actor who shot Lincoln. He must have thought it was funny, but it looked desperate. Brown said Reagan was an actor and implied he was a phony, mouthing words as an actor does from a script he hasn't written.

The last angered Reagan and led him to change his style. He stopped making speeches and started showing up all over the state standing at podiums and taking questions from audiences. It would be all Q and A, demonstrating more fully who he was and how he thought. It worked, and not only because it showed him to be up to the job of governor. It also worked because the questions were coming directly from audience members, meaning he wound up talking about what was really on voters' minds.

Brown wasn't. He thought he didn't have to.

Brown often said, in passing, that Reagan wore makeup. This irritated Reagan too because he never wore makeup. In his early days on the Warner Bros. lot, in 1937, a cameraman had told him he was one of those actors whose skin didn't take makeup well, didn't absorb it; he looked worse with it.

But Reagan couldn't run around saying, "I don't wear makeup!" So he ignored it until he and Brown showed up for a live debate on *Meet the Press.* When he arrived for the broadcast Brown was wearing makeup. So was every reporter on the panel. The only one in the room with a bare face was Reagan, who pointed it out. Then he told the story on the stump and made people laugh with it.

At three o'clock on the afternoon of the election Marion Jorgensen called Nancy at home. Nancy said she was nervous. "It's going to be a long day till the polls close at eight tonight," she said.

Marion said, "Well, what are you doing?"

Nancy said, "Nothing."

Marion said, "Well, wait a minute. Come on over at five-thirty. I'll get a few of your friends—we'll have a drink, we'll have an hors d'oeuvre or so before we all go down to the Biltmore for the party. Well, I did!"

She smiles and leans forward slightly toward her Cobb salad. Her voice is soft but definite and she manages to talk about the old days not with a sense of loss but of delight: *I was there, and it was wonderful.*

She tells me of the party. "Earle and I got—they came in the afternoon, we all had a drink, I got my cook to rustle up something. Veal stew, I remember that, a good veal stew with rice. And we just had a little something—hors d'oeuvres—and we had a drink. Just the other day I came across some pictures of that night, and it struck me how many people that were there aren't here. . . ."

Reagan won by a landslide, by a million votes—58 percent to 42 percent.

A. C. Lyles met him and the others at the celebration at the Biltmore, and what he remembers is what he saw in the back of the ballroom. "This young fellow was going around with a banner. And it said, REAGAN FOR PRESIDENT.

When Marion Jorgensen remembered that night, she smiled. The Reagans decided it was good luck to be with Marion and Earle on election night, and from then onward every election night was spent at the Jorgensens' home.

"What you have to understand," Mrs. Jorgensen says, "the key about Ronnie is this: I knew him as a movie actor, as a governor of the state of California, as president of the United States, and the thing about him is he never changed. He was humble. He had no sense of entitlement. It wasn't about him, ever."

It was after the voting, Reagan later said, that he realized something was happening in America. Brown, in defeat, said that Reagan's votes came from right-wingers and extremists, but the returns showed his votes came from middle-of-the-road voters in both parties. They were tired of high taxes, tired of the college upheaval spreading across the university system the state was so proud of and that people had sacrificed so much to build. Later he said, "It was a rebellion of ordinary people." They were tired of the fact that they worked hard and played by the rules and wound up losing thirty-seven cents of every dollar they made to one level of government or another, and worked harder and went deeper into debt. Tired of a welfare system that somehow didn't seem to be helping, disapproving of bureaucrats who kept programs going long after their use.

"There was unrest in the country and it was spreading across the country like a prairie fire," he said.

A. C. Lyles was sitting in the front row when Reagan was sworn in in the official ceremony as governor for the first time. "It was a dark, dank day in Sacramento," he told me, "just a foul day, heavy, overcast. And when he was sworn in—this is true, ask anyone who was there—a little spot in the sky opened, and the sun like a halo came down on Ronald Reagan, like there was a large bright light in heaven just shining down on him. It was scary. The same thing happened at the Inauguration—again, a little spot in the sky just opened up; it was like a halo coming down. It was eerie."

And so the citizen politician walked into the State House in Sacramento.

There's a scene in the old Robert Redford movie *The Candidate.* A handsome young man, relatively undistinguished but the son of a former governor, runs for the U.S. Senate in California and is elected because, essentially, he is telegenic, not some old statehouse hack. So he wins his hard-fought campaign and then he looks at his campaign manager and says, "What do we do now?"

Political professionals always remember that scene, because they've all seen it at the end of campaigns. The candidate thinks, "I wanted to win and did everything to win and now I've won and what am I living for? What exactly did I want to do with this job?"

In a way that happens with all politicians. The gifted political strategist David Garth once told me that from what he's seen, politicians usually start out with belief and end with mere hunger. And the hunger usually starts once they've won.

Reagan's problem, however, was not "What do I stand for?" or "What do I want to do?" but "I know what I believe in and I want to change things but, Lord, what do I do first?"

So he literally sat down and made a list. Number one: He wanted to attract a new kind of civil servant—not people who wanted high jobs in state government but professionals who didn't, who would have to make a sacrifice to come in and set things right. Number two: After hiring them, he'd provide goals he expected them to achieve and give them a framework for achieving it, a philosophy under which to operate.

The members of the kitchen cabinet found businessmen who knew how to do things and sent them to Reagan. Some were people like Caspar "Cap" Weinberger, a talented lawyer from San Francisco. Reagan met with him, liked him and put him in charge of the budget.

Reagan drafted a group of top businessmen to review every state program from the top down: How was it performing, what services did it provide, what did it cost, how many were employed by it, how much waste was there, should it continue or be blended into another program or agency, should it receive less funding or more?

The more he learned, the more bad news he heard. He hadn't known it when he campaigned, and Pat Brown hadn't told anybody, but California was broke. Brown's administration had concealed the fact through accounting tricks and continued spending, assuming a tax increase could come after the election.

Cap Weinberger told Reagan the state was spending more than a million dollars a day more than it was taking in—and had been doing so for a year.

It was California's worst financial crisis since the Depression. The day he was sworn in Reagan told California what he'd found out, and promised to do everything he could to turn the situation around.

He tried to do it with a hiring freeze, a 10 percent cut across the board in all agencies. The state sold its plane and stopped buying new cars, and it stopped construction. But more was needed.

So Ronald Reagan raised taxes. He had campaigned all through the state saying it was time to cut taxes, and here he was raising them, and by the biggest margin in California history.

He was criticized. He accepted the criticism because it wasn't unfair. He promised he would do everything he could to cut taxes as soon as he could.

And the people of California forgave him in the end, for three reasons. The first was they knew he meant it when he said he wanted to cut taxes, and they knew his reasons were rooted in justice: It's your money, not the government's. Second, they knew he wouldn't have raised taxes if he hadn't been forced to by the crisis Brown had let simmer. And third, they believed him when he said he would do everything he could throughout his term to cut taxes.

He'd go to work each day and said later it was like every day someone opened a new drawer with a new problem in it. He was at war with the Democratic legislature over everything. Jesse Unruh, the California Assembly leader, meant to unhorse the pretty actor. He couldn't, but Reagan wound up holding on pretty tight to his saddle.

"Do you know about his ulcer?" Nancy Reagan asked me. We were talking about his early days in the governorship. He came home a few months into his new job, looked at Nancy and said he didn't feel good. "He told me, 'I spent thirteen years at Warner Bros. and they couldn't give me an ulcer, but I think I'm getting one now.' And he was."

It was a sharp pain in his stomach that wouldn't go away. His doctor examined him and confirmed it. Reagan wasn't sure when it started, but he thought it was when he started to worry about running for governor.

He was embarrassed; he thought an ulcer was a sign of weakness, and he kept it a secret from everyone but the family and a few friends. It hung on for more than a year and got worse until one morning before leaving the house he reached for the Maalox and something inside him said: You don't need this anymore.

So he put down the bottle and didn't take his medicine before he left.

Later that morning he had a meeting in his office with a man from southern California who had a problem he wanted to discuss. As he left he turned to Reagan and said, "Governor, you might like to know I'm part of a group of people who meet every day and pray for you."

Reagan was taken aback, thanked him, said he also put a lot of stock in prayer. Later the same day he met up with another man, this one from North Carolina, and as he was leaving the governor, he turned around and said he met with a group of people who prayed for him daily.

Soon after, Reagan went back to his doctor for a checkup. The doctor poked and prodded and said, "I don't think you have an ulcer anymore." When more tests came in, he said there was no sign there had ever been an ulcer.

Later Reagan thought it was the power of prayer that had kept him from taking the medicine, that had told him he didn't need it anymore. It was the power of prayer that had healed his ulcer.

I asked Nancy Reagan if he really believed that and she said, "Oh yes, completely." She mentioned, as people who know Reagan always do, that he prayed a lot. "He was very spiritual and he believed in God, of course, and he prayed a great deal." I asked if he prayed on his knees, at bed, in the evening or morning. She said no, he prayed all the time and anywhere. "Wherever you are, whatever you're doing, if you want to pray you pray.

"He prayed every time a plane took off. He'd sit and look out the window and he'd look lost in his thoughts but he was praying. And aides would come to him to say something and I'd wave them off, and let him have his prayers."

The ulcer's going away came with more good news. The state's financial house was falling into order, he was using the line item veto effectively, he was learning how to negotiate with the legislature. Some conservatives complained about his willingness to deal, but Reagan thought he was being like FDR, trying everything he could to make progress, not having any expectation of making a hit every time he came to bat but trying for the highest possible batting average.

Most important, he was learning to take his case to the people. As a boy he had listened to FDR and his fireside chats, and they had made a great mark on him. As a man he had learned how to talk to regular people in his GE work, and had learned how to talk to a camera when he did TV. So he went over the heads of the press, just like FDR had, and went on television and radio and told everyone what he was doing and how things were going.

It worked. His support rose. He learned that if he could just make the public understand what he was facing and what he needed, they'd do the rest. They'd write letters, they'd call their assemblymen, they'd press for support.

One day in 1968 Cap Weinberger came into the governor's office and told him he'd been going over the books, and it looked like the state was going to have a surplus of more than a hundred million dollars in 1969. It was because of the tax increase and the cost cutting.

Reagan knew he had to decide what to do with the surplus before the legislature heard about it and came up with ways to spend it.

He said, "I already know what we should do with the money." He said they would give it back to the people in the form of a tax rebate.

This had never been done before. It was tricky, to say the least. He knew that if word got out the legislature would be all over it; he also knew that a taxpayer refund would have to be approved by the legislature. So Reagan decided to tell the people of California the good news right away; and he told them too that he wanted to give it back to them. He said that since the new surplus was expected to be equal to about 10 percent of the coming year's tax revenue, the best way to deal with it was for Californians, when they computed their income tax the next year, to send a check for only 90 percent of what they owed.

It was pure political genius. The legislature went wild but it was too late: The people knew everything, and the people supported it.

Reagan also in these days signed a bill that had been passed by both houses of the legislature that liberalized California's abortion laws. Reagan had little choice—the margins in both houses looked veto-proof—but he was never happy at having signed it, and he would in time become the most forceful and persuasive individual voice against abortion in the nation.

Reagan was by nature open minded and nonjudgmental, as we now say so often in our culture, on how people lived their lives and conducted themselves privately. He was by temperament charitable, and, as a man who had lived with artists and respected artists and wanted to be an artist, essentially live-and-let-live in his views, and always would be. Hollywood contributed to this part of his nature. It was a real mix, the home of many intact and successful families, of people of the most moderate habits and inclinations, but also the home of just about every form of deviant behavior known to man, of every scandal and sin that people can commit. He was not censorious, wasn't mean, made jokes and teased but thought people are people. "If men were angels . . . ," James Madison said, wistfully. Reagan knew they weren't, and that was all right with him.

But Reagan also had an intuitive or intellectually natural sense that though abortion would always exist and always be sad, to legalize it was to open the doors of hell. That was a living human, he thought, growing in the living womb of a woman who deserves respect. He said, "We cannot diminish the value of one category of human life—the unborn—without diminishing the value of all human life." He agreed with Mother Teresa when she said that "the greatest misery of our time is the generalized abortion of children." He thought there was nothing in the Constitution that granted that right, and he was indignant that the issue of abortion legalization was not, ultimately, decided by the people but by the U.S. Supreme Court. He passionately agreed with Justice Byron White's dissent in *Roe* v. *Wade,* in which White called the ruling an act of "raw judicial power."

And when he was president, he spoke about it. He did it most strikingly in his Evil Empire speech in Orlando, Florida. The majority of that speech was not about communism, it was about our nation's soul. And so it was also about abortion:

> More than a decade ago, a Supreme Court decision literally wiped off the books of fifty states statutes protecting the rights of innocent unborn children. Abortion on demand now takes the lives of up to one and a half million unborn children a year. Human life legislation ending this tragedy will someday pass the Congress, and you and I must never rest until it does. Unless and until it can be proven the unborn child is not a living person, then its right to life, liberty and the pursuit of happiness must be protected. You may remember that when abortion on demand began, many warned that the practice would lead to a decline in respect for all human life, and the philosophical promises used to justify abortion on demand would ultimately be used to justify other attacks on the sacredness of human life, including infanticide or mercy killing. Tragically enough, these warnings are proving all too true.

There were other things he did. One was a secret. He'd become governor just two years after the Watts riots and wanted to help heal the scars. He also wanted to reassure members of minority groups that he cared about them. And so, secretly, he began to visit families in black neighborhoods, and in the Mexican American barrio of East LA. He'd just disappear for a few hours and travel by private car and talk to people. Sometimes a family asked their neighbors over to meet him. He found out a lot this way. He heard black grievances that they weren't being given a fair shot at state jobs. He looked into it and found out they were right. He determined that the testing and application system was slanted and had it changed.

In East LA the parents told him their children were being left behind in school because their native language was Spanish. He asked them if they wanted to be able to go into the schools and visit their children's classes and make sure they were getting the instruction they needed. The parents were amazed: Only people with teacher certificates could participate in classroom functions. Reagan thought that was ridiculous, so he had the rule changed.

He became devoted to the idea of bringing more blacks and Hispanics into important jobs in the state government.

Around this time he got a call from several black leaders from the San Francisco area who said they wanted to talk to him about his treatment of blacks. He invited them in. They arrived with what he thought was a look of hostility on their faces. He disarmed them by asking, "Look, are you aware that I've appointed more blacks to executive and policy-making positions in the state government than all the previous governors of California put together?"

One of them said yes. But he asked Reagan why he wasn't telling people about it.

Reagan was startled. He told them that in appointing these people he was doing what he thought was right. He said it would have been cheap politics if he'd gone out and "started singing a song about it." Besides, he said, "They were the best people for the job; I didn't appoint them just because they were blacks. . . ."

The tone of the meeting changed. The black leaders told Reagan they thought he'd been quiet about it because he was afraid of angering his white conservative supporters. When they left the room they literally had their arms around each other.

He ran for reelection in 1970, this time against Jesse Unruh, the speaker of the Assembly who'd tormented him with style and vigor throughout his first term.

Reagan won easily, 53 percent to 45 percent, less than his first margin but comfortable nonetheless.

He finished his second term, was pressed to run for a third, resisted because he'd done what he wanted to do. A lot of his second term had been devoted to welfare reform, which he was satisfied with, and which presaged the national reform that would come about in 1995. It tightened eligibility and allowed fathers to live with their families without suffering a penalty. Some of his conservative supporters tried to pressure him into eliminating the entire statewide program, but he refused. He believed government must take care of people who through no fault of their own cannot take care of themselves. He just wanted to make sure they really needed the help.

In 1975, after his second term, he and Nancy left Sacramento and went to live on their ranch, a 688-acre spread in the Santa Ynez Mountains, just north of Santa Barbara.

It is often said of Reagan that part of the key to him was his love for the ranch. It was nothing in those days, a beat-up shack of a house and overgrown scrub with a pretty view. But he could ride his horse there, which was important because something in the loping, rocking movement and the slowly changing scene allowed his mind to relax and reflect. And in the relaxing he would consciously and unconsciously figure out answers to questions and problems.

He now faced a big one. His name had been put forth for the presidency in 1968 but it had been a small boomlet, and he knew he wasn't ready. Now Gerald Ford was president, and Reagan didn't like his policies much. Ford would be the incumbent nominee for the Republicans in 1976, unless, of course, someone challenged him. And everyone knew there was only one man who could do that.

He was sixty-five years old, in good health, prosperous. It was decision time. He got on his horse every morning, and tried to figure it out.

The Ranch

The psychoanalytic pioneer Carl Jung had a little country house on a lake in the woods outside Geneva. It was a place of isolation and simplicity; he did some farming there, and gardening. He liked to chop wood and did so well into his eighties, in his shirtsleeves or an old pullover. He'd wear socks with holes in them and old shoes. He'd stack the wood near a chopping block in the back, and he told his friends he was grateful that he had found a way to live "as part of nature." His biographer Ronald Hayman quoted Jung:

> Everyone, he maintained, "should have his own plot of land, so that the instincts can come back to life. To own land is psychologically important, and there is no substitute for it . . . Everything around me is part of me, which is why a rented flat is disastrous."

Big cities, Jung thought, were where uprootedness began. "Human existence should be rooted in the earth."

For Reagan, land integrated you into life. Love integrates you into life too, but it is abstract, or rather internal, you cannot hold it. Land you can hold in your hand, it gets under your nails. It's interesting to me that when people who worked with Reagan on his ranch talk about it they always say, "He liked to get dirty." He liked to be up to his elbows in it, dressed simply, sweating.

Ronald Reagan's ranch was the place he went to for peace, physical movement and thoughtfulness. It was where he daydreamed, let his thoughts go where they wanted. The renter's son who'd hopscotched through Illinois had a place of his own rooted in the earth.

In the last decades of his life it was his favorite place to be of anywhere on earth. It's also where he decided his future, during those days in the midseventies when he had to decide whether to move forward or stay put.

Rancho del Cielo wasn't his first ranch. That one was in Malibu and is now public land, absorbed into the state parks system. He'd bought it in the fifties, took his children there, and to this day Patti walks its trails. She'll be in the park, turn down a trail and suddenly she'll think *cows ahead*. Because that's where the cows grazed, or that's where the Tack Room was. Reagan gave the ranch up when it was too much to support, and for a short time he used another ranch, in Sacramento, when he was governor. But he didn't really like it. Patti was riding with him one day when he told her it was too flat and uninteresting. "When we were riding there, he said he didn't like being able to always see where he was going."

When he was governor he heard about another place, and he and Nancy drove there with their friends Bill and Betty Wilson, who had told them about it. It was north of Santa Barbara in the mountains.

This is what it's like.

You leave the highway and go up Refugio Road, passing little lemon ranches and avocado ranches. You're on a one-lane blacktop, you see California live oaks and scrub and grass and wildflowers and telephone poles. You pass little trailers, little avocado trees with their shiny light-green leaves. You pass a little stream with rocks and boulders. Now the blacktop is canopied by live oaks, but it's still a narrow old one-lane beat-up road. You pass a wooden fence that reads CIRCLE BAR B RANCH; it's an old guest ranch. Cary Grant used to like to go there, the locals tell you. But it doesn't look like a place a movie star would go to. It all looks so modest, and old. You ford a little stream, pass a few little houses and some more pickup trucks. None of it but the little ranches makes you think of California. Everything else makes you think of how you imagine West Virginia.

You pass little houses built in the forties and fifties. There's a scrubby place with a turn in the road and some trailers and it starts to get steep, and as you go up and up it looks like there's not much up here, and you realize you're going too high.

It's at this point that Nancy said, that day back in the seventies, "Honey, there's nothing up here; let's go back." But he kept on, urged by the Wilsons.

Suddenly you're up high enough to see that you're in a fabulous mountain range, you're up going toward two thousand feet above sea level and suddenly you're in the Santa Ynez Mountains, in a big rolling range. In late April the mountains are a beautiful lush green and if you look down one way you're looking into a beautiful valley, and on the other side you look toward the light blue ocean, and the Channel Islands just beyond.

You keep driving upward, past madroña trees—multitrunked, with big leaves, white blooms, a little like a magnolia. The trees are rusty looking until it rains and then they turn smooth and red. You go past a stone wall and a black gate. You look out the car window and see a dark green ridge of mountains and then a lighter green ridge rolling beyond and then the beautiful untouched ocean. It's like what a settler would have seen from these hills long ago, and you understand for the first time why the Spanish named everything they saw here for saints. That's Saint Barbara below and Saint Monica beyond, near the place of the Angels.

Reagan later said that when he would ride in this area he would, inevitably, think of scripture. "It casts a spell. There's such a sense of seclusion, and I suppose—I think of the scripture line, 'I look to the hills from whence cometh my strength.' " Judge William Clark told me Reagan called it "an open cathedral."

The ranch also made him think, irresistibly, of his oft-stated views on American exceptionalism, the idea that America was created in a way unlike other countries, deliberately and for an exceptional purpose. In a videotape he made about the ranch after his presidency he said, "I've always believed that there was some plan that put this continent here, to be found by people from every corner of the world who had the courage and the love of freedom enough to uproot themselves, leave family and friends and homeland, to come here and develop a whole new breed of people called American. You look at the beauty of it. God really did shed his grace on America, as the song says."

It's a half hour trip up the road from the highway. You can't go more than about twenty miles an hour most of the way.

There is a point on the road—within range of mountains, the ocean, the fogbank, the Channel Islands, Santa Barbara—where you see the coastline below running east and west. The sun rises on one end of the beach and sets on the other. You are stunned with the beauty of the place, and now you know why they called it Rancho del Cielo, ranch in the sky.

It's a section of land, 688 acres, right on the top of the mountain. You enter a gate and there is a dirt road, and as you drive along you hear rocks crackling and sticks snapping.

You pass horses, Arabian and quarter, and a few Texas longhorns, and an old gray burro named Wendy, who lived here when the president did.

Now there's a wooden sign hanging from a wooden bar on a wooden fence. It reads RANCHO DEL CIELO, R. REAGAN. He built the fence.

You can imagine the expectations of Gorbachev as he was driven up this road. He knew about capitalism and how capitalists and powerful men live in America. And the expectations of the queen of England, who knew something of how the famous in America lived.

And they saw: a shack.

And they thought: This is how staff lives!

This was nothing like his dacha, her castle.

It is a little one story house with stucco and adobe walls. They are painted white. There's a red tile roof.

There's a little patio; Reagan tore out an old aluminum-enclosed porch and put in an overhang, tiled it beneath. Within the overhang there's a little entry door with an Irish tile on it that says O'REGAN. And an official-looking sign that says ON THIS SITE IN 1897, NOTHING HAPPENED.

When you open the door you enter a porch room. To the right there's a hat stand with his favorite baseball cap, "United States Mounted Secret Service," blue and gold. He wore it all the time. There's a cowboy hat too, and Indian memorabilia. The room smells cool, like wood. There is a vinyl floor. On the wall an Indian blanket, and mounted near it the horns of Old Duke, his favorite bull. There's a sombrero, Indian peace pipes, Indian portraits, a potbellied stove, which provided the only heat in the house when he bought it.

His books are still on the shelves: *Odyssey of a Friend* by Whittaker Chambers, *A Very Strange Society* by Allen Drury, a first edition of *Witness* by Chambers, *Poverty Is Where the Money Is* by Shirley Scheibla, Drury's *Advise and Consent, The Kennedy Promise* by Henry Fairlie. *Inside Football* bears an inscription: "To Ronald Reagan, a great governor, George Allen." *Lonesome Dove* by Larry McMurtry, *The Book of the American West,* edited by James Monaghan, four volumes of *Arizona Highways, The Great Democracies* by Winston Churchill. A book of Irish traditions, a history of the U.S. Cavalry, a book about Indians and horses. *Jeb Stuart: The Last Cavalier* by Burke Davis, *The Treasury of Modern Humor,* edited by Martha Lupton, *Practical Horse Breeding and Training,* by Jack Widmer, a book called *Only an Irish Boy* by Horatio Alger.

He read up here. He'd be out all day and come in at five, before dinner, and sit in his favorite chair in the porch room.

The furniture is modest brown wicker, and scattered about are collections of things—little elephants, kachina dolls from the Hopi tribe of Arizona, little Indian spirits from the spirit world. There's a painting on the wall called *The Lame Horse*—a cowboy walking next to a horse in the rain, holding the bridle.

To the right there's an eating area, a plain wooden table that seats six. For Thanksgiving they would move young Ron's bumper pool table next to the wooden one to make enough room.

Move deeper into the house. A chain of titles is framed on the wall. In August 1898, Jose Jesus Pico owned this land, in 1900 Jose Jesus Romero, in 1902 Belasano Robles, all Latino American ownership until the 1940s.

Near it are leather boxes and leather panels, hand tooled. They were made by Bertha and Buzzy Sisco, two fans of Reagan's who took care of a young man named Sam, who was disabled. Bertha and Buzzy made and sold leather work to Reagan to support Sam. Reagan would draw out for them on a piece of paper what he wanted, including size and design specifications, and in time they paid local doctors for Sam and horse doctors for their horse with the notes the governor and then president had drawn. When Reagan found out, he drew more.

In the living room there's a Sharps rifle, and other firearms in a firearm cabinet.

The kitchen is small, with GE appliances, a GE stove circa 1974 and a refrigerator in the light mustard color GE called Harvest Gold. A small Formica sink area, a spice rack, a small little window overlooking the pond and a trailer. He built the pond, and built the dock that leads to the water.

It looks like a little kitchen in Indiana in 1950.

Turn from the kitchen and you see the famous jackalopes on the wall. You take a jackrabbit's head and ears and glue on vicious looking fangs and glue little antelope antlers on the head, and you mount them on the wall and tell your city friends, your eastern friends, the tale of the jackalopes, which roamed the mountains terrorizing all with their legendary speed and ferocity. Reagan had two on the wall. He liked to tell the press about them and once *The New York Times* is said to have almost run a piece on their existence. Reagan staffers stopped them, sadly enough.

In a tiny wet bar area there's a framed copy of the front page of *The New York Times* for February 6, 1911, his birthday. It headlines the latest in the Mexican Revolution, a rebel victory near Juárez. There's a turn-of-the-century U.S. Cavalry recruitment poster, and a beer stein with U. S. Grant on one side and Robert E. Lee on the other.

There's a private family room that only family was allowed into. Years later, after the presidency, Ed Meese went into it for the first time and saw that a painting Meese and the staff had given him had the honored place on the wall.

It was where they watched TV after dinner, *Jeopardy!* and *Murder, She Wrote.* He would always try to stay awake through the latter, and almost always fell asleep twenty minutes in. There's a longhorn steer hide on the wall. And a little box made by the Siscos with a note inside in Nancy's hand on how to use the remote.

The master bedroom is small, yellow walled—bright soft yellow was his favorite color. A modest old bathroom with a shower; the shower head is a liberty bell. There's a vanity for Mrs. Reagan, a small sink. There are a few religious icons on the wall, delicate icons of the

Virgin and Child; there are others scattered through the house, mostly gifts from Bill Wilson, who along with Judge Clark was always trying to convert Reagan to Catholicism. Reagan would listen politely and ask questions, but he'd already made his decision on that long ago.

The Reagans' bedroom is about twelve by eighteen feet, big for this house. Their bed was two twin beds pushed together, the bed posts tied to each other by rubber bands. A patchwork quilt on the bed, a little table with a rotary dial phone, a Westinghouse transistor radio, and a music box that plays "California Here I Come." It's odd to stand in this room years later, with it empty and no one living here, and wind up the little box and hear it play its tinny song. It sounds so old.

There's a small walk-in closet that was also turned into the safe room, with armored walls, when he was president. This is where the Secret Service would have secured the president if he came under attack. A few old work shirts hang inside, riding britches, Stetsons, cowboy hats and cowboy boots; Nancy's slacks and jeans and shirts. Her red robe and sun hats. Here's his membership patch from the Rancheros, a local riding group. And here's a beautiful silver spur with a small plaque. THIS WAS FLOWN ABOARD THE STS7 CHALLENGER, JUNE 18–24, 1983. PRESENTED TO RONALD REAGAN, PRESIDENT OF THE UNITED STATES. The *Challenger,* on its first flight.

The people who came to this house always described it the same way: humble, basic, simple, plain, unpretentious. And then they'd always say: Like him.

When he was president they had to add another little house on the property, a small stucco guest house—two bedrooms, two baths, and a small kitchen/sitting area. The ladies' guest room looks like a 1970s teenager's bedroom—nothing fancy, a wooden bed painted white. The gentlemen's guest room has a handsome antique bed and a Virgin of Guadalupe on the wall. The Gorbachevs, the queen, Mrs. Thatcher all used these rooms, but each stayed only for the day. There were never overnight guests at the ranch except for the Reagan children, and they not often.

There are a few unimportant paintings of Reagan in the house, not very good. There have never been good oil portraits of him, I think, because while he was handsome, with an open and attractive face, his features were uneven. There was an asymmetry to his face.

Artists seem to have tried to paint the thing they saw first, the attractiveness, and missed the asymmetry, and it doesn't ever seem to have worked. There are some excellent photo portraits of him. Either form, all kinds of portraits, tend to capture his happiness.

The stucco and adobe of the house hold whatever environment there is outside, and when it's cool it holds the cool. But like old houses its windows aren't big, and so it isn't a bright house, and when you walk out and step past the porch and into the sun, its force can startle you.

Out of the house, on toward the Tack Barn, you can look back at the hilltops where the media camped out when he was president. One time CBS News brought in a lens that was used to look at the moon, then used it to shoot videotape of the Reagans at their leisure. The cameras were so good with the lens they could see into the house. They often took shots of Reagan riding the trails, which they used on the news. Reagan didn't like this, thought it was a bridge too far in terms of the privacy he'd had to give up.

So one day, knowing they were up there with the lens, the president went out the front door, walked onto the patio, grabbed his chest and fell to the ground pretending to have a heart attack. He lay there for a few seconds as far away producers shouted and cameramen tried to load their film. They were grabbing their phones to the networks when Reagan got up, waved to them in a jolly way and clicked his heels.

His favorite horse when he was president was El Alamein, a white Arabian stallion, hard to control, given to him by President Portillo of Mexico before Reagan was elected president of the United States. His Secret Service men hated that horse. You had to be really good to ride him. Agent John Barletta would come up to the ranch a few days before the president visited and ride El Alamein to get the wildness out. Nancy's favorite horse was a handsome sorrel quarter horse called No Strings.

To get to the Tack Barn you walk past fences that Reagan made out of telephone poles, and up a few dozen graded wood and dirt steps. The Tack Barn is where he kept his saddles and spurs, the English saddles he favored and the western saddles Nancy used. English saddles are the smoother, flatter, lighter-weight ones that don't have that knob in the front you can hold on to. To ride English you've got to be in good shape because to stay on the horse you hold yourself in place with your thighs and calves. When things turn wild or surprising you use your body to control things. "That's why he had such a good posture," his longtime aide Dennis Le Blanc told me. "I mean, a seventy-eight-year-old man riding English!"

The physical work of this kind of riding tends to improve both posture and physical strength. This is part of why Reagan always liked to say, in one of his more cornball adages, "There's nothing better for the inside of a man than the outside of a horse." Riding was real exercise for him.

Western saddles, on the other hand, were bigger, with a big slope in front and back that you could fit into, and the knob on front. They were built, Reagan would say, for work, for cowboys who spent long days on the range and needed to be able to relax their bodies more. (They're also more beautiful, more ornamental—hand tooled with swirling indentations and accents.)

Reagan liked to trot, canter and gallop, but, Dennis Le Blanc told me, he had to give up the latter. "He couldn't gallop after he was president because the Secret Service would have to catch him, because he always rode in front. So there was a lot of trotting and walking. He sometimes jumped fences. But I remember Ed Meese telling him no more jumping when you're president, we can't afford to have the president flat on his back in the field. . . ."

It was in the Tack Barn that Reagan would saddle his horse and Nancy's. He didn't like anyone else to do it, liked to do it himself. When he was done he'd ring the bell, an old railroad locomotive bell, to tell her to come up from the house, and they'd go riding.

On the wall of the Tack Barn there's a big map that shows all the trails on the land, trails that wind through meadow and brush, ridge and gully, and have names like Sunrise and Hanging Tree and Rock Main, Snake Lake Trail and Valley Trail. They crisscross the property. He cut a lot of them. All those vacations past, during the eighties, when you heard on the news, "The president cleared brush today," that's what he was doing. I was a writer at CBS then and after a few years I thought, *Isn't he done yet? How the heck much brush is there?* And when you see it you realize: 688 acres.

Snake Lake was where they put the snakes that had hatched in profusion when they were building things up in the early days. Dennis Le Blanc, who also worked with Reagan on the ranch, told me, "One year we transplanted over a hundred eighty snakes from the house pond to another pond because they'd hatched underneath the trailer I lived in next to the house. The snakes were going from the trailer to the pond, so we'd go into the pond and have to grab them out of the water. And I hate snakes! But he wouldn't kill a thing. We'd put 'em in a gunnysack and take them to the other pond . . ."

There's a gas pump outside for the farm and ranch equipment, and for the Secret Service vehicles and jeeps. There are no gas stations nearby, and when Gorbachev saw it, he finally saw an opening. "Does every American have his own gas pump?" Farmers and ranchers do, Reagan said amiably. It's hard to drive a tractor to the local gas station.

The ranch was a place not only where he did hard physical work, but the place where he could see the results of his efforts. In other parts of his life it was hard to do that, but here he could see the fence go up sturdy and do what fences do.

He liked his guns. He liked his horses. He liked his rails, his bells, his dogs and cattle. He was a movie star and he was born in Illinois but he was a westerner at heart.

There was a small olive orchard.

There were Secret Service shacks but he had them taken out, all but one, when he left the White House.

He would ride the trails.

When he was president he would ride up to the helicopter pad, where Marine One landed. The helicopter pad was twenty-six hundred feet high and you could see the ocean on one side and the ranges and towns on another. He would ride the trails up there, but when he left the presidency he told them to pull it all out, the concrete landing pad and the hangar. It's empty now, the trappings of power are gone and the field is covered with wildflowers, which is the way he wanted it.

I have mentioned Dennis Le Blanc. He was a young man with the highway patrol in California when he was assigned to Governor Reagan in 1971. He was a security officer, and when Reagan bought the ranch in his last year in the governorship, in 1974, Dennis would go with him as part of his security detail. They had the same interest in the outdoors and in hard physical labor, and they both liked to make things; so Dennis came to work with him on the ranch. In time he left the highway patrol, joined Reagan full time, did scheduling and advance work, followed him ultimately to the White House, where he helped run the military office. During all those years if Reagan went to the ranch, Dennis went to the ranch, and he worked with Reagan there until they sold it.

He's fifty-five now and still looks sinewy, tanned and young. I talked with him one night in a hotel in Santa Barbara, just a few miles down from the ranch.

I told him people had told me he was like a son to Reagan, but Dennis demurred. "He was just good to me," he said. "He was very inclusive—eating lunch and eating dinner with them, and talking about family things.

"What the ranch was for him was a way . . . to rejuvenate himself. He really enjoyed doing the simple things in life—getting dirty, using his mind to create something. He totally loved being outside.

"When he was president he'd go there for Presidents' Day weekend in February, we were there Easter, in April, and Memorial Day, end of May. We'd go there in July for Mrs. Reagan's birthday, come back and then be at the ranch all of August. Then we'd go there for Thanksgiving, and we'd go back after Christmas. He had Christmas Day in the White House so the security agents wouldn't have to leave their families.

"He loved his life there. He would get up about seven-fifteen, seven-thirty. He'd go to the table in the dining room and sit with his back to the window, and that's where he'd have his Corn Flakes or Special K. And he'd have his briefing materials, couple of newspapers and news clips, and he'd work on that till nine or so. And then he'd go up to the Tack Barn. . . . They'd ride until noon. Then he'd go down and change his clothes from his britches and eastern boots into his jeans and work boots. . . .

"They'd fix lunch, and then he'd ring the bell down there and I'd come down with Barney, who was his driver and personal aide. We'd come down at twelve-fifteen and eat lunch inside or outside, depending on the weather. Then at one o'clock we'd go out cutting wood, rain or shine, until five. Except if it was really pouring, in which case he'd come up to the Tack Barn and help us clean saws or clean firearms. He kept rifles and pistols there. He loved target shooting, but he didn't do much after he was president. It made the security people nervous.

"When we were building the place there were groundhogs and gophers out there. Around quarter of five, when the sun starts going down, those guys would start coming up and we'd go out and sit on the fence and flick 'em off. He did that for safety purposes because the gophers would burrow holes in the ground. And at nighttime, if the horses were spooked, they'd just take off running, and if they didn't see the holes, they'd break their legs. So he did it to get rid of the gopher population.

"He loved the wildlife up there. Coyotes, mountain lions, bears, gophers, bobcats, deer—we saw a lot of them when we were first building it. It's only seven miles from the freeway but when you get up there, it's very isolated. Rattlesnakes, water snakes, gopher snakes.

"The noise from the chain saws usually scared 'em away. He'd see snakes when he was riding because horses don't make much noise so the snakes couldn't hear and leave when he was coming. At the ranch, some of the Secret Service guys would make the first round in their handguns a bullet that was like a shotgun shell, specifically for snakes, so if one got aggressive, there'd be a bigger pattern to the shot.

"When I first saw the ranch—well, the front part of the house was a screened-in aluminum porch, so we ripped that out and just made it an extension onto the house. And we extended his bedroom about ten feet. Before that you could barely walk from the edge of the bed to the wall. We modernized it. They built a two-bedroom guest house when he was president because they had no place to put visitors.

"We built the fences—the phone company has surplus telephone poles that sit in salvage yards, and anybody can have them, you just have to pay the trucking charges. He saw a ranch with telephone pole fences and he asked if I could help him get some. Each pole was thirty-two feet long; utility poles are tapered. Each rail was fifteen feet, so we'd get two rails out of one pole. Posts were six feet tall, so we'd get four or five posts out of one pole. This was his design, he designed the fence. The bottom rail was sixteen inches off the ground.

The fence followed the contour of the land, it didn't go straight, it dipped down.

"He loved concentrating on stuff like that. He was great at stuff like that, at how to make things. We poured cement up there—the Tack Barn and the garage area used to be gravel, we had it cemented in. The gravel was really dirty and full of oil. Trucks came up and he helped frame it in, smooth it all out.

"The fence building he learned from the foreman at his ranch in Malibu. He read books about it. And he learned from watching the home in Pacific Palisades, he went out there every single day to see it built.

"Dennis and Maureen came up twice overnight. Michael and his family came up maybe three times. People really weren't up to the ranch except at Thanksgiving time. That's how Mrs. Reagan ran the house.

"She lived for him and he lived for her. She's the most protective woman I've ever seen. But she knew that that ranch was Ronald Reagan's longevity, so she put up with it. She ended up enjoying it, but she did it for him. . . .

"She'd have her materials to read in the morning too. And she'd go riding with him. And when we were out working she'd talk on the phone or she'd go off for long walks. We'd have dinner about six-thirty or seven, watch TV until about nine, and that was it. He wanted to get to bed. I did too. It was very physical work! There were many times when he and I would be watching TV with Mrs. Reagan and we'd both start to doze off.

"It was a refreshing kind of tiredness, a physical tiredness. He'd have a smile on his face in the morning. When he'd go back to the White House he'd look great.

"Ranch life is simple. You work with your hands, you get dirty. And here's a gentleman who's got all the power of the world to tell someone else to go do that; you know, 'I'll sit here on the porch and watch you guys.' But he never asked anybody to do something he wouldn't do.

"We'd clear brush, clear away and cut a vegetation called greasewood. You can't drive through it; animals can't even get through it. Reagan cut his own trails, and that meant cutting the wood, the brush.

We'd clear it out. He liked to be able to ride about ten feet up in the air and he didn't want to bend down all the time, so we'd cut high on the trees, cut back the branches. We cut the greasewood with handsaws and sometimes gas-run chain saws. Handsaws have a small curving blade, and you saw with them. And we had pole saws to get the high branches down. We had six chain saws from thirteen inches to twenty-eight inches. It was me and Barney Barnett and the president. . . .

"The president was all inclusive. Mrs. Reagan was not all inclusive. He'd ask anyone up to help us.

"He'd chat like a regular guy. Regular guy things. Jokes. Dirty jokes. 'Have you guys heard . . . ?' Nothing political. Never talked politics. Politics had its place—his reading in the morning, a phone call, some conversation at the dinner table. But when he was out with the guys it was guy stuff, and that's the reason he enjoyed it. He didn't have the guy thing in Washington. He had friends and staff but in that environment they couldn't do guy things.

"He'd call me on the phone when we were back in the White House. He'd say, 'Dennis, it's not the same here, is it?' I'd see him in the halls and he'd look at me with surprise and say, 'Hey, those are store-bought clothes, aren't they?'

"He was a physical fitness nut. And he was in excellent shape. When he was shot he came very close to losing his life. One of the areas the bullet hit was around his stomach muscles . . . he had worked out so often the doctors had told him years before to ease off because his chest and stomach muscles were so developed they were afraid it would contribute to a hernia down the road. . . .

"But the stomach muscles helped slow down the bullet, and, of course, it stopped an inch from his heart.

"When we had people come up there, we told 'em do not wear anything white, do not wear a business suit, it's dusty or it's muddy, wear jeans. . . .

"When Gorbachev came it was like, 'This house isn't good enough for an important, powerful man.' I saw the reaction on his face when he came up to the ranch. No doubt in my mind, the people who went up there, they thought of Ronald Reagan as an ex-actor, he lived in Pacific Palisades, he is an ex-governor, he had money to burn. So when you're going up to his ranch it's 'Man, we're gonna see something really nice!' And Gorbachev, you could see—his eyes just sort of opened up and he looked around, and he saw how Ronald Reagan was dressed . . . and it set him back!

"But Reagan was—I use the word *simple,* as in *simplicity.* What you see is what you get, it's not phony. You see this motherhood and apple pie stuff—that is Ronald Reagan. I mean the guy cared about the country, he cared about people. He wasn't phony, just not phony. And a lot of people didn't give him credit because they thought, 'He's an actor.' But no, those were true emotions."

Once, four years after he left the presidency, Ronald Reagan was sitting with friends in the galley of a ship. They were sightseeing, in Alaska, and had been passing icebergs and glaciers and the wild lunarness of the scenery. It was Sunday morning and they were talking about everything in the world, politics and people, and Reagan said it was sad they couldn't go to church. He mentioned what they'd seen, and then he said of God, softly, these words: "His creation of this earth . . . is so beautiful."

It was so real to him, maybe the most real thing. His daughter Patti remembers that that's when he was really himself, that's when she could draw him out—when they were out riding or walking or being in the mountains. To draw him out she would always talk about God. Her father experienced God and nature as the same thing, or as two separate things that were full of each other.

He loved the beauty of all living things, of all things that grew in the soil and flew in the air and slithered and scrambled, all the wildlife, even homely old cows and burros. He saw the sanctity of ordinary things.

Reagan thought like his mother: God made them. He was by nature a conservationist because he believed what she told him: Man was made in God's image and given dominion over the natural things and it was a sin to destroy them or ignore them or dirty the world or be wasteful. Man had dominion, and if he didn't use it wisely or kindly or generously and thoughtfully, he wasn't much of a man.

He thought it eccentric, though, to see man himself as the problem and not the solution; he thought it eccentric to put the comfort of an obscure bug over the legitimate needs of human beings; he had no patience for self-proclaimed environmentalists who sometimes seemed to be trying to cloak a hatred for progress or wealth (or even humanity) with a loud love for snail darters. And he thought too that some people were strangely coming to think of nature itself as a god, a god in itself, and not something made by and part of His love.

He hated crudity, cruelty, selfishness and waste, thought the land is our paternity, the physical thing we leave to the next generations. So being cruel to nature was, to him, like—like setting fire to a cathedral.

Everything Changes

Even to those who differed with him and would come to oppose him, Gerald Ford was a good man. When he stepped into the presidency on August 9, 1974, he seemed a living antidote to the strain and trauma of Watergate. He was defined in part by what he was not: not a trimmer, not a strange-o, not a man hungry to get or keep power. A modest and moderate man.

Ronald Reagan liked Jerry Ford. In a way they went way back. He'd broadcast a University of Michigan football game in which young Ford had been a star player, and when Reagan was governor of California, Ford had asked him to join his cabinet. But Reagan wanted to finish his second term, and at any rate suspected Ford wanted to bring him into the administration so that he would be part of it and not a potential challenger.

A year into Ford's presidency Reagan concluded that the new president was as lost as Richard Nixon, not a forcer of international progress but a manager of international stress, a detentest like Nixon who was busy overseeing the humiliating end of Vietnam. His economic programs were weak and off the point, with "Whip Inflation Now" buttons that everyone laughed at. He seemed a low-budget liberal, his tax and spending policies in general accord with those of the Democrats of Congress, only a little smaller. But more than that, he seemed not to understand the forces that were sweeping his country, and the world.

For Reagan, for the young conservatives joining the party, it would not do.

Hardly a day passed that he wasn't called and told, *Run, Ronnie, run.* These were calls not only from California but from all over the country, and not only from acquaintances and longtime supporters but also from local powers throughout the country—state committeemen, party chairs.

Reagan would ride and think.

One of the things he might have been thinking about was this: Conservatives of a philosophical disposition sometimes feel a certain awkwardness about their desire for political power. Liberals can claim and announce their ambition with a fully revealed and fully felt hunger because it seems philosophically consistent. They think governmental power is a force for good, and its pursuit by definition constructive. Ted Sorensen, then a brilliant and sought-after young congressional staffer, tells the story of first meeting John Kennedy, who told Sorensen that he intended to move for the presidency. "Why?" asked Sorensen. "Because that's where the power is," Kennedy answered. Sorensen tells this story approvingly, and understandably so. Politics is about the flow of power; to be in politics and wish to win is to want the most power to do the most good.

But modern conservatives are devoted to limiting the government's power. Reagan was perhaps discomfited by what might have seemed the paradox of his ambition: rising up to seize the leviathan government for the purpose of making it . . . smaller. Presidents, congressmen—they all had too much power, he thought, and had taken too much power to themselves year by year almost since the century began but certainly since the Great Depression. To Reagan it may have seemed: *I have to maneuver like FDR and bully like LBJ in order to undo the overreaching that FDR and LBJ did. My ambition and desire for power must be very big so I can win leadership in an institution that I hope, from the minute I enter it, to make less powerful, less ambitious.*

But there was something new in Reagan's thinking this time, something very different from a decade before, when he had to decide whether to enter elective politics at all. This time he was listening, not dismissing or rejecting out of hand the summons of his supporters. The governorship itself had changed him. First, he had found he was more than up to the job of political leadership. Second, he had felt "the excitement and satisfaction" that comes from making helpful change. Third, but equally important, he had found as governor that the rules and regulations of the federal government were a central impediment to progress for the states. That was where change was needed now. He took to musing on James Madison and his 1788 warning that throughout history freedom has been most often taken from the people not in armed clashes but in the "gradual and silent encroachment of those in power." It was the concentrating of all power in Washington that was hurting America.

The federal government hadn't created the states, the states had created the federal government. Why then were they now at the mercy of what they had created? "Washington . . . was trying to turn the states into nothing more than administrative districts of the federal government," he said.

The federal establishment used money. They gave it to the states and localities and with the money came "strings that reached all the way back to the Potomac." The government in Washington didn't so much give money as create a bureaucracy that wound up telling states and localities how to spend and what to do. And the states and localities took the money—who wouldn't?—and became dependent on it, and now they needed it, which only encouraged the federal government to up the ante—more bureaucrats, more control, more strings.

This, he thought, was the gradual encroachment of power. It was spreading, and it had to be stopped.

At the same time, he reckoned, the federal government, in its ambition, was demanding and receiving more and more tax money from the citizens of the country, which made it impossible for states and localities to raise their *own* money to do things their *own* way. "We had strayed a great distance from our Founding Fathers' vision of America," he wrote. "They regarded the central government's responsibility as that of providing national security, protecting our democratic freedoms, and limiting the government's intrusion in our lives—in sum, the protection of life, liberty and the pursuit of happiness. They never envisioned vast agencies in Washington telling our farmers what to plant, our teachers what to teach, our industries what to build. The Constitution they wrote established sovereign states, not mere administrative districts for the federal government. They believed in keeping government as close as possible to the people. . . ."

These were his thoughts. He would ride his horse Little Man through Rancho del Cielo in the spring of 1975, enjoying the fact that he still, quite literally, could not see what was ahead, liked not knowing what bend in the trail was ahead. One day, he later wrote, he remembered something that he himself had said many years before and forgotten. "A candidate doesn't make the decision whether to run for president; the people make it for him." The people were certainly telling him, every day in letters and calls. The conservative rebellion was picking up speed. It would be hard to challenge an incumbent, and one who was a good man. The odds would not be with Reagan. And as for the Republican base, Republicans in those days tended to be orderly folk, by nature moderate and undramatic. Democrats loved a big fight, loved the fray, and the passionate call to arms. Republicans were more peaceful, saw loyalty as a high virtue. And Jerry Ford, by himself becoming the glue that helped keep the party together after the Nixon scandals, had earned their loyalty. Republicans also seemed to love it when things were boring. Reagan was going to mix it up and get things dramatic. Not everyone would appreciate it.

And even if he won, if he got the nomination, he'd be running for president backed by a broken and embittered party that had been exhausted since Watergate.

And it was a Democratic year.

He decided to run.

He put together a campaign team—Paul Laxalt of Nevada, now a senator but one with whom Reagan had been friends since they were both governors, would be general chairman. Stu Spencer, a wily old political fox who had helped lead Reagan's gubernatorial campaigns, had already been snapped up by Ford. Reagan hired instead the Washington lawyer and operative John Sears.

Reagan's strategy: Obey the eleventh commandment, "Thou shalt not speak ill of any Republican"; don't allow the fight to become personal. Score against big government and high taxes, make the case for a conservative shift, call the economy the mess it is, hit hard at the Democrats, show Republicans by these attacks that he was more their man than Ford.

His theme: *I'm an outsider, not part of the status quo, not a member of the Washington establishment. I am a choice, not an echo,* as Goldwater once said.

From the moment he committed, he campaigned hard. The first big primary was six months away in February, in New Hampshire. The day of the voting, 108,000 Republican votes were cast. He lost to Ford by 1,500—a heartbreaker. But it was a symbolic win: You don't come within a hair of taking down an incumbent without walking out looking like a winner.

The Ford campaign had whispered about Reagan's age, and reporters picked it up: Could an old man of sixty-five keep up with the demands of a campaign, of the presidency? Dennis Le Blanc remembers that the press talked about it for only ten days. "They never wrote about it after that. The reason is that he was always working hard." Before the campaign began he had been living a life in which he was on the road more than three weeks out of every month making speeches for others and building up IOUs. A presidential campaign seemed, in comparison, easy. "It was a piece of cake for him," Le Blanc told me. "It wasn't as hard as the life he'd been living."

After New Hampshire came the Florida primary, and Reagan was hopeful: A lot of conservative retirees from the Midwest lived down there, and some military people. He fought hard but the Ford people had woken up to the fact that they were in the fight of their lives, and they fought like it, hand to hand and precinct to precinct.

Reagan lost Florida.

Then he lost Illinois—his old home state, where he'd been born and had grown. He lost Massachusetts and Vermont. Five straight losses, and most weren't even close. Just two months into the primary season and he wasn't a winner anymore.

The press and party professionals wrote him off. His campaign was broke—$2 million in debt. The power structure of the Republican Party was against him, the polls were bad. Reagan's own campaign manager, John Sears, secretly met with Jerry Ford's campaign chairman to discuss the terms of withdrawal.

Even the accommodations were bad. They couldn't get good hotel rooms, and Dennis Le Blanc remembered the planes. "At one point we had a charter plane from Hughes Air West. We called it Hughes Air Worst. It was purple. Then came a turboprop plane. Then came the Flying Banana." That was a cramped plane so hideous to look at that it became a matter of general mirth.

The North Carolina primary was coming up in late March. Reagan stumped the state day and night but, again, the state polls were bad and his friends began telling him to concede to Ford gracefully and limit the damage to his reputation.

Every living former chairman of the Republican National Committee except one—George Bush, Ford's CIA director (who could not take an active part in politics)—told Reagan to get out. The money men of the party told him to get out. The *Los Angeles Times,* his hometown paper, told him it was over. Seven Republican governors called on him to end his quest.

Naturally, Reagan listened, and naturally, he didn't like what he heard. He was the only man left who really thought he could win. He was told that a man named Jimmy Lyon, one of his more ardent supporters from Texas, had offered to lend the campaign one hundred thousand dollars right away if it was used to buy national television time to show a replay of a Reagan speech in which Reagan had critiqued President Ford and Henry Kissinger's defense policies.

Should Reagan gamble on a hundred-thousand-dollar loan and shoot for Carolina? Or should he fold his tent, go out with class, wait back home and consider his options?

Reagan's men gathered with him in a hotel in Wisconsin, ashen faced, tired and ready to throw in the towel. They discussed the pros and cons. Reagan announced his decision. "I'm taking this all the way to the convention in Kansas City, and I'm going even if I lose every damn primary between now and then," he said.

His staff almost choked. There were still dozens of primaries ahead. And they hadn't been paid in weeks.

And tomorrow was the North Carolina primary, which they knew they were going to lose, and it wasn't going to be close.

The speech ran on North Carolina television that night. Reagan wasn't there; he was giving a speech out in the woods of Wisconsin. His aide and policy adviser Marty Anderson sat back and watched him and thought to himself, *This is the most attractive loser I have ever seen.*

Soon a network reporter, Frank Reynolds of ABC, shoved a crumpled piece of paper in Marty's hand and said, "Look at this!"

The paper said, "55–45."

Marty nodded. The North Carolina results. Good. Reagan would only lose by ten.

Reynolds said, "No, no, you guys got the fifty-five; Reagan is winning!"

It was an incredible victory, and given an added edge by the fact that before it Reagan had told the press that he was staying in no matter what.

So he rose from the ashes. And now it was a spectacular fight, on-the-ground political combat in over twenty states. It was a real race—and a trauma for Ford, who saw for the first time that Reagan could actually win this one by inches.

It came down—this is the last time in modern history that it happened this way—it came down to the convention, the 1976 Republican National Convention in Kansas City. There were still undecided votes, wavering votes, but he could put together a win if everything fell his way. Reagan spoke to every delegation, shook every hand, buttonholed delegates. It was a real convention, a true struggle with the outcome in doubt.

First ballot. He needed 1,140 delegates to win.

He got 1,070. Seventy votes short.

Ford won, with 1,187 votes.

He had come so close! Even at the end his people wouldn't leave. Walking onto the floor of the convention when it was clear it wouldn't work and their man would lose, his delegates still refused to go over to the winning side, to join Ford. That took courage; some of them earned for themselves the lasting enmity of the Ford forces, who were embarrassed at the closeness of the vote and trying desperately to peel Reagan's people away from him. But at the end, 47.4 percent of the total number of delegates stayed with Reagan. They went down with him, down with the ship.

The voting took place on the evening of August 18, 1976. The next morning, early, Reagan met with members of his delegation, the California delegation, and all of his staff to thank them and to say good-bye.

No one who was there will ever forget it. And when the old Reagan hands gather and talk about the great days, right after they mention the Goldwater speech they talk about this:

Ronald Reagan stood there without notes, twenty-five years ago, after a defeat more terrible for its closeness, and looked out at tough faces with tears on them, and he said,

> The cause goes on. It's just one battle in a long war, and it will go on as long as we all live. Nancy and I, we aren't going

> to go back and sit in a rocking chair on the front porch and say that's all for us.
>
> You just stay in there, and you stay there with the same beliefs and the same faith that made you do what you're doing here. The individuals on this stage may change. The cause is there, and the cause will prevail because it is right.
>
> Don't give up your ideals. Don't compromise. Don't turn to expediency. And don't for heaven's sake, having seen the inner workings of the watch, don't get cynical.
>
> No, don't get cynical. Don't get cynical because look at yourselves and what you were willing to do, and recognize that there are millions and millions of Americans out there who want what you want. Who want it to be that way—who want it to be a shining city on a hill . . .

Nancy Reagan stood there with tears in her eyes like everyone else, and a quarter century later her eyes would well up again when she was asked about it. "Oh, it was a heartbreaker," she said.

The next day they all got on a chartered United Airlines 727 jet, and during the flight Marty Anderson talked to Reagan. He was disappointed, that was obvious, but he didn't seem depressed. "Even then, he spoke of what was to come, not what had been." Marty asked Reagan to autograph his floor ticket to the convention. He wanted to frame it, put it on his wall. Reagan took it and looked out the window for a moment. Then he wrote, "We dreamed—we fought & the dream is still with us. Thanks."

And Marty Anderson knew what Reagan was going to do. He was going to run again.

Anderson later wrote, "On August 20, 1976, Ronald Reagan in effect began his third drive for the presidency."

Twenty-five years later, Ronald Reagan's advance man, Dave Fischer, who would become his personal assistant, the man who was with him from first thing in the morning to last thing at night, remembered those days. He was trying to tell me what they had meant for him and others.

He had been young, in his midtwenties then, and he was a political conservative who believed in Ronald Reagan. But he was new, kept his head down.

He remembered that last speech at the convention, to the California delegation. "I still remember it, everybody crying at the City on a Hill speech. And at the airport in Kansas City, when we were going back to California, the Secret Service agents who were saying goodbye to him there—they all turned away at the airplane and they were all very emotional, had tears.

"Reagan had walked the full length of the plane thanking everyone personally, and Mrs. Reagan did too. And when we landed in California we got off the plane and I went over to where his limousine was going to go by because I wanted to be the last person to see him. He knew I was an advance guy and that was about it; he barely knew me. And the limousine is slowly coming right past me and it's getting ready to go out the gate, and he sees me. And he leans over Mrs. Reagan and looks at me and did one of those things—he gives me a big thumbs-up. And I thought here is this guy who just went through this awful experience, and yet just like he did with those kids in Kansas City—the message he gave the kids there was 'We've only lost the battle, we haven't lost the war.' "

Reagan knew that it couldn't end here, wouldn't end here. He had devoted most of his adult life in one way or another to what he believed in, and for the past ten years to instituting his beliefs politically. He couldn't just walk away.

Even so, he played the good soldier, campaigning in twenty states for Ford. He started a newspaper column and a daily radio commentary. He spoke for candidates, spread his message.

He did what you do to vamp for time while waiting to see if the party wants you and your people want you. You wait to see if the fire will take, as you quietly fan it.

He wanted it, quite frankly—he admitted it to himself now, and to others. He wanted to be president. He was going to reinstitute the vision of the founders.

In 1978 he was visiting England and bumped into Justin Dart, one of his original California supporters. Dart said he'd like to get Reagan together with an interesting friend. Reagan agreed, and met Margaret Thatcher. Instantly, he later said, he felt she was "a soul mate." She was for smaller government: less money for the state and more for the people. After the meeting he met an Englishman who asked what he'd thought of her. She'd make a magnificent prime minister, Reagan said. The fellow said, A woman? Reagan reminded him of a queen named Victoria who'd done rather well.

He went to fund-raisers, built up chits and favors, got his name out there, kept it alive, tried to roll it into a sense of inevitability in the party: Of course Reagan would be the nominee in 1980; who else could be?

"What I remember from those days was his stamina," said Dave Fischer. "You know that he never took naps! All those years we were flying commercially I always slept on airplanes, I'd open a book and two pages and I'm out. And I'd wake up and he'd still be working. He could not sleep on airplanes. This is not a guy who ever took naps."

Reagan watched the new president, Jimmy Carter, closely. He thought Carter was producing an economic disaster—high unemployment, high inflation, interest rates going up—and a national security disaster. "While [the Carter administration] was cutting back on our military power, we were losing ground to communism in much of the globe. Our strategic forces were growing obsolete, nothing was being done to reduce the threat of a nuclear Armageddon that could destroy much of the world in less than a half hour's time."

Those are Reagan's words. Add to them the words of the writer David Frum, now a speechwriter to George W. Bush and author of the highly regarded history *How We Got Here: The 70's: The Decade That Brought You Modern Life—for Better or Worse.* Frum told me,

I think understanding [Reagan] means understanding just how terrible were the series of events Americans went through in the 1970s. And those events do tend to blur in memory under the gaudy visual memory of the seventies and also as you get farther away from events. . . .

But Alan Greenspan, who's not an excitable person, gave testimony in Congress in 1975 . . . in which he said we're at the decision point that decides whether the United States is going to remain a free market society or, if it continues on its current path, will cease to be.

Federal energy controls that were irrational, inflation that was terrible. Everything broke down at once, partly for related reasons, partly by coincidence. The cities broke down, the economy broke down . . . the beginning of the evangelical belief that the end is nigh. The plunge in the dollar, the rise in the value of gold. There was a complete market panic. It is not as severe as the first three months of 1933. But—and one shouldn't get carried away—but the only thing that it is like is the first three months of 1933—the last three months of the Carter presidency, they're half as bad. Gold prices skyrocketed because people lost faith in the dollar. . . . As a French art dealer said to my father, "Le monnaie, c'est merde."

A dozen conservatives came to Reagan and asked him to leave the Republican Party and run for president as the leader of a national conservative movement. They also told him that if he wouldn't they would look elsewhere. He told them he did not believe a third party was needed, that the majority of Republicans were now conservative. He turned them down.

Reagan had one worry, and that was his age. If he ran and won in 1980 he would be seventy years old just days after his inauguration—the oldest newly elected president in American history. But he was healthy, his energy and interest were undiminished, and his ambition since 1976 had only grown.

And so Ronald Reagan announced his candidacy for the presidency on November 13, 1979. It was a bear from the gitgo. There were seven other candidates, a crowded field. There was dissension within his campaign and a failure his first time out, in the Iowa caucuses, where he had been expected to win. Instead he'd been embarrassed by the superior organization and tireless stumping of George Bush, who soon took to jogging with reporters—he was still young enough to jog, his actions seemed to say—and claiming that he had "the Big Mo"—momentum.

Humiliated, Reagan hit New Hampshire hard. He could not afford to lose two in a row, and everyone knew every man who wins the presidency wins New Hampshire first. Once again fate handed him an opportunity. He was to meet with George Bush in debate, just the two front-runners. The *Nashua Telegraph* newspaper sponsored it, Reagan's campaign paid for it. But the other candidates protested: They wanted to be part of the debate. So Reagan's campaign agreed, and allowed them in.

The night of the debate, February twenty-sixth, the Bush campaign saw the other candidates, and balked. So did the newspaper sponsoring the debate: We had a deal, they told Reagan's team. But Reagan put his foot down: Everyone ought to be able to take part!

Bush and Reagan walked on stage. Bush sat frozen in his chair; Reagan saw that the crowd was confused and restless. A lot of his supporters were there, but a lot of supporters of the other, less important candidates were there too. He decided to tell them what was happening. He began to speak, but the editor of the *Telegraph,* angry, told the sound man to turn Reagan's mike off.

Reagan was indignant, stood, sat and said the first thing that entered his mind: "I'm paying for this microphone, Mr. Breen!" (He never said, but I always thought—and many journalists of the time did—that Reagan's mind had quickly gone to Spencer Tracy's line as the beleaguered presidential candidate in the movie *State of the Union.* Tracy, being cut off while he made a speech, barked, "Don't shut me off! I'm paying for this broadcast.")

Reagan's words electrified the audience, which roared its approval. Bush looked weak, Reagan strong. He thought afterward he might have won the primary, and the nomination, at that moment.

Reagan won New Hampshire with its crowded field with 51 percent of the vote, which was just about what he needed. He sailed through the rest of the primaries. At the GOP convention in Detroit he announced George Bush would be his vice president. He accepted the nomination with a speech that broke modern precedent by asking the delegates, and those watching, to bow their heads and silently pray with him. I remember being there, in a little studio off the floor, for CBS Radio. All of us, the writers and producers and technicians, we watched him, and listened to the silence when he asked for the prayer, and I'll tell you, most everyone around me thought it a moment of almost inexpressible corniness, and I understood how they felt. It *was* corny. But it also seemed to me powerful, because it seemed truthful. I could sense that he meant it, and thought he knew that he was taking a chance on being called cornball, a manipulator. That's why he said, "I'm almost afraid to do this, but I'd be afraid not to." He knew what he was doing, and why, and took a chance. I liked him so much at that moment.

He hit Carter hard throughout the 1980 campaign, decrying double-digit inflation, double-digit unemployment, interest rates over 15 percent. He said, "Recession is when your neighbor loses his job, depression is when you lose your job, and recovery is when Jimmy Carter loses his job."

He went after U.S. military decline and neglect. The Soviets were modernizing their forces on a massive scale, while half the ships in the American navy couldn't leave port because of lack of parts or crew; half our military aircraft couldn't fly for lack of parts; our enlisted personnel were high school dropouts and we paid them so little they were on food stamps. The Soviets in Afghanistan, communism spreading into Central America and Africa. In Iran, more than fifty Americans being held hostage in the American embassy.

His theme was what he believed: Tell the truth, announce the facts, explain what to do about them and pledge to do it. Insist on what you believe: We don't have to accept the idea of an America in decline, we can change it. Together through our actions we can bring America back. America's best days are ahead, not behind. "We have the power to remake the world."

It all came together.

Four years before, Jimmy Carter had attacked Gerald Ford using the new term "the misery index." Carter's people had added the rate of inflation with the rate of unemployment and said it was high, 12 percent, and called it the misery index. Reagan remembered the phrase. He added Carter's rate of inflation and unemployment rate and announced that it came to more than 20 percent.

When he finally forced Carter to debate, on October 28, 1980, a mere week before the election, again there was a famous Mr. Breen-like moment. Carter claimed Reagan opposed Medicare benefits for Social Security recipients. It wasn't true. Reagan shook his head, half smiled and said "There you go again." It's hard twenty years later to communicate why that was a powerful moment, but it did what Reagan had to do—show he was at least Carter's equal, maybe his superior. There was something in his soft disapproval, like an older but also wiser man correcting a younger, perhaps too eager one.

Reagan tied it all up in his closing statement when he asked the American people, "Are you better off than you were four years ago?" He said that if their lives had gotten better, vote for Carter. If they had not, vote Reagan.

He found out he'd won before everyone else. It was the afternoon of Election Day, and he was taking a shower at home in Los Angeles. He and Nancy were going to a party later—the traditional election night gathering at the home of the Jorgensens. Nancy, who had just bathed, came into the bathroom wrapped in a towel. She shouted above the running shower water that Jimmy Carter was on the phone.

Reagan got out, threw on a towel, picked up an extension in the misty bathroom, listened and said, "Thank you, Mr. President." He turned to his wife and said, "He conceded." They hugged, hard.

The polls wouldn't close for two hours in California, so they kept it to themselves. He wrote later of the surprises of history. "Standing in my bathroom with a wrapped towel around me, my hair dripping with water, I had just learned I was going to be the fortieth president of the United States."

And then the Reagans did what they always did on election night. They went to dinner at Earle and Marion Jorgensen's; they had a house just up the road in Bel Air. It was a buffet, and their friends were there—Irene Dunne, the Salvatoris, the Tuttles . . .

That night at dusk when she knew they were coming, Marion had stood at the end of the driveway to wait for Ron and Nancy to drive up. A Secret Service detail had already arrived, and one young agent approached Marion. "Do you know how to do this?" he asked.

"Of course," she said, drawing herself up. "I've done it many times."

"No, you haven't," he said. "You haven't greeted the president of the United States."

And suddenly it hit her: Everything had changed.

The Reagans drove up and he got out of the car first. It startled Marion because he always followed Nancy out of the car. But the agents had told him: The president has to get out first, he can't be a sitting duck. That was the way it would be for the next eight years, and as Marion told me, "He hated it! He hated that he had to get out first, before any woman, before Nancy."

Marion greeted him. When I asked her twenty-one years later what she'd said to him, she said, "Something stupid like, 'This is just great, congratulations.' He gave me a hug and a kiss. And they walked in, and as he walked in everybody applauded. They knew then that he was president."

He greeted everyone in the living room. "He just smiled and kissed everybody. He talked to everyone. He had on a dark suit, what else? You know, one does that. He looked wonderful. He had such a nice way with people, he was truly friendly with people."

Margaret Thatcher, one year a prime minister, was one of the first to find him at the Jorgensens', and to congratulate him. "It was all very informal," Marion Jorgensen said. "And we all went over then to the Century Plaza." For the victory speech.

"It's just hard to believe," she said. "Nothing ever changed him. He was always the same. He had humility, he didn't think he was better than anyone else."

"Nothing ever changed him." That is what people who knew him for decades say, that whatever he was—movie star or SAG president or celebrity or governor or president—it was always an external fact. Nothing internal, within him, changed. Reagan had an extraordinarily continuous nature; his character seemed to be an unbroken line that didn't waver or soar too high or low. He was not given to conceit, didn't play with people when he had the chance, didn't show up places late because he's the most important and interesting man invited, so the fun will have to start when he gets there.

And he was incapable of asking people to do things he thought it was his job to do for himself.

In December of 1980, one month after being elected by the American people to what they consider to be the greatest office in the world, and just before he left his California home for Washington, Reagan called his aide, young Dave Fischer, from his home and asked him to come out and help him do something important. Fischer arrived wondering what his great mission would be. They went outside the house. There were Secret Service men and political aides standing around talking. And Dave Fischer and the president-elect laid out the strings and checked each light and then they put the Christmas lights up on the house.

Fischer said, "There were Secret Service there but that wasn't their job. It was a husband and father's job to do it for his family, to the house they shared. So he asked me to help out. That's what we did that afternoon."

The Things They Carried

Ronald Reagan entered the White House with a wife named Nancy, with children named Patti and Ron and Maureen and Michael and a whole history of choices and efforts, failures and triumphs. A whole history, that is—a past, parents, a ranch, a governor's mansion, misunderstood children. He brought it all in with him. His presidency was hard on the entire family. In the political life it is always hard for the entire family.

This is how his daughter Patti Davis summed up her experience when I asked her what it was like. "When my father went to the White House I knew it was an ending and a beginning, and it was so huge. But then, of course, my rebelliousness kicked in and I thought, 'Oh this isn't huge, I can handle this.' When the best thing I could have done would be to go to New Zealand and wait it out. And keep my mouth shut! I didn't do that," she said.

Most of all there was the wife who'd changed his life. He loved her. He believed, as his friends said, that she was the best thing that ever happened to him. He thought she was beautiful, a listener, a nester, a woman who kept the machine around him humming. He thought she protected him from cynical people and operators and people who would use him. He wasn't always good at figuring out other people's motives. He knew this, in part, because she sometimes pointed it out.

Good was the secret of it. She could tell he was good, solid as a rock, and that's why she married him. That's why she loved him. He reminded her of her stepfather, not the father who had left her mother but Dr. Loyal Davis—loyal Loyal, who loved her actress mother and had made it possible for her to settle down in comfort, with status. Loyal treated Nancy like a princess when he wasn't at work or distracted.

When Nancy wed Ronnie she knew they would, together, be members of the Hollywood starocracy, the local establishment of show folk past and present. The Reagans would be members in good standing of an interesting community. She would be a Hollywood wife, a Pacific Palisades or Bel Air or Malibu wife; they would have a circle of friends and get the kids to school when it was their turn in the car pool and Saturday night they would go to a dinner party or Ciro's or The Brown Derby or Slapsie Maxie's.

That's what she expected. It's what she *wanted.*

She didn't know that when she married him she was entering history, didn't know what she was getting into, could not have imagined.

We sit at lunch in April of 2000, outside at her table in the garden of the Bel-Air Hotel. All around us birds are singing, hopping from branch to branch, and people are taking discreet cell phone calls at their tables. I think of something I read recently, that members of the Audubon Society have noted that certain birds have begun to sing differently, have changed their birdcalls in a way that seems to imitate the ring of portable phones.

I am with Mrs. Reagan, who is handsome in a bright pantsuit. I want to talk about things like birds and cell phones, and so, I suspect, does she. But we talk about the past, about what happened to her years ago. I ask her about something I've always puzzled over. I say, "You thought you had married a movie star and instead you walked into history. How did you . . . cope with all that?"

She laughs and says, "I had no idea I was walking into history."

So how did you learn to do your part?

"Oh, Peggy, you take it each day and you learn along the way. You know, somebody at the hospital recently, when Ronnie broke his hip— Someone told me, 'We were afraid to tell you about it, that his hip was broken, we were afraid it would be too much for you.' You know, I looked at them and I said, 'Listen, think back on my life for a moment. I've seen my husband shot, I've seen his two cancer operations, I've seen him thrown from a horse, I've seen his brain operation. And if I didn't fall apart for any of

those, I'm not going to fall apart for this. Don't worry about telling me what you have to tell me.' "

I nod at this, as if it tells me what I want to know.

I go at it another way. "How did you take the criticism that comes with the job? You never thought forty years ago that you would have to be handling so much, how did you learn to deal with it?"

"With criticism? You just do, that's all, there's nothing you can do about it. You hope eventually people will get to know you and understand you."

"But things like the Joan Didion piece years ago really hurt you, didn't they? Or am I wrong in thinking that was important?"

"Oh, she was mean." Her face changed. She looked out at the restaurant and shook her head and said softly, "That was mean."

Was the president aware of your difficulties, of the shots you took?

"He tried to cheer me up of course."

"What kind of things did he do?"

"I don't remember."

I asked her if it's still difficult for her sometimes. She said, "I just know I can get through most anything as long as I have Ronnie."

She was never going to be a big star. She was pretty, with clean sharp looks, but she wasn't beautiful. She lacked the kind of glamour that suggests mystery, or the kind of mystery that suggests glamour. She looked the way producers imagined housewives and young matrons looked, so that's how they cast her. She was not of the first order as an actress; in the few movies I've seen her in, I've wondered if she wasn't really thinking, in the romantic clinch with James Whitmore, "Did I take the chops out of the freezer? Is the dress in the cleaners?"

She was in many ways a person of average gifts trying to do a public role, wife of the governor, then wife of the candidate, then wife of the president.

She tried hard to do it well, and had a lot of things going for her. She likes to meet people and she was friendly and charming with strangers. She had energy and commitment. She believed completely in her husband. She has an intuitive sense of discretion, not something political relatives always have, and a natural sense of dignity. She knew how to hold herself, how to be a lady in the old-fashioned sense of looking and comporting herself in a certain way, and also in the more modern sense of having a certain elegance or élan. She understood and enjoyed the entertaining inherent in the job, and tried hard to be up to the media requirements.

Jackie Kennedy was a glittering hostess who famously and understandably balked at some of the requirements of first ladyship—the endless chatting with the boring governor's boring wife, the endless receptions. She'd go hide out sometimes with a book. But Nancy took to it with a vigor that suggested she not only enjoyed some of it but was also convinced that she was helping Ronnie, who was the darling of her life.

In other ways she had no gift for it. She did not have deep political interests, was not a person of surprising depths, was not always patient, which is probably the biggest thing a politician's spouse has to be—patient with everyone's conflicting needs, patient with reporters, patient with problems because you know they will pass, and soon there will be new things to be patient with, so why not just . . . maintain an even strain, as the astronauts used to say.

Nancy believed strongly in one thing, her husband. She more than anyone else had seen his struggles, knew he was an honest man, ethical and sincere and serious. He would be a good president. So she tried to help him in her own way.

Here she is now. It is 1999, and we have been at a small dinner at a restaurant in New York. Nancy seems small, vulnerable but also strong. She is nearing eighty but is still chic, with jewelry, and big brown eyes and dark hair. Outside a car hums, and Secret Service agents with wires in their ears wait for her. We have talked of her life and her husband and later, as we all walked outside and said good-bye, I thought suddenly that there is a thing she never says—an unspoken plea. There are words that she will never say about something that may never be understood. These are the words: *Do you know what price I paid? Do you know what it cost me to be Nancy with the laughing face, to be the focus of so many critical eyes? Do you know what it was to be best friend and protect him and surround him with people who knew how to help him? The conservatives never liked me, but do they know that without me and the price I paid there was no* him? *He was frail—all men are frail! He needed encouragement and support, he needed stability, and peace. He got it. It came from me.*

It had all gone pretty well for her until June 1968. That's when a short one-page profile of the wife of the governor of California came out in the *Saturday Evening Post.* It was written by Joan Didion, a brilliant woman who was not known for finding conservatives or conservatism congenial. If you read the piece now you sense that Nancy was trying to show the famously intellectual Didion that she too was bright, not someone taken with the trappings of power but a sophisticate who gets the joke.

Joan Didion looked at her and saw exactly what she was: a big fat target. She picked up her acute and unforgiving shotgun.

"Pretty Nancy," she wrote, says things with spirit. "Nancy Reagan says almost everything with spirit, perhaps because she was an actress for a couple of years and has the beginning actress's habit of investing even the most casual lines with a good deal more dramatic emphasis than is ordinarily called for on a Tuesday morning on 45th Street in Sacramento." Nancy speaks banalities, Didion continues, "with the air of someone about to disclose a delightful surprise." Nancy's trills of laughter suggest "a set . . . perfectly dressed, every detail correct." Nancy is playing out "some middle class American woman's daydream, circa 1948." There are two dogs, two children, the house is perfect, her smile is perfect.

Didion's Nancy speaks like a Stepford Christian. "'Having a pretty place to work is important to a man,' she advised me." Nancy says the arrival home from school of son Ron Junior, ten, is "the pivotal point" of her day. But when he arrives home he scoots in silently without saying hello and when his mother tries to draw him out—there is the strong suggestion Nancy is trying to impress Didion with her closeness to her son—Ron Junior is reluctant, stands in a doorway and balks at his mother's invitation to converse. Didion notes it all, quoting Nancy at the end, "I don't believe in being an absentee mother, I just don't."

By the journalistic styles and standards of 1968 it was a startling piece, beautifully observed and quite deadly. It drew the attention of the Washington journalistic establishment, which understood what it was being told: Nancy Reagan is a Plastic Phony Living a Clueless Life. This became the journalistic cliché that would ever after be applied to her.

Nancy was hurt. Her husband saw her humiliation and felt not only immediately protective but also guilty: He'd gotten her into this mess. She wouldn't have been attacked like this if it hadn't been for his ambition.

Years later when I became curious about her, watching her from the other side of the White House and wondering what was going on in there, I asked a friend about Nancy's anxieties, what seemed to me her worries over this or that. I was talking to a close friend of the Reagans from the California days, who gritted her teeth. "It was that mother," she said. "That mother who left her alone all her childhood."

According to her birth certificate she was born Anne Frances Robbins on July 6, 1921, in Sloane Hospital in New York City. Her mother was Edie Luckett, an actress in stock companies and road shows, and her father, Kenneth Robbins, Edie's husband, a life insurance agent and veteran of World War I. Edie nicknamed her daughter Nancy and chose as her godmother her old friend, the silent screen star Alla Nazimova.

When Nancy was two her parents separated and then divorced. Her mother returned to the stage and Nancy was sent to live with her mother's sister and her husband in Bethesda, Maryland. Nancy lived with Aunt Virginia and Uncle Audley until she was seven years old. The house was small; she slept on the porch. She was once seriously ill and cried for her mother, but her mother was not there. She was in New York working, and trying out for roles. She visited when she could. So did Nancy's father. But it was an unusual childhood, and is frequently pointed to by journalists and biographers as the reason for what seemed sometimes a nature marked by loss.

Nancy Reagan herself doesn't see it that way. She was, she tells me, a happy child. And when I asked her last spring if she had felt abandoned by her parents, particularly her mother, she denied it with some warmth.

"I was not abandoned by my mother!" she said, and she gave me a look that said This Is Important. "I was not abandoned by my mother. People say that but I never felt abandoned. She had to go out and work. And she did, and she was on the road, and it's not as if she left me with strangers, she left me with *family.* And we had a wonderful time. I can remember the Fourth of July, we had a little dog named Ginger and we'd put a little red, white and blue scarf around it and red, white and blue on our bicycles. Mother would come whenever she could. And sometimes I'd go to New York."

It was there, she remembered, that she would visit whatever play her mother was working in and dress up in her costumes backstage. She would put on her mother's makeup and act in front of the mirror.

Edie Luckett was touring Chicago when she met a doctor named Loyal Davis, who was recently divorced and on his own. They married in 1929; Edie announced she was leaving the stage forever. Nancy went to live with them. She came to see Loyal Davis as her father and eventually took his name.

Everything you ever hear about Edie Luckett Davis tells you she was an American original—pretty, witty, glamorous, irreverent. She and her husband rose in Chicago society and she lived to see her son-in-law become president, but it never changed her bawdy style.

"She could tell the naughtiest jokes, they'd embarrass Nancy to death," A. C. Lyles, who knew Edie, told me. "She was like the Katzenjammer Kids. She would call me—she'd never say hello, she'd just start talking. It'd be 'A.C.—sweetheart, darling. I just talked to Mamie Eisenhower'—she was a great friend of Mamie Eisenhower. She'd say, 'There's a story on the front page of the papers saying Jimmy Carter had an operation for hemorrhoids.' She said, 'A.C., sweetheart, did you read the story this morning about Jimmy Carter?' I said, 'I did, Edie. I did.' She said, 'Well, it can't be true.' I said, 'Why?' She said, 'How could he have a hemorrhoid operation when he's been a perfect asshole all his life!'

"The Secret Service loved her. She could be pretty risqué!"

Loyal Davis on the other hand was committed to the medical profession, talented, disciplined, and maybe a bit of a grump. But he wasn't a grump when his wife was around, and she didn't have to tour anymore when he married her. They appreciated each other, were grateful to each other, protective of each other.

Which is exactly how Nancy Reagan felt about her husband.

She tried to protect her husband by separating the wheat from the chaff. There were those who were attracted to his power and celebrity and wanted to serve him. Fine. There were those who wanted to use him. Not fine. There were those who would take a bullet for him. Good, keep them close. There were those who would duck: Lose them. She did her best, made a lot of smart judgments and made some mistakes: thought some wheat was chaff and some chaff, wheat. She made her calls and did her best, alone, because she didn't have anyone to figure it out with her. The only person she talked to about such things was Ronnie, and he was the one she was trying to protect.

She kept him from some people who would have been bad for him. She kept him from some people who would have been good for him too. He would have benefited from more access to original thinkers, to historians, academics, serious men and women. He liked people who were trying to figure it all out, people with sharp powers of observation, people with data from past and present.

But that kind of person, in Reagan's day, seemed usually to be one of two types, neither of which was, to her, interesting. There were the academics and writers who were liberals, and really, Ronnie felt he had little to learn from a John Kenneth Galbraith, who had taken to writing of the Soviet Union's unsinkable economy. And there were the academics and writers who weren't liberals but who, inevitably, tended to be social, journalistic and academic nobodies.

It took good radar to find the kind of people who could and would help him, and amuse him. There were the Buckleys, Bill was very smart and Ron liked him a lot, and Pat, his wife, who was like a living definition of fun, outrageous and fashionable. Jerry Zipkin, the New York socialite, was fun, really amusing and informed. He had the best gossip, pedigreed gossip, knew all the stories not only of the people all around him but of their families; he knew and could recount generations of antics. She liked some of the Hollywood crowd, liked Frank Sinatra, who was fun and full of fizz.

Will Durant was not fun. Ariel Durant was not fun.

Charlie Wick was fun, and Mary Jane, and the Bloomingdales and Jorgensens and the Walter Annenbergs. They got the joke, they could be silly, they were high up so not overly impressed by the high up, such as the new governor and then the new president.

They were, essentially, like the men and women John Kennedy kept around him, the Dave Powerses and Bill Walton, the Red Fays. And the social and aristocratic people Jackie brought with her—the Bunny Mellons; her sister Lee and her husband, Stas Radziwill. They were fun too, full of laughs, and easygoing with their friend the president; easygoing *for* their friend the president.

JFK wanted from them what Nancy wanted from her friends and that her husband found pleasurable too. It can be captured by a nice old phrase from the Kennedy era that people don't say much anymore, "a few laughs." Let's get together, have a few laughs.

Chris Matthews of *Hardball* once mused aloud to me about Bebe Rebozo, Richard Nixon's best friend, "Why would a guy like Nixon want to be with him?" Meaning why would an intense and intelligent leader want to hang out with an unintellectual, uninvolved, relatively uninformed businessman.

And I thought, as Chris spoke: Everyone needs a Bebe, someone you can just be no one with and have the kinds of conversations that don't have a point or a purpose; someone you can trust not to talk about what is said, or observed. Every leader needs a Bebe. Or Bebes.

Nancy wanted to be with social Somebodies and have fun, in part because it made up for all the things she didn't really want to do but did—all the staff recommendations and personnel decisions she kept her eye on, all the passing on of ideas and directives.

But there was another reason she chose the Somebodies in Washington. She had judged the town with a practiced eye and wanted to help her husband.

"She's the one who made friends with Kay Graham and the Democrats in this town," the Reagans' friend and aide Robert Higdon told me. "She was the one who had Bob Strauss in the White House and said, 'What do you think, what's your view, you been here a long time ol' man, tell us.' Democrats weren't left out. The Reagans helped make this a real bipartisan working town."

She was not deep and did not pretend to be, liked to talk about people not policy, liked stories about politics mostly to the degree that they were stories about human beings, their foibles and frailties and surprising grace.

And she yearned. Reagan veteran Mike Deaver once said he always saw her as a kid with her nose pressed up against the glass, looking at the people inside at the party. She was curious about Brooke Astor and Kay Graham. But while she liked discovering their world she also stayed close, through the White House years and after, to their friends the California people, the ones from business and show business and politics.

She didn't always understand intellectuals, thought they were ambitious for themselves when sometimes they were ambitious for ideas, and sometimes the ideas were good. She didn't understand the Christian conservatives, I don't think. I always got the impression she thought they were somewhat exotic folk who possibly scourged themselves in private. She didn't understand conservatives in a textured and sophisticated way, or liberals either. She was more like a Republican than a conservative.

The difference between Republicans and conservatives:

In 1986, after I had left the White House as a speechwriter for the president, I went home to Virginia, where I lived, and began to write a book. I wanted to capture a time that I could see receding like a wave, the Reagan era, for I felt it had been big and historic. At the same time I wanted to capture what it was like to work in the White House, what it was like to be a young woman there with no importance but eyes, and with feelings. When I thought about what it was that I wanted to describe, my mind always went to a picture: the way early in the morning on a blustery day, on the stark black-and-white-tiled floors of the Old Executive Office Building, where I worked, everyone's big black open umbrellas would be placed outside their offices on the floor, and how beautiful the round shape of the umbrellas looked as they silently dripped on the marble. Silently, as other umbrellas had for generations, when they had covered the heads of the secretary of John Foster Dulles and Jimmy Forrestal and Rosemary Woods . . .

I was happy to be working on such a great thing, a book. But I was out of the White House. And when I would meet with former colleagues at a party or symposium they would look at me and say "What are you doing now?" And I would say with pride, "I am writing a book." And they would look at me appraisingly, as if I'd said, "I'm in physical therapy to heal a badly fractured leg."

And they'd say, "But what are you—*doing*?"

I told a friend about it, a tough, shrewd man. I said, "Why do they do that, why do they think writing a book isn't doing something?"

He said, "Because they're Republicans. Democrats respect books because they respect ideas. Conservatives respect books because they respect ideas. Republicans respect money."

Ah, I said.

He told me the next time someone asked me what I was doing I was to answer, "I got a huge advance for a book." He said they would be impressed. And you know, I think they were.

So that's the difference between Republicans and conservatives.

Ronald Reagan didn't much care what social circle he was in; I'm not sure he noticed what social circle he was in. He didn't ever seem to care about the standing or status of the person he was talking to as long as the conversation was interesting and as long as he was learning something.

A digression: It is not true, as has often been said, that Reagan wasn't curious. He just wasn't curious about what you'd expect a man like him to be curious about. If he was talking to a doorman at the Mayflower Hotel about how they park and retrieve the cars on a busy night, he'd be learning something and be truly interested. If you were a professor back from China or the Sudan and had real-world observations, anecdotes and history, he'd eagerly take it all in. If you told him about the history of the visitations of the Blessed Virgin he'd be rapt. If you told him that Margaret Thatcher's mother had been a part-time seamstress he'd be fascinated and ask, "What kind of things did she sew, did she design them on paper and cut the cloth herself, how long did it take her to make a dress, what did she sell it for, what kind of profit was there for all that effort, did it help keep the Thatchers going during World War Two?"

But if you told him that the respected pundit David Broder had recently said he was clearly stupid, he wouldn't care beyond five seconds of a furrowed brow. If you told him an economist at Yale said his tax theories were foolish and regressive, that wouldn't rate a furrowed brow at all; and if you told him the visiting president of Ireland was struggling with growing religious tensions he'd nod, listen, be mildly bored because . . . visiting presidents of Ireland are always struggling with religious tensions. That's like saying, "Sometimes water comes from the sky. We call it rain."

He was interested in the concrete, especially when it connected in some way to the abstract or lent itself to metaphor.

He loved understanding how the world worked, from the internal laws of nature to the external laws of how men govern themselves. He was not, as I have noted, a cynic. He never thought the worst about people, or events. That was his father's way, which he'd rejected, and at any rate he sensed that cynics were maybe embittered romantics, unrealistic people for whom things hadn't turned out right.

But Reagan was a skeptic—he had a detached doubt. For instance, he did not think that people with great degrees or great success were necessarily smart. He had little interest in credentials. He once told me—he told a lot of people—that an economist was a person with a Phi Beta Kappa key on one end of his watch chain and nothing on the other. Meaning: A lot of them don't know what time it is.

He didn't dislike intellectuals, and to the extent he had heroes a lot of them *were* intellectuals—Madison, Jefferson, the founders—and in his own time Milton Friedman, Friedrich Hayek, Whittaker Chambers. But in general he did not favor the intellectuals of his time because he found so many of them to be high-IQ dimwits. He had a natural and instinctive agreement with George Orwell's famous putdown that a particular idea was so stupid only an intellectual would believe it.

He thought that intellectuals, especially the great liberal academics of the latter half of the twentieth century, tended to spin themselves into great webs of complexity, great complicated things that they'd get stuck in, and when they got out they'd spin a new web to ensnare themselves or mankind.

He thought these intellectuals were the natural heirs to the intellectuals of the beginning of the century, the Bloomsbury group, for instance. He thought they were among the most brilliant stupid people who had ever lived. Of course, in thinking like this he was, paradoxically, thinking like Nathan Glazer or Irving Kristol or George Will or James Q. Wilson—all intellectuals.

The writer Marie Brenner wrote in *House of Dreams,* her biography of the Binghams, the great newspaper clan of Louisville, Kentucky, of the closeness of the patriarch Barry Bingham and his wife, Mary. They were "like two halves of the same whole." Their union was so intense, their relationship so consuming of the other's self that . . . it left their children out. There was no room for them in their parents' completion. Barry and Mary were The Relationship, and The Relationship took the oxygen out of the room; their children went elsewhere to breathe.

The same, essentially, has been said of the Reagans. Their marriage was a small house with one room and it was theirs. All of the Reagan children have spoken of this in one way or another, that they felt at different times and to varying degrees kept away, kept out, and it is no doubt true.

Ronald Reagan hadn't had much of a father and he absorbed that fact and perhaps turned it into energy that fueled his rise. But he was brought up in an age when not so much was expected of fathers. His father had been limited, he had done all right. Reagan became a limited father and married a woman who had had limited parents, and was limited in turn.

Together they were limited parents. Like a lot of parents. But their children grew up in an age when a lot was expected of parents and you noticed if they didn't come through.

The Reagans' children were under pressures their parents could not have dreamed of. Their father was governor and then president; he was controversial, the focus of both great derision and great love. They got attention they didn't always want and questions they resented. *Why aren't you a big star like your mother, Maureen, or a big political force like your dad? Patti, are you a Fascist like your father; do you, like, share his politics? Ron, you gonna what, choreograph right-wing ballets? Michael, how come you're never on Air Force One?*

It wasn't easy for any of them. And their parents didn't fully understand, maybe *couldn't* fully understand. Because they thought their children had grown up with everything.

Ronald Reagan was perplexed. He had given his children everything his father hadn't been able to give him. He was sober, earned a reliable income, owned a home, even a ranch. He was not at the bottom of Dixon but the top of America. So his kids had it better, didn't they? And they got what they needed: If one of them had bad eyesight the kid wouldn't have to wait until he was twelve and accidentally put on Nancy's glasses to find out! They'd notice.

Ronald and Nancy Reagan had bent themselves to their parents' needs, with Dutch ultimately supporting his family with good humor and understanding, and Nancy acting the part of a happy girl to make her mother feel better about the facts of their lives. Dutch and Nancy must have assumed their children would do the same, for them.

And there is more, of course. There is the great sadness of the political life, which is the great sin of all persons of intense ambition. Robert Lincoln didn't always speak of his father, Abraham, with great affection, and didn't much like his mother. FDR wasn't really an attentive father, Eleanor a fairly unusual mother. Robert Kennedy loved his children so much he would kiss their hands as they walked by, but when the choice came between bringing them up in an air of relative calm after their uncle's assassination or gambling himself for the presidency—in a dangerous time when they were killing people like Jack and Martin Luther King, Jr., and Medgar Evars—he gambled, and ran. And he too of course was killed, leaving ten children to be brought up by an overwhelmed mother in a home marked by loss.

Washington is full of people who work at the office late and go in on Saturdays and Sundays to prepare and argue over child-friendly welfare bills and child-friendly education initiatives and Head Start programs and reading programs for impoverished children. They are doing good work at HHS and the Department of Education and in the OEOB. It is work that is important to our country. And sometimes at their desks they think of their own children and look up and promise themselves, "Next week we'll go on a picnic, or to a ball game."

And their children are home watching TV or pushing a rock with a stick in the driveway thinking, "Where's Dad? Where's Mom?"

Washington, of course, isn't the only city this applies to, nor people in politics the only professionals. My son has pushed that rock with a stick. Maybe yours has too.

This is what professional ambition does: It takes you into the world and away from your family. You can make a lot of people's lives better that way, but you can make the lives of those around you worse. It's one of the great traps, the great strains of trying to make the world better, and I don't mean that ironically.

One of the things Nancy Reagan did for her husband was to absorb. She absorbed things that he was feeling, took the heat, bore the brunt. Reagan had a temper, and everyone who worked with him has a story about it. Dave Fischer, who spent more time with him than most, was once standing next to the president on a road trip. They were in a hotel room, it was nighttime, and Reagan had picked up something, a memo or newspaper, and didn't like what he read. He made a sound like a grunt, threw it down on the table, and Fischer was so startled he jumped. This almost made Reagan jump. Then they both started to laugh and Reagan said, "Why did you jump?" and Fischer said, "I don't know, I thought you were gonna hit me!"

When Reagan got angry he'd take his reading glasses off and throw them on the table. Sometimes he'd swear, sometimes he'd purse his lips and shake his head. He had to get really mad to get mad but when he was mad he was mad.

"He would just blow," said their longtime friend Robert Higdon. "She would let him just get it out. And then she'd say, 'That's okay, honey, we'll take care of it.' He'd walk in their bedroom and throw down the schedule and say, 'Damnit, why is this on the schedule!' He'd get irritable. 'Damn this!' And she'd give you those eyes.

"She didn't usually take him on, she'd pick her fights, not a lot. He would let his irritability show with her. He would put up with a lot from everyone and then finally he'd go boom. And he'd do it in front of her. And she'd listen, and the listening helped him. 'I know, honey, I see, honey, calm down, we'll take care of it.' She'd divert him to something. 'Honey, go lie down, go relax.' And then she'd turn to us. 'Why is this on the schedule, why is that on the schedule, what the heck's going on here?'"

He added, "She knew him. She knew not to push him, knew to let him be himself. She knew how to help him be the best in all situations.

"Some of the imagery stuff that was done in the White House—don't forget she had to okay it. She would always okay what we were doing—if you knew what would work for him, how to pitch the ball so he could hit it out of the park.

"She didn't swing the bat for him, he did that. But she tried to make it so he was pitched to right."

"A lot of people were afraid of her in the White House," Dave Fischer said. "The first thing I learned about dealing with Mrs. Reagan was she would ask questions of people, and some people weren't smart enough to know that if they didn't know the answer just say you don't know the answer but I'll get back to you. She knew that I always would give her the answer or get back to her. But I often say she was the only person I know that could make my hands sweat, just because if she asked a question it was something she wanted to know, and you had to make sure to get back to her quickly.

"Because of that a lot of people were unfairly afraid of her. People didn't get to see the tender side, the real Nancy Reagan."

He felt the real side was the tender side. Fischer remembered once when a piece ran about Nancy and made mention of her legs, saying they were piano legs. Fischer walked in to see her, and he knew she was upset. She had a very sad look on her face. He went up to her and hugged her and held on to her for a long time. "It was personal, and petty, and it hurt her. I got to see a different side of her."

My read was that she was so anxious that things go well because she considered herself to be the last bulwark against trouble headed for Ronnie. She had to take care of him because she felt he had needs he would not look out for himself. And sometimes it all made her tense.

And she looked like an aging movie star. So you add tense to movie star and you get: Evita.

*Nancy recognized that he gave everybody the benefit of the doubt and she was better judge of character

Which is what I called her in my first book. We young ones in the White House used to compare her to Gloria Swanson in *Sunset Boulevard*. "I'm ready for my closeup, Mr. De Mille." We called her "the Hairdo with Anxiety."

Once when I saw her coming my way in the White House, I hid behind a pillar, and wrote about it in my memoir of those days. I don't blame myself for having hidden, she was scary. She was scary to a lot of us.

Years later when I knew her and wondered what she thought of my criticisms, I asked her what it was like to take shots from people, from supporters, from those who worked in her husband's White House. "Like me!" I said merrily.

She started to laugh, and I did too. "Yes, that does happen now and then," she said.

And that was all.

I was grateful when we became friends. It was the result of the sweet assistance of her friend Jerry Zipkin, who had become my friend and who thought it silly that two of his friends didn't understand each other. This was in the early nineties, when the Reagans were back in California. When I would see Jerry Zipkin in New York he'd say things like "I told Nancy that wonderful thing you said about Ronnie." And then he said the next time I bumped into him, "I was just talking to Nancy, who said to be sure to say hello to you." This surprised me so much my mouth dropped open, and Robert Higdon, who was with us, burst into laughter. Then Robert invited me to dinner with her and I saw her—the president had only recently been diagnosed with Alzheimer's—and everything somehow was changed, and I just wanted to put my arm around her and appreciate her. Because suddenly I saw what it had cost her, had always cost her. And I wanted to say: Thank you.

The price she paid for loving him and being his wife was high. She lost all privacy, lived in a photo op like most major politicians' wives but more so with him because he was a real leader, truly powerful. The loss of privacy hurt, as it does all first ladies. But she had a harder time than most, and we forget it. The editors of *The New York Times,* a great newspaper, made a mistake and put on their front page the charge that she'd had an affair with Frank Sinatra. Biographers inspected her sexual practices, if any, as a young starlet. When she fought with her children it was headline news. When her children and stepchildren showed their unhappiness, it made the gossip columns.

She lost him to work, to the distractions and preoccupations of his office. And what she got was not bad. She got fame and celebration and beautiful photos on the cover of *Vanity Fair.* This was not burdensome to someone who wanted to be a famous actress and on the covers of magazines. She got an interesting life. She got success, social acceptance, affluence and standing.

But if you ask her what she got, as I did, she will tell you, "Ronnie." And she will mean it.

You know what else I think? I think her mother was elusive, her father had left and the stepfather was wonderful but distracted and preoccupied. I think she found the somewhat elusive and often distracted Ronald Reagan and thought, "I'm home. I know this zip code."

But to keep the elusive man she had to make herself central to him, and to do that she maybe consciously and maybe not kept some others away from him. And he let her be in charge of the family and the friendships. He owed it to her, in part because of all they both thought she'd sacrificed to be his wife. Their children were about as hurt and shunted aside as any children in an unusual family. And there are a lot of unusual families.

I'm not sure any of his children fully understood him, or he them. The members of his family are still trying to figure it all out, understand it all. They're like people who've been in a field that has been bombed, rushing about to save each other. And years later, concussed by history, they're trying still to orient themselves, to understand everything that happened to them in their unusual lives.

They are all good people; they are all people you'd like to have for your neighbors. They sometimes found it hard to be each other's neighbor. Just like so many families, maybe most. But theirs was interesting because, again, within it was a great man.

When I think of Patti Davis, I think of this phrase: The things she carried. Because once when I was talking to her about her father she veered off into a consideration of what was the best book about Vietnam: Tim O'Brien's *Going After Cacciato* or maybe *The Things They Carried*.

She is approaching middle age now, but doesn't look it. She was famous at twenty. It's more than two decades since, and she's different, of course, more mature, not the rebellious young woman. She is bright, aware, theatrical—I see her in my imagination as a kind of Stevie Nicks, in a shawl, twirling.

She is wry, ironic, tries to have friends, be funny, be wise, get attention. She writes for magazines, and she's still trying, like all of them, to figure it out.

She tells me, "My first memory of my father was one my father was surprised that I had. I asked him once about a blue-eyed horse at Dick Powell's ranch in Mandeville Canyon. 'We were standing,' I said. 'You were holding me by a fence and there was a horse with blue eyes.' I think I was three. I can still picture this horse. Dappled brown and white, with blue eyes.

"I don't remember my father as a movie star. I remember when he was on TV. I wasn't allowed to see his last movie, *The Killers,* because they decided it was too violent. I really wanted to see it and it was a big thing but now I could rent it and it never enters my mind.

"I went to school with Pat Boone's children and Jamie Lee Curtis and with Lorna Luft. I went to Star Kid's School. Leslie Caron went to the parents' meetings; Tony Curtis was there. It was John Thomas Dye School in Bel Air. Then I went to boarding school, where I repeated eighth grade. They had skipped me in third grade.

"I was an angry girl, and had discipline problems. And also I had decided what I wanted to learn and what I didn't want to learn. I wasn't interested in science, in little frogs in formaldehyde. I wanted literature and poetry and writing. So I flunked the courses I didn't like.

"I was terribly rebellious. I think my anger started in childhood. It's hard for me to look at young pictures of myself. I'm sure it puzzled my father and I know it pained him; I know it really confused him. He couldn't understand it.

"Remember the book *Black Like Me*? When I was twelve I would have given my right arm to find that stuff and turn myself and my entire family black. Because I wanted to show solidarity with people I thought were oppressed and who were in fact oppressed, and some still are. But also I felt so guilty about being white and privileged. I felt very guilty about it." I asked if the guilt she felt ever lifted in her childhood. "I always felt . . . not deserving. Poor people too—I wanted to be one of them by showing my solidarity.

"I had this who fantasy—I remember sitting out there in Arizona at the golf course, at my grandparents', sitting out there in the sun reading *Black Like Me*. I thought things would have been so much better if I could turn myself black and turn my whole family black."

I ask her about the kind of father her father was. She says:

"I think you come to a peace with it when you realize at a point that he did the best he knew. He was the child of an alcoholic. Where would he have learned how to be a conscious parent? Where would he have learned how to be an emotionally available father? It wasn't in that era. It wasn't like parenting magazines were sitting there on the coffee table. They didn't talk about those things. Expectations were low.

"It's very typical of a child of an alcoholic that it hurt too much to talk about intimate things. Later, knowing that enabled me to—to forgive myself for the things that I carried around: 'If only I had been better, if I had been different, if I had been a Republican.'" She laughs. "I could have gotten closer to my father, I could have traveled that distance.

"You know what I've come to realize? A lot of things he taught me as a child I didn't reject, but I didn't take them on big time until I got much older. He did have something special with God; he talked to God all the time. It didn't mean that he was any more special in God's eyes or that he believed that. We all are special with God. It's not that God's speaking to anybody more than anyone else, it's that some people choose to listen. And talk back. And my father talked to God. That's what I got as a child, I got that he just talked to God all the time. He just had conversations with God.

"And that's the way I talked to God when I was a child. My idea of prayer was never that you sit down, clean up your room, clean up your act before you can talk to God. Never. It was always that I knew I could take my mess to God, I knew that I could just get down and talk to God like my father, all the time.

"When we'd go horseback riding at the Malibu ranch, just the two of us, I knew the way to get him to talk and to have a conversation was to talk about God. And talk about heaven, ask him about heaven—'What do you think God thinks of this,' 'What do you think heaven is like?' If I went to that place we would have these wonderful conversations. . . . And he would just tell me sometimes, 'Well, I asked God about this and this is what he said back to me.'

"My father told me that my whole life. You ask God something and he will answer you, he will answer very specifically. Might not be the answer you want to hear, but God will give you an answer. It's why he felt confidence about the big decisions in his life—Hollywood and running for office . . ."

Her mind goes to something that happened when she was eight or nine years old:

"When I was a kid and my fish died—I had a black fish which I creatively called Blackie. And Blackie was at the bottom of the fish tank for a day, and I thought he was sleeping. My father said fish don't sleep like that. He was dead. And he gave me a fish funeral. Just Blackie and me. We went out to the yard. I had just seen the movie *Joan of Arc,* where they lash the two twigs together as she was dying. So I said, 'Daddy, you have to take two sticks and lash them together into a cross for the little fish grave.'

"He made the cross out of twigs and string, and he said a prayer, and I remember him telling me my fish—I asked, 'I know he's in the ground but where is he now, where is his soul?'

"And he said, 'In heaven. Where he can swim and swim and swim, and he can see all these other fishes, and nothing will ever eat him, and he'll live forever there in this clean blue water.' And it was this beautiful picture that he painted. So I wasn't sad for the fish. I had so much fun at the funeral I thought, can another one die? Maybe we can kill one!

"He was such a brilliant father for young children. But when we got older and the questions got sort of more gnarly, and we got more complicated and more screwed up and all that stuff that goes along with growing up, he was just befuddled. He didn't know what to do.

"He didn't know how to navigate the more turbulent waters once it got to that. But both of us, as we started getting older, it started getting more complicated. It's complicated to raise a child.

"He was out of his element—his element as a father was that brilliant part of childhood, of make-believe. But what's interesting to me now is I've come sort of full circle and I've come back to that time of childhood and it's such an area of richness in my life. Spiritually that's where I've gone back to for sustenance. Of everything that I've learned and studied and believed and come to and continue to come to spiritually—I can trace it back, and the beginning of that thread, the beginning of that weave was him. And the things that he told me as a child. He was the dominant parent in terms of the formation of my inner being, and my own creativity.

"I cried when he left to go to the White House because I had never wanted him to be president. I always knew that he would be, from the time I was a child I knew he would be. I always knew he would be. From the time I first learned about Lincoln being shot when I was a child, it's like I saw my father. I remember being at John Thomas Dye School and learning about Lincoln being shot, sitting in Ford's Theatre and everything, and thinking—just seeing my father. . . . It was just that leap, I just saw it. After my father was shot a friend of mine reminded me, he said to me, 'Do you remember when your father was running for president you said I'm so scared because I think he's gonna be shot?' I said, 'I said that to you? I know I felt it but I didn't know I said it to you.'

"I will never understand my father. He will forever be a mystery. He was elusive everywhere. I think he was elusive with my mother. I don't think—I don't think my mother even really got to totally figure him out. Somewhere in my mother's heart she knows. . . ."

I told Patti that an aide to her father had told me recently of something he saw on inauguration day, the Sunday inauguration in the White House in 1985, the private swearing-in that preceded the public swearing-in the next day. At the swearing-in inside the White House, the Bushes were there and the Reagans were there. The aide thought to himself, "Here's the Bushes, here's the Reagans. George Bush is surrounded by a real family—kids, vibrant, not perfect but vibrant; they have a relationship with each other. And then I looked at Reagan and thought, 'This great man, the most important work a man can do, making a family, and he doesn't have it together.' "

Patti said, "I feel enormous sympathy now for my parents for that. And for my father's—listen, in some ways I think maybe my father is still here now in order to see—I mean there's a soul there that doesn't have Alzheimer's, there's a soul in there that isn't ill. So his soul is inside watching everything going on. And I've thought sometimes maybe he is still here on this earthly plane to see my going up there and to see us together in a room without bitching at one another and kvetching at one another. . . . We die when our souls are ready to die, when God is ready to take us. That's the truth of it. But I do wonder about it . . . and it has occurred to me that my father looks out sometimes and sees me sitting there with my mother. And when Ron goes up to the house, my father is so vocal. You can't really understand what he's saying but—it's like something about Ron just energizes him.

"And he's—you know, he missed everything. He didn't really have a sweet father-daughter relationship except when I was young; he didn't really have a good father-son relationship in the ways that fathers and sons can really bond. . . .

"The truth of the matter is, it was like sibling rivalry but America is the other sibling. And America is always gonna win. America will always win. America will always have bigger crises than a kid, and more immediate-seeming crises. And America elected him. America is always going to be the most important member of the family."

She never came to share her father's politics. Even as a child to the extent she understood his views she did not agree with them.

"Already even at the time of the Goldwater speech I was not in agreement with him, not so much ideologically but, you know, Vietnam was starting. And I just never responded as a child to my father's anti-Communist stuff. It never made sense to me.

"He would show us maps where all this area was red, and he'd say—it was a flattened-out map, and all this area of the Soviet Union seems rather large, and he'd say, 'See how close they are to the United States?' Because the ocean on the map seemed really small. 'See how close they are? They could just come over here and we'd have to be red too.'

"And I thought, 'Why do they want us? Don't they have enough land to take care of on their own?' It just wasn't logical to me. I'd look from our house in the Palisades and I'd look at the ocean and I'd think, 'So, like, the Russians would land there, so then what?'

"He probably really tried to explain what communism was, but I think it went over my head as a kid. What I remember taking from it was that all the cities are gray in the Eastern bloc countries and all the people are unhappy.

"But I couldn't quite make that jump to—I'd think, 'Okay, if all of the people are hungry and unhappy, then how do they have enough money to come over here and take us too?'"

She laughs, remembering their conversations. "They're hungry and weak. It was like, 'How are they gonna get across the ocean? Do they have boats? They can't travel across the damn ocean, much less take us over. I mean, take us over with what? They'll just land here and paint the cities gray?"

This is what happens in modern fame. You can go through your whole life thinking your father is a mystery, unfathomable. And as an example you give the revelation, in Edmund Morris's biography *Dutch*, that Ronald Reagan and Jane Wyman had had a child who lived only a few hours. Patti told me Ron had called her in amazement, had said, "Did you know we had a half sister?" He said the book was dedicated to her. But Ronald Reagan talked about the tragic birth of that child in his first memoir, *Where's the Rest of Me?* It wasn't a secret. He talked too about how his absence from home and his relentless interest and engagement in Hollywood union politics led his wife Jane Wyman to leave him.

And yet Patti knew none of this. *Because you forget what's in the books written about a famous father.* When I asked Nancy Reagan if anyone knew the story she'd told me about her first meeting with Ron, she told me she thought it was in her memoir, but wasn't sure. This is the nature of modern fame. You talk to your family in your books, and they may not read them, or remember them, or absorb the facts put forth in a way that incorporates the information into their emotional experience of who Dad was, or who Mom was.

All famous families are like this to some degree. Ted Kennedy once told me about one of his sons' allergies, and I said that was the same one Jack had. He blinked with surprise: Really? How do you know? I read it in a biography of him, I said. It was data to me but obscure and forgotten information about a late elder brother to him.

Executive Mansion

They got used to the Executive Mansion on their own. The Carters had broken with recent tradition and not given the Reagans a tour of their new home. The end of the 1980 campaign had been hard, with Carter suggesting Reagan was a warmongering nuclear cowboy and the Reagans' son Ron responding by calling Carter a snake. The Carters greeted the Reagans a few days before the inauguration and then turned them over to staff. In the limousine on the way to Reagan's swearing-in, Carter was silent, exhausted and depressed after a night dealing with last-minute snags that threatened the release of American hostages in Iran. They would be freed moments after Reagan was sworn in, a final humiliation for the outgoing president. Reagan had thought Carter rude but later changed his mind: It is painful to leave the presidency, more painful still to be voted out, and replaced by a man you don't respect.

The inauguration too broke precedent, being held on the west side of the Capitol for the first time in history. Reagan wanted to look west, toward Illinois, where he had been born, and California, where he had become a public figure—toward the country that had chosen him in a landslide. The usual tens of thousands of people showed, a great expanding pool of humanity. There were flags and bunting, choirs and cannon. He saw in the distance, at the far end of the Mall, the glittering dome of the Lincoln Memorial.

It was overcast. But as Reagan took his place behind the podium and looked at the chief justice of the Supreme Court, the sun burst through the clouds in what he remembered as "an explosion of warmth and light." He could feel the heat on his face as he recited the oath of office. His left hand was on his mother's Bible, which was open to 2 Chron. 7:14: "If my people, which are called by my name, shall humble themselves, and pray, and seek my face, and turn from their wicked ways; then will I hear from heaven, and will forgive their sin, and will heal their land." Next to the verse were words Nelle Reagan had written in her shy script, "A most wonderful verse for the healing of the nations."

Ronald Reagan's first inaugural address was not soaring and lyrical but declarative and explanatory: Government, which is not the solution to our problems but rather the great problem itself, must be tamed; so, by inference, should the elites who would use government to order us about; and in the taming will come a greater portion of freedom for individual Americans, and with that freedom they will make their own lives, and our country's life, better.

He watched the inaugural parade from the grandstand that had been set up on the front lawn of the White House and waved to the Dixon High School band. The parade over, he and Nancy entered the White House for the first time as its occupants.

The Executive Mansion had always had something of a mystical aura for him. He had first walked into it when Harry Truman was president, as part of a delegation of motion picture labor leaders. He had visited the White House again when he was governor of California, when LBJ was president and then again when Nixon was president.

But now it was his, or rather the mansion was the place where he lived, at the sufferance of the people.

They held hands, took an elevator up to the second floor, to the residence. They stood holding hands in a long hall with a high ceiling. They walked down the central hall and suddenly it hit home. "It was only at this moment that I appreciated the enormity of what had happened to me." He was the president now.

Their eyes filled with tears. They walked through each room. The Lincoln bedroom . . . the Treaty Room . . . the Truman Balcony. And later he peeked into the Oval Office, and stood and said a silent prayer. His aide Michael Deaver was with him now, and Reagan sat at the great desk he had chosen to use, JFK's desk. The new president said, "Do you have goose bumps?" And Deaver laughed and said, yes, he did.

And that night came the inaugural balls. As he dressed in white tie and tails he turned to one of his children and comically clicked his heels. "I'm the president!" he said.

The Reagans danced at each of the ten balls.

After their first night in the White House a funny thing happened, or rather, didn't happen. It was years before he realized it hadn't happened.

For decades, Ronald Reagan had had a recurring dream. In it, he was looking at houses. He entered a big house that had high ceilings, white walls, big rooms. An impressive place. He stood and looked at it and thought to himself, "A house that is available at a price I could afford." And the dream would end.

From the day he entered the White House to live he never had the dream again. Only when he lived there did he understand what it meant—that it was information from his subconscious: You can have the White House if you want it, you can meet its costs and demands.

The next day he walked into the Oval Office, looked at his schedule, looked at his aides—Mike Deaver and Ed Meese from California, from his governor days, and Jim Baker of Texas, the talented and shrewd campaign manager for George Bush—and thought: This is like my first day as governor. He looked at the schedule: meetings with legislators and staff. Just like the old days.

He established a routine. Up at seven or seven-fifteen. Read the papers, drink Sanka or brewed decaf. Into the office at nine, work straight through—speeches, meetings, appointments, briefings, no stops—in the office until five or six P.M. Then up to the residence for paperwork, phone calls, an early dinner on trays with Nancy, more homework—letters to heads of state, speeches to read, decision memos—and then to bed, by ten or eleven if he could. Those were his favorite nights. But often he would leave the office at the end of the day and go to the residence only to change for a dinner, a speech, an interview, an appearance.

His days always began, and in time this became famous, with jokes. He had a repertoire of them, perhaps a thousand on call in his head at any time, and something—workers in the Rose Garden or something

Deaver said when he walked into the office—would make him think of one and off he'd go.

From the beginning there was one huge fact, which also harkened back to his experience in California. The country was in economic crisis. Interest rates were the highest since the Civil War, the prime interest rate at an astonishing 21.5 percent. High unemployment, high inflation.

Reagan and his men had been putting together an economic recovery package since the day after the election. And now, his first day on the job, the subject of his meetings was tax reform—his desire to reduce federal income tax rates from top to bottom, for all taxpayers. This was his thinking: If we get tax rates down it will stimulate the economy; a stimulated economy will produce growth, which will produce jobs; this will get both interest rates and unemployment down. And with more jobs and with a growing economy there will be more people paying taxes, which will eventually make up for the decrease in tax revenues that will follow the tax cut.

He would talk to his aides about his thinking and they would dutifully take notes. Some of them—Ed Meese, for instance—agreed with him. Others—Mike Deaver, for instance—would keep their eyes on establishment opinion to make sure that the eventual tax plan did not go too far in a direction that would arouse the passionate opposition of the American media and Wall Street CEOs. Baker would be dubious of big cuts, but he understood the boss's wishes. Reagan would refer to a fourteenth-century Muslim philosopher named Ibn Khaldoon, who wrote, Reagan said, of the tax structure of ancient Egypt: "At the beginning of the dynasty taxation yields a large revenue from small assessments. At the end of the dynasty, taxation yields a small revenue from large assessments." Meaning: When rates are low, revenues are high, and when rates are high, revenues eventually become depressed because high tax rates discourage economic effort and dampen energy.

The newspapers and various political philosophers and economists called it supply-side economics. Reagan was bemused. He didn't think he was creating any new theory and he didn't think it had any new name. Everything he knew about practical economics came from four things. He learned basic economic theory at Eureka College, where he had majored in economics; he earned money as an American worker from the 1930s through the 1980s and experienced tax rates and the individual changes in behavior they encouraged or discouraged; he had read the economic and philosophical canon from Friedrich Hayek to Milton Friedman to Michael Oakeshott and Edmund Burke; he had for eight years governed the nation's largest state and handled its tax demands, tax revenues and tax spending. He had learned what he knew, that is, from concrete and personal experience, from reading abstract theory and from political and governmental work.

His economic background was broader and more layered than that of any modern president. Unlike FDR, Kennedy and Bush, he had not been born to wealth; unlike Eisenhower he had not spent his life as a salaried member of the armed forces; unlike Johnson, Nixon and Kennedy he had not left a young manhood in World War II to enter the state-salaried life of politics. The only modern presidents who came close to Reagan in terms of economic experience were Harry Truman, who had been a small business owner and had later found his calling in politics, and, ironically, Jimmy Carter, who after spending his early adulthood in the navy had run a business in Georgia. But Carter had inherited the family peanut business and ran it essentially as his father had. He had not consistently been forced into the scrambling and risk taking of the entrepreneur, had not experienced the stress of the self-made, of those trying to invent for themselves a business or profession.

Reagan, the independent operator—radio freelancer, radio star, movie actor, movie star, television host—knew what it took to go it alone and had not only a natural respect for entrepreneurs, whom he thought created the economy, but also a protectiveness toward them. They should pay their fair share, he always thought, but they shouldn't get clobbered by taxes just because they turned their guts into a business that makes money.

His sympathies too were with the sort of men and women he met on the line in the 1950s in his General Electric plant tours. Why would they jump at the offer of overtime when Uncle Sam was going to tax them so much more heavily for their extra effort?

His feelings and thoughts about inflation too were grounded in a sense of what is decent in the way the citizenry is treated by the government. Inflation, he always said, is a thief. It silently, invasively erodes the take-home pay of a father supporting a family. The father doesn't do anything to lose purchasing power, he just keeps coming home with the paycheck and it just keeps buying less and less. Reagan thought this especially cruel to the old, who lived on savings that would not grow. And he thought there was an important moral element to inflation for those who were young, and just beginning to form their economic habits. When you are young and working hard and bringing home money . . . and you put that money in the bank like a responsible citizen saving for a house or a car . . . and in that bank the value of your money day by day falls because its purchasing power falls . . . well, that encourages the young not to save but to buy, and now, right away. It changes the character: Inflation says, "Live for today, don't plan for tomorrow." Inflation encourages the young to be heedless because the heedless choice seems the prudent one.

A month into office he sent the Congress a bill containing an across-the-board tax cut of 30 percent over the next three years. And he launched a program to cut those governmental rules and regulations that seemed born not to meet the needs of consumers who needed protections but bureaucrats who needed to be busy.

The day Reagan walked into office the federal budget deficit was at roughly $80 billion—high, and growing. He could have eased its rate of growth by taking an ax to American military spending. Instead he increased it—as he had promised throughout the 1980 campaign.

America needed to be safe. The Soviets were building nuclear and conventional forces at an astounding rate, actually spending 50 percent a year more on weapons than the United States. Our soldiers and sailors and marines were underpaid, and treated with insufficient respect. Vietnam had ended six years before but the country wasn't over it, not nearly. Some in the armed forces had become so dispirited that they didn't wear their uniforms when they went to town. And there were the problems with parts and personnel: We had ships that couldn't sail and planes that couldn't fly.

Reagan met with the Joint Chiefs of Staff and told them he would turn it around—improve funding, encourage respect for the professionalism of the men and women who protect us. He told them he wouldn't accept a second-rate army and navy and air force. He asked them what they needed to achieve military superiority over potential enemies.

Most important, perhaps, he told them that when he had campaigned for the presidency he had been asked time and again what he would do if he wound up forced to choose between national security and more growth in the deficit. He told them he had always replied that it was easy—he would come down on the side of national defense. He told the chiefs he would put that promise into practice.

This was all in the first few months of 1981. He thought that if he worked hard, made the right decisions, took the right chances and got some breaks, he could increase military spending, cut taxes, ignite the economy and get a balanced budget by 1983.

He was hopeful but not naïve. He took to quoting Lincoln to the effect that events controlled a president more than a president controlled events. He was about to find out just how right Lincoln was.

Grace Under Pressure

Two weeks before, he was at a ceremony at Ford's Theatre, looking up at the flag-draped box in which Lincoln had been shot. He thought to himself as he gazed at where the shots had rung out that even now, more than a century later, even now with all the security a president has, he can still be shot by someone who really wants to get him.

This, oddly enough, is what John F. Kennedy was thinking one evening when visiting Texas as president. His biographer William Manchester reports that Kennedy, in his hotel room one night, mused to his aides how easy it would be for a man with a rifle to shoot him. The next day, November 22, 1963, he would go to Dallas.

It was the afternoon of March 30, 1981, and the president of the United States, in office just nine weeks, was wearing a brand-new blue pinstripe suit. There was nothing special about the day. Spring had come but Washington was overcast, with a mild chill. The president's afternoon would be dominated by a speech to the Construction Trades Council at the Washington Hilton, just a mile from the White House. Sitting presidents had gone to the Hilton 110 times since the first president to go there, Richard Nixon, in 1972, so there was no sense of event, no air of anxiety among security personnel.

The Construction Trades Council was a union group with which some of Ronald Reagan's policies were not popular. Union leaders in the 1980s sometimes experienced a disjunction with their membership on the subject of Reagan. The personal conservatism and middle- and working-class insights and experiences of a lot of members made them like Reagan, understand him. But Reagan was not in general considered sympathetic to union-supported legislation by union leadership, so most union leaders opposed him, as did their unions, officially. How the members voted, however, was something Reagan had a hunch about. He liked the rank and file, felt the same kinship with them he felt for the men and women on the line at the GE plants, and thought they felt a kinship with him too.

The president departed the White House in a small motorcade, arrived at the Hilton and soon walked onstage in the downstairs ballroom. The speech went fine, receiving semihardy applause. He waved, nodded, smiled and left.

The president and his party left the hotel through a side entrance and passed a rope line of press photographers, TV cameras and reporters. With Reagan was a small group of aides, including Dave Fischer, Mike Deaver, press secretary James Brady, and a larger group of Secret Service agents, including the head of the detail, Jerry Parr. Parr wasn't supposed to be there; it was a simple assignment and he'd meant to give it over to another agent, but that morning he changed his mind and decided to go.

Reagan was walking toward his limousine when he heard someone shout a question. It was Mike Putzel of the Associated Press.

"Mr. President!" he cried out. "Mr. Reagan!"

He was going to ask a question about Lech Walesa and the Solidarity movement in Poland.

The president began to turn toward Putzel. Mike Deaver reflexively did what he always did, which was to put his hand on the press secretary's back and press him toward the reporters. Jim Brady began to move toward Putzel and the rope line.

Dave Fischer, who was usually with Reagan from the moment he stepped out of the elevator in the morning until he stepped back in at the end of the day, had also heard Putzel. He had been walking with the president toward the door of the presidential limo. (You can see him, a young man of thirty-one with brown hair and a mustache, in part of the historical footage used in a scene in the movie *Forrest Gump*.) But for no reason, Fischer turned from the president's side and walked to the back of the limousine, by the trunk.

He stood there for a split second and thought, "What am I doing here? I'm usually right there next to him."

And at that second, at 2:27 P.M., as that thought passed through his mind, Ronald Reagan heard what he thought were firecrackers. Two or three of them just over to his left, a small fluttering *pop pop.*

Mike Deaver knew they weren't firecrackers. He was close enough to the shooter that he smelled sulfur. His immediate thought: gunshot.

Mike Putzel, thirty-eight years old, knew too. He had covered Vietnam for two and a half years. When he heard the *pop*s he knew: Those aren't firecrackers. He didn't see a gun and didn't see the shooter but he knew what he'd heard.

A split second later Reagan is turned toward the sound and says, "What the hell's that?" At the same moment, Jerry Parr and Agent Ray Shattuck grab the president, bend him at the waist and throw him "with a tremendous lunge," as Parr put it, into the back of the limousine. Reagan landed hard, on the transmission bump in the middle of the floor in the backseat, Jerry Parr on top of him. Reagan felt sharp pain, the "most paralyzing pain" of his life.

Before the shooting began Agent Tim McCarthy had already opened the president's car door. He was two or three feet from Reagan, watching the crowd as the shots rang out and Reagan was thrown into the car. McCarthy stood with his arms out between the shooter and Reagan. It was his job to take the shot. He was punched into the air by a bullet that hit him in the chest.

In the car, Reagan snapped at Jerry Parr to get off him. Parr told the driver, Drew Unrue, "Get us out of here!" Unrue hit the accelerator and headed for the White House.

This is how fast it all happened: The six shots were fired in less than two seconds. The door of the limousine was slammed shut by Ray Shattuck a second later. The president's car was moving within five seconds.

"We are trained all of our lives for moments like this," Parr later told me. "Every agent understands: Cover and evacuate. You hear a shot you don't go for your gun, you don't curse, you don't yell, you don't go after the assassin—you cover the president with your body and you get him out of there."

Reagan tried to sit up. Parr pushed him into a sitting position. He saw the bullet mark on the car window, and had seen the bodies down on the sidewalk as they'd pulled out.

Reagan lurched back as the car shot forward. They made a left turn at Connecticut Avenue. Reagan told Jerry he thought he might have broken a rib when he was thrown to the floor of the car. Parr examined him wordlessly, running his hands under his coat, over his chest, his hair, his neck. Parr radioed Shattuck: "Rawhide's okay, let's head for Crown." The White House. Then total radio silence.

At Dupont Circle, Reagan took something from his pocket—a handkerchief, he later said; a napkin from the union lunch, Parr remembered—and coughed into it, hard. It filled with red, frothy blood. Reagan said, "I think I cut the inside of my mouth." Parr looked, saw bubbles, barked at the driver to change destination, get to George Washington University Hospital.

Parr told me, "I saw distress in his face. He didn't say very much at all. I saw the blood. I took one look at it and I made the decision to take him to the hospital, knowing full well that if it was a wrong decision it would be a very big deal. There was just something about the way he looked, an intuition. He was growing pale, grayish, not looking well." But Parr wasn't wrong about what the blood suggested. Like all agents, he had, during his training, taken a course they called Ten-Minute Medicine—it taught the basics of how to keep people alive. Things like, "For a sucking chest wound you take cellophane or a shirt and cover the wound because the more air, the worse the bleeding."

The Secret Service called the hospital emergency room to tell them to be ready. But the nurse on duty thought it was just a practice run—the kind of thing a good advance team does when the president is moving around. There was "a little dialogue," as Parr put it, and finally she realized this wasn't a dry run.

Reagan was having trouble breathing. By the time they got to the hospital, just three minutes later, he felt he couldn't get enough air. The handkerchief or napkin was filled with blood, and now he was filling Jerry's handkerchief.

The limo pulled up short by the walkway to the emergency room. The agents sprang out, opened doors. Parr offered his hand but Reagan pulled himself out on his own, and stood. Twenty years later Mike Deaver still marveled over what Reagan did then. He always remembered it as the Reagan Moment.

Reagan stood up straight, sucked in his abs, pulled up his pants at the belt and buttoned his suit jacket. He was getting himself together, as he always did. He would walk into the hospital as a president of the United States. He'd walk in as a gentleman.

Dave Fischer jumped from the car behind Reagan's and ran up to him. Fisher looked into the president's eyes and saw a funny look, "a distance inside,"as he told me twenty years later to the day.

Reagan walked toward the entrance of the emergency room, agents to his right and left. They walked about twenty or thirty feet to the door. Reagan later remembered a nurse at the entrance coming toward him. Deaver and the others remembered doctors, nurses, staff. Reagan walked toward the nurse at the entrance and said he was having trouble breathing. Then his knees buckled and he began to fall.

They caught him, the two agents, the nurse and the doctors. They stretched him out in their arms and ran with him. Soon they were carrying him at shoulder height, carrying him as if he were "a football after the winning game," in Mike Deaver's words. And as they ran they were tearing off his clothes, so by the time they got him on a gurney in the ER the president of the United States was completely naked.

Within seconds the room was bedlam.

They brought Reagan to trauma bay number five. Parr set up a security perimeter. "You start with the president's body and you turn off all access to it."

They started checking his blood pressure, heart rate. Both were faltering. He was going into shock.

Now it was up to the trauma team. "They were magnificent. They sloshed blood into him," said Parr.

Reagan was lucky again: A meeting of the entire hospital staff, with all of their top doctors and personnel, was taking place upstairs. When they got word everyone who thought he could help ran downstairs.

The doctors and aides did a quick exam. They ran their hands quickly over his body, turned him, looked closely. No gunshot wounds; he must have had a heart attack. It made sense: high and sharp stress, seventy years old.

Reagan had passed out as they carried him in but he came to on the gurney in the ER. They put a tube down his throat but he still couldn't get enough air. He stared up at the white ceiling tiles as everyone yelled and barked orders and he started to pray.

Then he lost consciousness again.

"All hell broke loose" in the ER, according to Fischer. "The place exploded, total chaos. You had all these medical people who were just streaming into this room where he was. Here's the president of the United States and he's naked. They covered him up but he was naked, and I said to Jerry Parr we have to get some control. And I found a head nurse and Jerry worked with her and we started saying, 'Is this person necessary?' and if they weren't, they were out. And then we wouldn't let anyone in unless they were part of a medical team."

Soon the ER looked like a battlefield. When James Brady was wheeled in, he was conscious, raising his head from the gurney. When Mike Deaver saw him he had to hold the wall to keep from fainting. Brady had raised his head several times on the sidewalk in spite of the bullet in his head, and now the nurse was saying, "If I don't intubate you, I don't think you can live." But he resisted as she forced the tube down his throat. Tim McCarthy was wheeled in too, also conscious and in great pain.

Fischer shouted to a military aide, "Where's the vice president?" No one knew. They had to get word to him, had to make sure that wherever he was, he got back to Washington right away.

It is May 4, 2001, and former president George H. W. Bush calls me from his cell phone in a car in Houston. He is on his way to the airport; he is going to South Africa, where he will make a speech and spend some time. Along the staticky line he tells me what he remembered of that day twenty years before.

"Well, with my aging mind and my aging body it's hard to remember," he laughs. "I remember I was down in Fort Worth, and I remember someone telling us Reagan was shot, and I remember some calls on Air Force Two as we flew back. Haig called in, and others. There was thought there might be a conspiracy, you know. I don't remember too much except as we flew back to Washington we kept getting calls that were speculative."

Meaning, he said, that no one knew if the president was going to make it.

"But finally at one point I was reassured that he was all right. So we landed [in Washington] and I went to the VP's house and then went down to the situation room of the White House. What I determined to do was not act like I was president. Not act like he wasn't all right. That wouldn't help. My feeling was my friend has been shot. It wasn't a question of 'the awesome burden of the presidency' falling on you or any of that. This man I liked very much was hurting. And that was my feeling."

He was talking about a big and serious thing, a tragedy for the republic, the shooting of a president—the hours in which it became quite possible that he might suddenly be elevated to the presidency. And he was trying to adopt a tone suitable to the subject. But it was hard because right now he was so happy. He and Bar had just spent two nights in the White House with George and Laura, he tells me. I laugh and ask him if he is enjoying being the father of a president.

"Oh yes, I don't know how to describe it; it's wonderful. It's awesome. Or cool, that's another way to describe it." He talks these days like a man with a lot of teenage grandchildren.

A friend of his would later tell me that he had greatly enjoyed his visit to the White House, had visited all the telephone operators and gone through the West Wing, sticking his head in and calling hellos to surprised staffers.

He reiterated that what he essentially remembered about that bad day in history is that it was personal: His friend was hurt, and was hurting for him. And that was about all. He laughed now and rang off, "Best to your son; good luck with the book!"

A few months later I spoke to his son, the new president. What struck him most when he remembered that day, he told me, is that you can't help but forget for a moment that Reagan had been president only nine weeks when he'd been shot. "It's hard to believe—*hard* to believe—because it seemed like he'd been president a couple of years when it happened. But it was just a few months."

People always think Reagan had been president for years when he was shot. I think it's because we learned so much about him so quickly that it seems, looking back, that it must have taken place over years, and not mere days.

When George W. Bush heard about the shooting, he was in Texas but not with his father. He thinks he was in Midland. But he didn't expect the worst; he thought Reagan would make it. "No. I had—I'm one of these guys that doesn't expect the bad until it happens. So I always thought Reagan was going to survive. I don't know why."

He didn't remember if he had called his father on Air Force Two.

It just didn't seem possible to him that Reagan was going to die. That old man was strong and lucky, and he was going to go on.

"Who's holding my hand?" Some time had passed; he didn't know how much. Ronald Reagan was semiconscious and aware that someone, some wonderful person, a woman, was holding his hand. "Who's holding my hand?"

No one answered. He continued in and out of consciousness. He came to again with the same woman holding his hand and he said, "Does Nancy know about us?"

He was never able to find out who she was, but ten years later he was still grateful. It was a wonderful feeling, he could never afterward find the words to explain how reassuring it felt when she held his hand tight. It was like the time thirty years before when he'd had pneumonia and wanted to give up breathing and that unnamed nurse coaxed him to take each breath.

His blood pressure was plummeting. They didn't know why. His lungs were filling up with blood and he was going to die if something wasn't done to stop the bleeding, but they still thought he hadn't been shot, so they didn't understand about the bleeding and didn't know what to do.

"They couldn't find the bullet," said Parr. So they searched every inch of his body again, X-rayed him again and finally found the entrance wound, a neat and bloodless little slice under his arm.

They rushed Reagan into the operating room, put him under, opened him up, tried for the bullet and missed, kept trying. Finally they got it and put it in a cup.

It was a devastator bullet, designed to explode within its target. And it would have exploded if it had had the muzzle velocity it required. But Hinckley had had a short-barrel gun. The devastator bullet needed a muzzle more like a rifle's.

As the first hours passed, what had happened outside the Hilton became clear.

The first shot had hit James Brady in the head, left temple.

The second shot had hit District Patrolman Thomas Delehanty in the neck; he had been turning toward the president when the first shot rang out, and he was in the hospital now.

Then Hinckley had paused.

Jerry Parr: "Hinckley saw two people go down and not the president. We are bending the president over, throwing him in the car. Hinckley is firing combat style now, holding the gun with two hands, in a crouched combat position. He began to shoot again. The third shot hit Tim McCarthy, who was standing with his body wide between the shooter and the president. The fourth shot hit the window of the president's limousine. The fifth shot ricocheted off the armor of the limousine, flattened out like a dime, went through the half-inch space between the open door and the car and sliced into the president, hitting him under his left armpit."

The bullet had tumbled onward, then turned, tearing through muscles into the president's lung and finally resting one inch from his heart.

When he was in the ER they told Reagan who'd been hit. They wheeled Brady by him at one point and when Reagan saw him he said a prayer for his life, for the lives and safety of everyone who'd been shot. And then he thought: "I can't ask God to heal Jim and the others and at the same time feel hatred for the man who shot us," so he asked God to help the man deal with whatever demons had made him shoot them.

As he waited to go into the operating room he thought of that moment two weeks before at Ford's Theatre when he'd looked at the box where Lincoln had sat. He had been saved by two Secret Service men, Jerry Parr and Tim McCarthy. They'd both put their bodies in harm's way to save him, and one of them, McCarthy, had literally taken a bullet for him, had stood like a small granite wall in a gray suit, and turned, arms wide, toward the shooter.

Jerry Parr told the doctors he wanted an agent in the room with the president at all times. "I feel when he sees an agent it may give him a sense of comfort," he told them. And so day and night an agent was there, until the day he left. "We'd been with him in 1968 and 1976," he said of the first two times Reagan, as a possible candidate and then as a candidate for the presidency, had required Secret Service protection. "He was familiar with the agents, and he liked us."

He did. Reagan liked his Secret Service agents a lot, respected their professionalism, and they loved him. This isn't always the case with presidents and agents, of course, but with Reagan something special was going on. Some agents became his friends after the presidency, like John Barletta, who rode with him every day when he was at the ranch.

Reagan liked them because he understood what they did for a living. He knew this was their job: to be cool and brave. It was their job to be calm in crisis and do the right thing when there was no time for a wrong thing. It was their job to see a bullet aimed at him and move to stop it with their bodies. And they were men he understood because they were masculine men of the old school, so many of them. They liked man things, as he did, and clung to them while manliness, in many circles, was going out of style.

They knew what a gun was and respected it, knew what a fence was and how to build it. Few of them were from the West but they were all westerners of the heart, as Reagan was. And because they spoke the same language and lived in the same world, he gave them a gift they weren't always used to from presidents. He treated them with equality. He preferred talking with them to talking to the politicians who were in the backseat of the limo with him on the way to the rally. He liked to swap jokes with them and he liked to tease them. There was an old unused outhouse at the ranch, and he would tell the new agents with a face that betrayed nothing that that was for them. They'd nod, yes, sir. And he and the experienced agents would start to laugh. At the ranch he'd walk with them and see a snake far away and pull out a gun and hit it with ease. New agents would think he was the deadest eye in the West until he'd finally tell them he was using a shotgun shell with a big footprint. They were just his kind of men. And now they'd done what he knew they would do in the circumstances: They had saved his life.

While they had been trying to figure out why Reagan was, in effect, dying, a hospital official came to Dave Fischer with the president's personal effects. There wasn't much—no cash because presidents don't need cash and no keys because they don't need keys. There was his watch, though, and the nuclear launch card all presidents must carry with them and which Reagan had carried in an inside breast pocket of his suit. And his cuff links. He loved those cuff links, which were gold and shaped like the golden bear of California. Only there was only one of them. "Where's the other one?" asked Fischer. The official was embarrassed. "Don't worry, we're launching an investigation and—"

"You're telling me the president's cuff link was stolen as he lay there bleeding on a gurney?"

Apparently, said the official.

They never found the other one, never found out who stole it. Dave Fischer got a goldsmith to make a new one.

In the moments after the president was shot, as he lay on the gurney in the ER, the country found out what had happened.

This is part of how they found out.

Mike Putzel, of the Associated Press, the reporter who had shouted questions to Reagan, was in the reporters' pool that day with Dean Reynolds of UPI, Judy Woodruff, two television crews, a radio tech with a long mike, photographers and Walter Rodgers of AP Radio. They had all covered the president's speech and then rushed to the rope line to catch him between the hotel and the car as he left.

Putzel had positioned himself well on the rope line, up front near the president's limo. He wanted to have a view of the president and he wanted the president to see him when he shouted his question about Lech Walesa. There had been a new escalation of tensions in Poland, concerns the Soviets might move against the Polish government or Walesa himself.

I talked to Putzel in the spring of 2001 and he told me, "The door [of the hotel] opened and I had one of those little micromini cassettes attached to my belt, so as the door opened I flipped on the tape recorder." But because of what would happen in the next few minutes, he soon forgot about the recorder.

Which picked up everything.

And now Mike Putzel played for me over the phone the sound of the shooting of a president. Most of us have seen the videotape of Ronald Reagan walking toward his car as the shooting began. But you almost never get to hear the sound of it. The audio is more chilling than the video.

Mike pressed PLAY, and I listened with my ear glued to the receiver. And into my ear came history.

There is a *bong* sound that no one who hears the tape can ever identify. Then a woman's voice. Then you hear Mike Putzel's voice over the others. He is calling out, "Mr. Reagan—"

And then you hear two shots, *bop bop.*

And then four shots in rapid succession.

For a split second, quiet. Then screaming. A woman screaming, "Oh, oh!," women shouting, the sound of crying, Secret Service agents and police shouting furiously, "Get back, get back!"

The tape makes you "see" what you don't see in the videotape: fifteen seconds of mayhem and the beginning of horror.

At the end of the fifteen seconds you hear a muffled voice.

The voice says "Get a telephone."

It was Mike Putzel talking to himself.

Putzel had seen Jerry Parr grab the president and throw him into the car. He saw Parr dive on top, saw the door slam, saw the door locks automatically click shut. He saw the car shoot forward. He would never forget the right back tire suddenly spinning.

He knew by instinct not to go to the pool van but to sprint into the lobby of the hotel and find a phone—these were the days before cell phones, the days when reporters had to get to a pay phone to file a bulletin. He had to call the AP Washington bureau and file what he knew.

Putzel dashed into the hotel lobby. He went barreling in. It was crowded—no one knew yet what had happened just outside, but there was a milling lobby of people checking in and out.

He ran ahead trying to remember where the phones were. He'd been there a hundred times but now couldn't remember where they were! And just as he thought this he realized he was running past a bank of pay phones. He stopped short, dropped a quarter in and dialed the Washington bureau of the Associated Press.

Doran Howard, working the news desk, picked up the phone. Putzel still didn't remember the tape on his belt that was picking up everything.

He continued to play it for me on the phone. You can hear an urgent man's voice:

"Doran, this is Mike Putzel, get me Lee Byrd real fast."

Byrd was the A.M. supervisor.

Doran's voice: "Okay. Lee, Mike Putzel."

Byrd picks up, Putzel begins to file, Byrd sets up a header for a Bulletin, coding it with the number of the story.

Putzel's voice again, urgent and loud:

"Several gunshots were fired at President Reagan—"

Byrd was typing to put it out on the wires as a Bulletin. In the big-story pecking order there was an Urgent (very big news), a Bulletin (big news), a Flash (a headline or heads up for newsrooms, not to be published). When JFK was shot it was a Bulletin; when he died it was an Urgent. There hadn't been a Flash since "Man Lands on Moon."

"—as he left a speech in a downtown Washington hotel." Putzel's voice is urgent but collected. "There was no indication he was injured," he continued.

Byrd sent the Bulletin.

Between Mike Putzel's yelling, "Mr. President!" to Ronald Reagan and Mike Putzel's finishing his telephone report to the Associated Press, fifty-three seconds had elapsed.

Putzel beat everybody.

Putzel's wife of five years was the reporter Ann Blackman, also of the Associated Press. She was in the AP's cavernous newsroom working at her desk when she heard a commotion. Someone said the president was shot. Someone said people were down, a press guy was down. Ann Blackman was pretty sure her husband was in the pool. She stood and walked quickly to Lee Byrd's desk. There was a big plastic garbage can that people threw used wire copy into, and as she passed it she leaned over and quietly vomited.

Then someone told her Mike was filing. She picked up the phone and heard his voice and caught her breath. She asked if he was all right, he said, yes, and then he told her to get over to George Washington

University Hospital. She hung up and ran. The AP newsroom was at 2021 K Street. GW was three blocks away. She and another reporter ran all the way and when they got to the hospital she saw the president's limo parked under the overhang. "We were among the first persons there, and the most startling thing was to see the presidential limousine with bullet holes. Things were chaotic. Some people were saying he had walked in, others said he collapsed, others that they carried him."

She knew for the first time that Reagan was there.

She ran down the block to find a phone—she didn't need one yet but she would. She found a pay phone outside a bar and she did what reporters used to do at moments like this. She unscrewed the part of the phone that you speak into and took out the transmitter. She put it in her pocket and ran. It would be her phone now.

She saw Sheila Tate, the first lady's press secretary, collared her, told her the White House had to talk to the press, that there were rumors all over—the president's dead, Brady's dead. Which she didn't precisely know to be true but was the kind of thing that would elicit a response. So Lyn Nofziger was sent out, and he said the president was about to enter surgery, his condition was satisfactory.

Ann Blackman ran to her phone now, but there was a drunk crumpled inside the booth. She couldn't move him. So she ran into the bar, commandeered the bar phone, called the AP and reported that the president was shot and was going into surgery.

She beat everyone too.

Back at the hotel, Putzel walked back to the scene of the shooting. Emergency personnel had just taken Brady and Delehanty away after doing shock trauma on the sidewalks where they lay. He was walking around looking for witnesses when an FBI agent overheard him telling someone where the shooting had taken place. "You're gonna have to come with me," the agent said to Putzel.

"I'm working," Putzel said.

The FBI man said they were doing a crime scene reenactment, and he would have to detain him. Putzel refused to be detained. So the FBI agent arrested him. They had started to take him and a few others into the hotel when an ABC News correspondent saw what was happening. He didn't know what was going on but he thought Putzel might see something newsworthy, so he got himself arrested too.

Mike Putzel had just gone from reporter heaven—beating everyone on a major story—to reporter hell—being confined in a room for hours with witnesses to a crime who were not allowed to talk to one another because the FBI didn't want them comparing notes. They kept him there for hours.

"Funny How History Works"

Mike Deaver sped to the hospital in a car behind the president's, and when he got there and saw Reagan on the gurney he began to set up a mini-White House. "I really saw my job as opening up a connection with the situation room," he told me. "I stayed on the phone full time. There was mayhem in there, in the ER, so I just commandeered a phone on a desk and called Jim Baker. He transferred me down to the situation room, where they'd set up a command post. I just hung on the line, the White House operator had me and I just held an open line. And I would tell them what was happening. The president's doctor came out at one point and I said, 'What is going on?' He said, 'I don't know. We think it could be his heart.' I said, 'His heart? It's strong as an ox!' "

Nancy Reagan had not accompanied the president to the Hilton when he made his speech. Instead, she had gone to another official luncheon across town. But she felt off somehow, something was bothering her and she didn't know what.

"In the middle of lunch I had an overwhelming desire to get back home," she told me. "I just had to get home and I didn't know why. So I left, I went home and I went up in the solarium."

She was talking to the White House chief usher, Rex Scouten, and the decorator Ted Graber when the head of her Secret Service detail entered the room. "He made a gesture with his forefinger as if to say 'Come here.' He'd never done that to me before."

She went to him. He said there had been a shooting, but the president was not hit.

And twenty years later as she recounted that moment her face turned stony.

"Well, I heard that and I am in the elevator, I am going to the hospital. The head of the detail said again, 'He isn't hit.' And I said, 'I am going to the hospital and either you get the car or I am walking.' "

They got the car. She felt an urgency that she did not understand, even though she knew people were telling her what they thought was true: that the president was safe.

When she got to the hospital the first person she saw was Mike Deaver. She wanted to get in to see the president and the doctors said, "No, he's fine but we're working on him and you can't see him right now."

She said, "I've got to see him. He has to know I'm here."

A doctor came up to her and said, "The president was hit. He has been hit."

Deaver was standing with her and she turned and gave him the full force of her fear in the form of anger. "I thought you told me he hadn't been hit!"

"I didn't know he'd been hit," Deaver explained gently.

After Nancy Reagan told me what she'd said—"He has to know I'm here"—she stopped speaking. This was the spring of 2001, and as we talked her eyes filled with tears.

"I said, 'I've got to see him.'

"The doctor said, 'I'm sorry. He's all right, not now.'

"I said, 'I've got to see him. He's got to know I'm here, you don't know how it is with us."

But now the president was being operated on, and she waited, in the halls and in a little side room, with Mike Deaver and other aides walking in and out. At one point Deaver told her there was a chapel in the hospital and asked if she would like to go. They found it, but it wasn't empty. Secret Service agent Tim McCarthy's parents were in there, praying. "They all embraced, and then they all sat quietly together," Deaver said.

They walked back to the small room where they had been waiting. The TV set was on, and they looked up to see anchorman Frank Reynolds of ABC reporting that James Brady was dead. Nancy gasped. Then they watched as Reynolds came back on a few minutes later to say he was wrong, he'd been given incorrect information. He had an understandable flurry of temper on the air.

I told Deaver, twenty years later in his office, that I'd never forget that moment either, that I was at CBS News then, working on the radio side for Dan Rather, trying to track down John Hinckley's parents. I looked up with everyone else in the newsroom to see, on the ABC monitor, Frank Reynolds announcing Brady's death. Everyone in the newsroom at CBS jerked straight with the electric shock posture of journalists who are hearing that a story is getting much worse and bigger, and who are hearing the competition beat them to it, live. And then Reynolds blew his stack, and we all knew just how he felt, and felt sympathy and relief: Brady wasn't dead. And we hadn't been beat. Except if you were looking at the CBS in-house monitor, where Dan Rather had just announced Brady's death and was asking for a moment of silence . . .

There were tough moments for everybody those first hours. While the president was being operated on, two-man FBI teams started going through the hospital interviewing everyone who had witnessed the shooting. One would ask questions, the other would take notes.

They took Dave Fischer aside in a private patient's room and their first question was "Mr. Fischer, would you tell us why you were out of your normal position with the president?"

And it hit him, and his eyes filled with tears. He lost his composure for a moment and snapped, "What, do you think I knew he was going to be shot and I got out of the way? That's a terrible question."

Nancy Reagan had trouble reaching the family and at first they couldn't reach her. Her son Ron was touring with the Joffrey Ballet, Maureen and Michael were in LA, and Patti Davis was meeting with a psychologist at an office in his home in Santa Monica Canyon.

They were in the middle of their meeting when there was a knock on the door. The startled psychologist said, "Come in," and the door opened and it was one of Patti's Secret Service agents.

"My first reaction was absolute fury," she later said. "I thought damnit, now they're interrupting my therapy sessions!" She hadn't gotten used to constant Secret Service protection, was struggling with being the daughter of her parents and the daughter of a president. "But then I saw his face, and the guy's face was just white, pale. And he looked at me and he said, 'I have to talk to you.'

"I went over to the door and he said, 'There's been a shooting in Washington. We don't think your father's hurt but we need to take you back to the residence.' Meaning my apartment."

They took her back to her bungalow in Santa Monica. The phone was ringing off the hook with friends but she couldn't reach anyone in the family, tried and couldn't get through to the hospital. She was the president's daughter but she didn't know anything more than anyone else who was watching television. "And it was like 'Jim Brady's dead, Jim Brady's not dead,' 'President Reagan hasn't been shot, yes he has been shot.' I mean everything, everything. I mean I watched the whole thing."

Patti, Michael and Maureen met in Los Angeles. They wanted to fly immediately to Washington but were told they couldn't take a commercial flight, because of the possibility of a conspiracy. By evening they were on a military air transport carrier, one of those big hollowed-out planes. They gave them ear mufflers and a box lunch.

With the time change, they got to the White House in the middle of the night and set Patti up in a little room off her parents' bedroom.

She slept for three hours and had nightmares. "I remember these horrible dreams—I remember dreaming that I was seeing my mother's face and it was cracking, like it was porcelain and it was cracking. I remember it, I can picture that, her face was cracking."

She woke up early and crept to her mother's bedroom door to see if she was up. She was. Nancy told her she had slept with her father's shirt. "She slept on his side of the bed, and she slept with his shirt in her hands, for the scent."

Hours before, in the recovery room, Ronald Reagan had started to come to. When he opened his eyes Nancy had been with him, looking down at him, and he did what he did when she was upset. He repeated the joke "Honey, I forgot to duck." That's what the great fighter Jack Dempsey said to his wife the night he was beaten by Gene Tunney for the heavyweight championship.

Everyone—nurses, doctors, agents, Nancy—started to laugh. It was the beginning of something extraordinary that the whole country was soon going to hear about, and think about, in the way you think about a friend who hit a crisis and really came through.

When they told him he was going to be operated on he looked up at the doctors and said, "I just hope you're all Republicans." And a doctor, in a moment of great grace, said, "Today, Mr. President, we're all Republicans."

Dave Fischer spent the night with him. "He was remarkably upbeat. I don't think many people would react the way he did. I think you really find out what people are made of in that kind of situation, where you're helpless. He couldn't even talk, he had to ask questions by writing. . . ."

He had some bad moments. At one point, hours after the president came into the recovery room, with the tubes in his throat, he croaked to Mrs. Reagan, "Can't breathe." He was frightened. Nancy turned to a nurse and said, "He can't breathe." Young Ron Reagan, who had just arrived, leaned in and said, "Dad, it's all right, it's like when I'm scuba diving, the machine sort of breathes for you, you just sort of put it in your mouth and breathe, it's okay, it's like scuba diving."

It was a closer call than the American people were told; he was harder hit than they knew. He'd been harder hit than a lot of people in the White House knew too. And he was seventy years old. He ran infections, his temperature spiked. Because the bullet had gone through lung tissue, there was a buildup of blood and phlegm in his lungs; doctors loosened it by pounding on his back and getting him to cough and spit. At one point Maureen Reagan walked into a hospital waiting room and saw Nancy Reagan by herself, hunched over, alone. Maureen, who had not always been close to Nancy, sat down next to her, and they said nothing as they listened to the president cough and get pounded and cough. From that time onward they were closer than they'd been, and understood each other better.

Everyone who worked with him has a particular story they think of when they think of him, and this is mine. When I try to tell people what Reagan was like I tell the bathroom story. A few days after he'd been shot, when he could get out of bed, he wasn't feeling well one night and went to the bathroom connected to his room. He slapped water on his face, and water slopped out of the sink. He got some paper towels and got on the floor to clean it up. An aide came in and said, "Mr. President, what are you doing? We have people for that." And Reagan said oh, no, he was just cleaning up his mess, he didn't want a nurse to have to do it.

But mostly there was the extraordinary thing going on in the recovery room, where he did something else regular people don't do. Ronald Reagan, intubated, postoperative and recovering from shock and trauma, started writing funny notes to people. Actually he'd begun with a few notes back on the gurney in the ER, and some croaked comments too. When his top staff all came in late in the afternoon, he'd said, "Who's minding the store?" And when they assured him the government was running as usual he said, "What makes you think that would make me feel better?"

But most of the notes were from the recovery room, and they had a kind of magical effect on the people there. After a while it didn't feel like a trauma recovery unit, it felt like a quiet celebration, with doctors and nurses coming and going and getting his notes and laughing, and his friends and family laughing with the over-the-top relief people get when someone doesn't die.

Reagan couldn't laugh but his eyes sparkled because he was: alive. His life had been spared and he was grateful. The medical staff was happy because they'd successfully kept a president from dying. His aides were happy because the boss wasn't dead. And the country was happy too for the same reasons and also because they were hearing about what had happened in the ER and was happening in recovery. They knew because Reagan's aide Lyn Nofziger told them, and then everyone in the room started telling them. But Nofziger wrote later in his memoirs that he'll always be grateful to the unnamed, unremembered reporter who said at the end of a briefing, "Did the president have anything to say?" And he realized he should tell them.

So we all heard about the famous notes, but in time a funny thing happened. They started disappearing. Some people held on to them, saying the president had written them personally, to them. But when Nancy Reagan realized that they were authentic history, that they contained within them the moment when the American people started to understand Ronald Reagan, she got them back.

And one day when we were together in Bel Air she said something cryptic that at first I didn't quite catch. It sounded like "I understand you're looking for something." I nodded. She said, "I heard you wanted to see these." It was an eight-by-twelve-inch manila envelope. Inside were the notes, the real ones. I held them in my hands in the sun as the birds sang.

When Reagan could not speak, nurses and doctors gave him pads of white and pink hospital forms that said GEORGE WASHINGTON UNIVERSITY HOSPITAL on the back. He held them, and in black felt tip pen and in pencil he wrote out his notes.

Nancy looked at them again and handed them over. She'd say "Oh, look at this" and "I remember that."

A note: "I am aren't alive aren't I?" I read it aloud and she corrected me: "I am alive, aren't I?" she said. It was his first note, and her eyes filled again. One of the president's aides had told me once, long ago and not joking, that when Reagan first came to, in that first moment he saw a white ceiling in a white room with a pretty nurse dressed in white gazing down at him, he thought he might be in heaven. So he wrote the note asking if he was alive.

Another: "How long in the hosp?" Below that, "I left something out I do have an allergy . . ." and I couldn't decipher the next few words.

Another note, on pink clinical record paper: "I thought it was still afternoon." Below, "I've done a remake of Lost Weekend"—a reference to the classic film in which Ray Milland portrayed a bingeing alcoholic who loses all sense of time. (The young woman who tries to save him is played by Jane Wyman.)

Another piece of paper: "Could we rewrite this scene beginning about the time I left the hotel?" Below that: "What happened to the guy with the gun?" "Was anyone hurt?"

Another, this one in black felt tip pen on white hospital forms: "Send me to LA, where I can see the air I'm breathing."

This one in pencil, on lined clinical hospital form paper: "All in all I'd rather be in Phil." For Philadelphia. The famous words the comic W. C. Fields wanted put on his gravestone.

Another note: "If I knew I had such a talent for this I'd have tried it sooner."

Another note: "If I had this much attention in Hollywood I would have stayed there."

Another pink piece of paper: "Will I be able to do ranch work, ride etc."

You can tell because of the rough handwriting, the abbreviations and the syntactical failures that the words are being written by a man under duress or coming out of anesthesia.

Another note: "Winston Churchill said nothing so exhil as to be shot at without result." "Exhil" of course is "exhilarating." Another: "I was just saying goodnight."

The things that happened that day affected many lives. For a long time David Fischer couldn't stop feeling a sense of guilt and a sense of mystery: When the shots rang out he was in the wrong place, not next to the president as he always was but near the back of the president's car. Why was he in the wrong place?

He had nightmares for a long time. "The nightmares all had—there was one in particular. I was in Moscow. I had never been to Moscow in my life. But in this dream I was in Moscow, and I was crossing a busy intersection, and shots rang out. And everybody hit the ground."

And he would wake up, afraid.

He told me it had taken awhile to figure it all out in a way that made sense to him. "I've told very few people, but I really feel I was moved out of the way that day. No question in my mind. Because I'd thought of it when the shots rang out, 'Why am I here?' And then when [the FBI] asked the question it hit me."

Mike Deaver would become emotional in the weeks after the shooting, but he knew why, there was no mystery. When the shots rang out he had just put someone in harm's way. James Brady would never be the same, and it was his fault. "I was on the phone in the emergency room when they brought Jim by me. . . . He was laying there with blood all around his head. And I almost lost it at that moment."

Because of what he'd done. "When we were walking out of the hotel and Mike Putzel fired the question, I grabbed Brady and moved him. And I'd let the press person field the question, and I'd take his place with the president and we'd get in the car. I heard Putzel, I moved Brady. And Reagan was waving, and I went around the back of the car just as a shot crossed my right shoulder. A shot right across my shoulder. I ducked down and then immediately got in the car and looked back and it was like a war zone.

"And I had weeks and weeks and weeks of anguish. I would break down, I was in such anguish over Jim. I'd think, 'My God, I'm the guy who put him there.' "

Deaver struggled along. His wife Carolyn suggested he go to the neurosurgeon who had operated on Brady and saved his life. "Why him I don't know," Deaver said. "But I went to see him and I went through this thing and told him I was having a tough time."

The doctor listened, thought about it. When Deaver had told his story the doctor asked, "How tall are you?"

Deaver was startled. "I told him, 'I'm five foot nine.'"

And the neurosugeon said, "Jim Brady is six feet tall. And if he'd stayed there where he had been before you moved him Ronald Reagan would be dead. Because Brady took the bullet that would have killed Reagan."

If it had been Deaver standing where Brady was, the bullet would have gone over his head and hit the president. Hearing that made Deaver see it all in a different way, and he started to recover.

Nancy Reagan remained haunted. "I never got over it," she told me. "You know they show that film all the time on television, the film of his being shot. I can't watch it, ever, I always turn away." But she saw it once, early on. "Did you ever see the expression on his face just after he's been shot? There is complete bewilderment on his face."

She had bad dreams too. There were dreams that someone was coming after him, in darkness. "The threats increase after an assassination attempt, because there are nuts out there who think 'Oh John

Hinckley didn't get him, I will.' Every time he went out to speak I just died. I didn't have any peace until he came back. I did a lot of praying, at all times. I prayed, 'Please Lord, keep him safe.' "

Mike Putzel had a bad time too. When he got out of the FBI witnesses room, he returned to the White House, and as he was walking near the press secretary's office he saw a colleague, a competitor from another news service. The colleague said, "So, Mike, how does it feel to be the guy who got Ronald Reagan shot?" It hadn't occurred to Putzel: He'd called the question, the president had turned, the shots rang out. It hadn't occurred to Putzel that he might be responsible. Was he?

It took him awhile too to realize that there was just no telling—maybe if Reagan hadn't turned the bullet wouldn't have hit the tough muscles of his abdomen, maybe if he hadn't turned the bullet wouldn't have stopped an inch from the heart, maybe if he hadn't turned the bullet would have hit his heart. . . .

After the shooting and the hospital work, by the evening of the day Reagan was shot, Jerry Parr went to the FBI and filled out a deposition on everything he had witnessed and experienced. Then he reported in, late that night, at the White House. He met up with Ed Hickey, the head of security, and they went to the White House mess. Parr hadn't eaten, and he ordered.

What did you order? I asked him.

"A straight vodka," he said.

Parr had dreams after the shooting too.

One occurred the second night after the shooting, which was the first night Parr slept. "I dreamed that my tractor—I lived in Potomac and I had a tractor—I dreamed that my tractor started without me and I was running after it, I was trying to catch it. Then I had a dream my car started on its own and I ran and tried to catch it."

He knew what they meant. "These are dreams about being out of control. It was about trying to keep control of the X zone." The X zone is how agents describe the area that has the president at its center and that radiates ten yards in all directions.

Almost a year after the shooting, Jerry Parr went to the president and Mrs. Reagan and told them he had been promoted to assistant director of the Secret Service. It would mean leaving the White House detail, leaving the president's side. He talked to them for an hour, told them he'd been there eighteen years and wanted the new position, but he wouldn't take it if they asked him not to. They told him to take it, wished him well, asked him to make himself available if they ever felt they needed him. He promised he would.

Parr was sent to the Federal Executive Institute in Charlottesville, Virginia. He was there when the first anniversary of the shooting came. That night, on the anniversary, he fell into a deep sleep and dreamed he was out in an open boat with no oars.

"I grew up near Miami. I'd go out fishing with a buddy. But in this dream I was out of sight of land, on a broad ocean. It was very calm, but I had no oars. Suddenly I see a rogue wave begin bearing down on me. This was like an 'Oh, Jesus' experience. There is nothing I can do about this but watch it come. And as it came my boat started rising as it lifted me up, carrying me up higher and higher. And I could hear [the wave] hissing as it curled over, the white at the top. I was poised at the top of it—and then I woke up."

Parr knew a man who was doing research on danger at a naval hospital. "It was a big investigation into the nature of dangerousness, it was in the hospital's mental health unit, and I was supposed to have lunch with a guy who was working on it. So I said, 'Let me tell you, you're a shrink, let me tell you this dream.' He listened. He said it was a dream where it all came together—the surprise, the fear of the shooting. He said, 'It was a dream where you rode it out. It was big and scary but you rode it out.' "

Parr thought about that for a long time. And a few years later he suddenly realized what he had seen at the end of the wave in the dream, what he saw that was beyond the wave. "It was all a level sea. So I thought, maybe the experience lifted me up to another level of awareness, another level where I am in my spiritual life, in my life in general."

And every once in a while he still has the dream. But the way he said it, I knew it wasn't a dream about fear anymore.

There were plenty of personal stories woven through the drama of the day of the shooting. Jerry Parr's wife was an attorney with the IRS, and she had never seen the new president. Parr told her to look out her office window the next day at noon, the president had a speech at the Hilton, which was right across the street from her office. But she forgot about it until after noon that day. Then she threw on her coat and walked over and waited with the crowd outside the hotel. She'd see the president and maybe Jerry when they left.

She was waiting outside when she heard the shots, saw men begin to fall and saw Jerry and the president jackknife into a car that jerked away at breakneck speed. She thought Jerry had been shot and began to cry, "My husband, my husband!"

When I heard this I realized: She was one of the women on Mike Putzel's audiotape.

A Secret Service agent saw her and called, "He's in the car with the Man," and she ran back to the office and called their children to say their father was okay. She got the principal at the grade school and passed the word, but by the time she got her daughter in college she had already heard an agent had been shot and was terrified.

Mike Putzel and Ann Blackman's children were frightened too. Their two children, aged five and two, were at home watching *Sesame Street* when the shooting occurred. *Sesame Street* is on PBS, which scrapped its programming and went live with the shooting. The girls saw it. They knew Daddy was there because he worked with the president, and they thought he'd been shot. The elder is twenty-four years old now and still feels it, remembers those moments. . . .

And within about twelve hours, by late that night, the talk on television had turned to politics, to how the shooting would affect the political landscape. And that too was all good news for Reagan. His supporters were newly reinspired by their affection for him, and his opponents by their respect for him—not many men get shot and joke their way through the trauma room and buck up the country like that. And those who were meanest about him lost the quiver of their meanness, because you can't be mean to such a gallant old man without seeming churlish and childish. A friend called me that night at CBS, and said, "I'd hate to be in Tip O'Neill's shoes right now," and we laughed, because Reagan's shoes were suddenly a better place to be.

Later Reagan would say he was sure someone was looking out for him that day. Which is precisely what Pope John Paul II himself would think, when, eight weeks later, he too would be the victim of an assassination attempt. The pope, who was Reagan's ideological and philosophical comrade, felt that he had been saved by the intercession of the Blessed Mother. It was the feast of Our Lady of Fatima, and the pope was a Marian devotee. When he survived he said that the rest of his life was owed to God, would go to God.

Eight weeks earlier, across the sea, Ronald Reagan in recovery also said that whatever time he had left was God's, would go to God.

It would change Reagan's life forever.

Mike Deaver told me, "I know from conversations he and I had after the assassination attempt that there was no question in his mind that his life had been spared. He absolutely believed it. He felt the Lord had spared him to fulfill whatever mission it was that he was supposed to fulfill. And he was gonna make sure that he lived his life to the fullest and did whatever he considered to be the right thing for the rest of his life."

When he had recuperated enough, they got the president on a weight-lifting routine. He took it to heart—he was a physical fitness buff anyway—and he'd work out after he went home at the end of the day. He was proud of the fact that he had actually added to his chest measurement and his biceps. Deaver told me, "He'd show people, he'd say 'I've been lifting weights, I added an inch here and two inches there.' He was very proud of that. He was in good shape anyway but he was actually in better shape after he was shot because he got into weights."

There were dumbbells and a Nautilus machine upstairs in the residence. Soon, Mrs. Reagan was lifting too.

In time the Secret Service and everyone else learned about the man who shot the president, and why. John Hinckley was twenty-five years old, the unstable, drifting son of an affluent Colorado couple. On the evening of March twenty-ninth he was staying at the Park Central Hotel, just three hundred feet from the headquarters of the Secret Service, in Washington. He woke up there the morning of the thirtieth, read the president's schedule in *The Washington Post* that day and walked to the Hilton to wait for him. Hinckley had been in the crowd outside the Hilton when the president and his party arrived. The president and his aides had passed within thirty-five or so feet of him, but for some reason Hinckley had decided to wait, to shoot the president when he came out. The Secret Service learned of Hinckley's presence when they reviewed all the tapes and film of the event.

John Hinckley later said he had wanted to be like the character Travis Bickle in *Taxi Driver.* He wanted to impress the beautiful girl in that movie, the character played by the young actress Jody Foster. To impress her, he would be Travis and shoot a political leader. That was why he was going to shoot a president: to impress a character in a movie by becoming another character in the movie.

But there's more, and it's even more fantastic. In one of those oddities with which history is replete, John Hinckley was not the only person that day whose fate had been shaped by a film. One day many years before, when Jerry Parr was a boy, he saw a movie called *Code of the Secret Service,* starring a young actor named Ronald Reagan. Reagan played the heroic agent Brass Bancroft.

When young Jerry Parr saw the movie he was hooked. "That's why I became a Secret Service agent," he told me. He told President Reagan too, one day after the shooting, when they were both out at the ranch. "I told him, 'By making that picture you became the instrument of your own destiny.' And he thought about that."

"I internalized Brass Bancroft," said Parr. "Hinckley internalized Travis Bickle. It is strange how history works."

The Power of Truth

There are a number of special challenges when you try to capture the work of a great leader, a president or prime minister or revolutionary. When you work for such a man, when you're in the thick of it each day, you don't as a rule talk about it in a fully forthcoming way to friends and family and reporters and curious people. Part of the reason is loyalty: Discretion is a way to demonstrate the loyalty you feel, or to show you feel it to people around you who might be watching. Part of the reason is sheer busy-ness—people who have some role in a White House, for instance, are so consumed with their part of the drama, with smoothing over the scheduling problem or planning the summit, that they don't take time to observe as much as they later wish they had. Or if you do observe, you tend to see mostly your small area and can't always connect it to the big flow of events around you. You're too busy to keep a diary (or, now, too afraid of subpoenas). Or you might find that you're often on overload: Too much data come into your head each day when you work in a White House, and your brain may constantly wind up hitting DELETE on seemingly nonpertinent information when you mean for it to be hitting SAVE.

Another challenge for those who try to capture an administration: By the time people feel free to be "indiscreet" they have often gotten very old. Many of the men and women who served with Ronald Reagan were in their fifties, sixties or seventies in those days; now they're in their seventies, eighties and nineties. When the historians come knocking on their doors they start telling a story and halfway through they become frustrated. They're blocking on the name of the NSC adviser, or the country that is the focus of the anecdote or can't remember if the conversation with the first lady took place in Cairo or Cleveland. I have wondered sometimes, when I talk to them and they pause in the middle of a story, if they're not thinking: "Wait, did I have that conversation with the president or did someone tell me twenty years ago that he had the conversation with him, and I got the two confused?" . . . And then they grow quiet and say, "Well, it's all in the books. . . ."

Once, in the mid-1990s, I was asked by the University of Texas at Austin to take part in a lecture series in which various historians and authors were asked to speak about the personal character of a specific modern president. I was honored to be included with Doris Kearns Goodwin, who spoke on Franklin Roosevelt, and David McCullough, who spoke on Harry Truman, and Hendrik Hertzberg on Jimmy Carter, for whom he had been a speechwriter, and Michael Beschloss on George Bush the elder. I would speak on Reagan.

I reasoned, as I began my work, that one way to judge the character of a president is to see if he came through on the things he said he'd do when he ran for office. My impression was that Reagan had, on all the big issues. But as I researched it, comparing what he promised in 1980 with what he'd done by 1988, the sheer mounting of fact upon fact left me not only pleased but, in a way, moved.

In 1980, on the campaign trail he promised he would cut the inflation rate. It was running at 12.8 percent then, the last year of the Carter administration. It had reached its peak of 14.8 percent in March of that year. By 1983, Reagan had taken the actions—tough, politically damaging actions such as backing a tighter monetary supply and taking a recession in turn—that produced an inflation rate of less than 4 percent. Most important, inflation remained at 3 to 4 percent throughout the Reagan presidency. So he'd cut inflation by more than half almost since the beginning, and by the end it was less than a third of what it had been.

He said he would cut taxes. The day he walked into office the top tax rate for individuals was 78 percent. The day he walked out, he'd cut it down to 35 percent. Stephen Moore of the Cato Institute has said that no act in the past quarter century had a more profound impact on the economy of the eighties and nineties than the Reagan tax cut of 1981. "The nation was in quite a deep hole of economic collapse when Reagan was elected. We were in the midst of the worst economic depression in 1980–81 than at any time since the Great Depression of the 1930s. . . . Reagan's tax cuts—combined with his emphasis on sound money, deregulation and free trade—created a mighty economic expansion. . . . This expansion carried through the 1990s as well—creating America's greatest sustained wave of prosperity ever." How high a wave? The economy grew by more than one third in size; it produced a $15 trillion increase in America's wealth. And from 1981 to 1989—which is to say, from the beginning of the Reagan era to the end—every income group in the country from the richest to the poorest saw its income increase.

Reagan said he'd get the economy going again. See above. And see this: The Dow Jones, which was at less than 800 at the beginning of his first administration, was at more than 2400 by the end of his second administration.

He said he would decontrol oil prices. He did, and they began to plummet.

He said he would reduce unemployment. It was high when he went into office, 7.4 percent. When he left it was down more than 30 percent, to 5.4 percent. As important, or more so, the number of new jobs began to rise.

He said he would lower interest rates—and he did, cutting them to less than half what they were when he began his presidency. He said he'd reduce federal regulation, and he did. The Federal Register, which had eighty-seven thousand pages of rules and regulations under his predecessor, was cut back to a low of forty-seven thousand pages by 1986. He said he would cut the federal bureaucracy and he did.

He said he would cut the budget, and did. He didn't get nearly the cuts he hoped for, but in the words of the historian Michael Barone, "The budget cuts by themselves did not reduce government spending drastically, but they signaled that it would no longer be allowed to grow faster than the economy. The annual rates of growth in federal outlays would turn out to be slowed down from 17% and 15% over the period 1979–81 to 10%, 8%, and 5% during 1981–84."

He said he'd name a woman to the Supreme Court; he said he'd oppose racial quotas; he said he'd appoint conservatives to the federal bench; he said he'd oppose abortion; said he would try to create a defense system against incoming missiles; said he would rebuild the armed forces; said he would move toward a six-hundred-ship navy. Done, done, done, done, done, done and done. Every bit of it.

He said he would not bow to the Soviet Communist state, and vowed to speak truthfully both of and to it.

This he did most dazzlingly, most movingly of all.

A wonderfully cynical old German diplomat of the nineteenth century once said that it's no trick to fool a man who thinks himself clever, but an honest man, well, it can be a real challenge to fool him.

That's what I think of first when I think of Ronald Reagan and his dealings with Soviet totalitarianism. The clever men and women of his time were, more often than not, fooled by the arguments and maneuvers of the Soviets. But Reagan, who didn't think himself clever, was not.

That is a fact, and I'll support it in a moment. But facts, which are good things, are often dry. You have to extend a fact to look at its impact on people, and then it can sink into your brain and your heart. That's where facts settle in, accumulate, come together and yield, finally, a truth.

Here is a truth.

There was a man named Anatoly Shcharansky, a brilliant man who was in prison in Russia because he would not bow to the demands of its dictatorship. Shcharansky was trouble, a Russian intellectual respected in the West and a colleague of the great Andrei Sakharov, another inconvenient man who would not stop telling the truth.

Shcharansky was in prison—specifically, in Permanent Labor Camp 35 in the Ural Mountains—when Ronald Reagan became president. And what Ronald Reagan said to the world about the Soviet Union after he became president liberated Shcharansky. First, it liberated his spirit, because Reagan's words thrilled him and the other prisoners with their stark truth—and this gave him and the others in the gulag the one thing they needed to live each day, and that was: hope.

Shcharansky and the other prisoners would hear—sometimes it was something overheard, one guard talking to another, or sometimes it would come from the radio as part of a propaganda broadcast showing the Russian people what a warmonger the American president was—what Reagan said in his speeches about freedom. And the one who heard it would pass the word to the other prisoners.

Years later Shcharansky told me there are ways "even in the gulag" that prisoners can communicate with each other. Sometimes he and the other men would empty out the toilets and the sinks and whisper to each other through the pipes. Sometimes they used code, from cell to cell. And there were other ways he didn't want to talk about. But he wanted me to know that there were times when Ronald Reagan spoke that the gulag would explode with a great racket of taps, knocks and whispers as they heard what he said and passed it on.

I will tell you of two important things Reagan said that changed the world, but first I will put them in context. The context has to do with Reagan himself, with who he was as a man, as an individual.

Ronald Reagan loved the truth. We all do or say we do but for Reagan it was like fresh water, something he needed and wanted.

He loved the truth for a number of reasons, a primary one of which is that he thought it, in our current political circumstances, uniquely constructive. He thought that by voicing it you were beginning to make things better.

He thought the truth is the only foundation on which can be built something strong and good and lasting—because only truth endures. Lies die. He thought that in politics and world affairs in his time there had been too many lies for too long, and that they had been uniquely destructive. And so his public career was devoted to countering that destructiveness by speaking the truth, spreading it and repeating it.

He wanted to put words into the air that were honest and have them take the place of other words that were not.

He wanted to crowd out the false with the true.

So now let me tell you what he said, and then I will tell you more about Shcharansky.

In June 1982, Ronald Reagan went to England. It was a hard time for an American president to go abroad because a U.S. economic recession had begun. The Democrats of Congress, many in the press and many voters blamed Reaganomics—the tax and budget cuts Reagan had worked to implement.

But Reagan felt this was the time to move forward in foreign affairs, and that the economy would right itself, and so he went to England.

On June 8, 1982, he spoke to the British Parliament in the Palace of Westminster in London. It came to be called the Westminster speech.

He later said of this speech, and of the one that would follow, the famous Evil Empire speech, "I wanted to do some things differently, like speaking the truth about [the Soviets] for a change, rather than hiding reality behind the niceties of diplomacy." He said it was one of the most important speeches he ever gave, that "what eventually flowed from it became known as the Reagan Doctrine." Which he defined, simply, as a commitment to support "those fighting for freedom and against communism wherever we found them."

He felt that previous American leadership had not taken on the principles of Marxist-Leninist philosophy because we had feared to offend. But Reagan was not inhibited in that way. He thought: We can scarcely make the Soviets worse, and the truth might make things better. Or at least establish the only platform on which things can become better.

And so he took some deep breaths, stood straight, put his shoulders back, walked to the podium of the great wood-paneled room and this is what he said (I'm going to give you a lot of this speech, because it is an important historic document and because it captures so much of who the old man was):

> My Lord Chancellor, Mr. Speaker:
>
> The journey of which this visit forms a part is a long one. Already it has taken me to two great cities of the West, Rome and Paris, and to the economic summit at Versailles. And there, once again, our sister democracies have proved that even in a time of severe economic strain, free people can work together freely and voluntarily to address problems. . . .
>
> This is my second visit to Great Britain as president of the United States. My first opportunity to stand on British soil occurred almost a year and a half ago when your prime minister graciously hosted a diplomatic dinner at the British Embassy in

Washington. Mrs. Thatcher said then that she hoped I was not distressed to find staring down at me from the grand staircase a portrait of His Royal Majesty King George III. She suggested it was best to let bygones be bygones, and in view of our two countries' remarkable friendship in succeeding years, she added that most Englishmen today would agree with Thomas Jefferson that "a little rebellion now and then is a very good thing."

From here I will go to Bonn and then Berlin, where there stands a grim symbol of power untamed. The Berlin Wall, that dreadful gray gash across the city, is in its third decade. It is the fitting signature of the regime that built it. . . .

We are approaching the end of a bloody century plagued by a terrible political invention—totalitarianism. Optimism comes less easily today, not because democracy is less vigorous, but because democracy's enemies have refined their instruments of repression. Yet optimism is in order, because day by day democracy is proving itself to be a not-at-all-fragile flower.

From Stettin on the Baltic to Varna on the Black Sea, the regimes planted by totalitarianism have had more than thirty years to establish their legitimacy. But none—not one regime—has yet been able to risk free elections. Regimes planted by bayonets do not take root.

The strength of the Solidarity movement in Poland demonstrates the truth told in an underground joke in the Soviet Union. It is that the Soviet Union would remain a one-party nation even if an opposition party were permitted, because everyone would join the opposition party.

America's time as a player on the stage of world history has been brief. I think understanding this fact has always made you patient with your younger cousins—well, not always patient. I do recall that on one occasion, Sir Winston Churchill said in exasperation about one of our most distinguished diplomats, "He is the only case I know of a bull who carries his china shop with him."

But witty as Sir Winston was, he also had that special attribute of great statesmen—the gift of vision, the willingness to see the future based on the experience of the past. . . .

We have not inherited an easy world. If developments like the Industrial Revolution . . . and the gifts of science and technology have made life much easier for us, they have also made it more dangerous. . . .

There is first the threat of global war. No president, no congress, no prime minister, no parliament can spend a day entirely free of this threat. And I don't have to tell you that in today's world the existence of nuclear weapons could mean, if not the extinction of mankind, then surely the end of civilization as we know it. . . .

At the same time there is a threat posed to human freedom by the enormous power of the modern state. History teaches the dangers of government that overreaches—political control taking precedence over free economic growth, secret police, mindless bureaucracy, all combining to stifle individual excellence and personal freedom. . . .

Historians looking back at our time will note the consistent restraint and peaceful intentions of the West. They will note it was the democracies who refused to use the threat of their nuclear monopoly in the forties and early fifties for territorial or imperial gains. Had that nuclear monopoly been in the hands of the Communist world, the map of Europe—indeed, the world—would look very different today. And certainly they will note it was not the democracies that invaded Afghanistan or suppressed Polish Solidarity or used chemical and toxic warfare in Afghanistan and Southeast Asia.

If history teaches anything, it teaches self-delusion in the face of unpleasant facts is folly. We see around us today the marks of our terrible dilemma—predictions of doomsday, antinuclear demonstrations, an arms race in which the West must, for its own protection, be an unwilling participant. At the same time we see totalitarian forces in the world who seek subversion and conflict around the globe to further their barbarous assault on the human spirit.

What, then, is our course? Must civilization perish in a hail of fiery atoms? Must freedom wither in a quiet, deadening accommodation with totalitarian evil?

Sir Winston Churchill refused to accept the inevitability of war or even that it was imminent. He said, "I do not believe that Soviet Russia desires war. What they desire is the fruits of war and the indefinite expansion of their power and doctrines. But what we have to consider here today while time remains is the permanent prevention of war and the establishment of conditions of freedom and democracy as rapidly as possible in all countries."

This is precisely our mission today: to preserve freedom as well as peace.

It may not be easy to see, but I believe we live now at a turning point.

In an ironic sense Karl Marx was right. We are witnessing today a great revolutionary crisis, a crisis where the demands of the economic order are conflicting directly with those of the political order. But the crisis is happening not in the free, non-Marxist West, but in the home of Marxist Leninism, the Soviet Union. It is the Soviet Union that runs against the tide of history by denying human freedom and human dignity to its citizens. It is also in deep economic difficulty. The rate of growth in the national product has been steadily declining since the fifties and is less than half of what it was then.

The dimensions of this failure are astounding: A country which employs one fifth of its population in agriculture is unable to feed its own people. Were it not for the private sector, the tiny private sector tolerated in Soviet agriculture, the country might be on the brink of famine. These private plots occupy a bare three percent of the arable land but account for nearly one third of meat products and vegetables. Overcentralized, with little or no incentives, year after year the Soviet system pours its best resources into the making of instruments of destruction. The constant shrinkage of economic growth combined with the growth of military production is putting a heavy strain on the Soviet people. . . .

The decay of the Soviet experiment should come as no surprise to us. Wherever the comparisons have been made between free and closed societies—West Germany and East Germany, Austria and Czechoslovakia, Malaysia and Vietnam—it is the democratic countries that are prosperous and responsive to the needs of their people.

And one of the simple but overwhelming facts of our time is this: Of all the millions of refugees we've seen in the modern world, their flight is always away from, not toward, the Communist world. Today on the NATO line, our military forces face east to prevent a possible invasion. On the other side of the line, the Soviet forces also face east—to prevent their people from leaving.

The hard evidence of totalitarian rule has caused in mankind an uprising of the intellect and will. Whether it is the growth of the new schools of economics in America or England or the appearance of the so-called new philosophers in France, there is one unifying thread running through the intellectual work of these groups—rejection of the arbitrary power of the state, the refusal to subordinate the rights of the individual to the super-state, the realization that collectivism stifles all the best human impulses.

Since the exodus from Egypt, historians have written of those who sacrificed and struggled for freedom—the stand at Thermopylae, the revolt of Spartacus, the storming of the Bastille, the Warsaw uprising in World War II. . . . In the Communist world . . . man's instinctive desire for freedom and self-determination surfaces again and again. To be sure, there are grim reminders of how brutally the police state attempts to snuff out this quest for self-rule—1953 in East Germany, 1956 in Hungary, 1968 in Czechoslovakia, 1981 in Poland.

But the struggle continues in Poland. And we know that there are even those who strive and suffer for freedom within the confines of the Soviet Union itself. How we conduct ourselves here in the Western democracies will determine whether this trend continues. . . .

We cannot ignore the fact that even without encouragement there has been and will continue to be repeated explosions against repression and dictatorships. The Soviet Union itself is not immune to this reality. Any system is inherently unstable that has no peaceful means to legitimize its leaders. In such cases, the very repressiveness of the state ultimately drives people to resist, if necessary, by force.

While we must be cautious about forcing the pace of change, we must not hesitate to declare our ultimate objectives and to take concrete actions toward them. We must be staunch in our conviction that freedom is not the sole prerogative of a lucky few, but the inalienable and universal right of all human beings. So states the United Nations Universal Declaration of Human Rights, which, among other things, guarantees free elections.

The objective I promise is quite simple to state: to foster the infrastructure of democracy, the system of a free press, unions, political parties, universities, which allows a people to choose their own way to develop their own culture, to reconcile their own differences through peaceful means.

This is not cultural imperialism, it is providing the means for genuine self-determination and protection for diversity. Democracy already flourishes in countries with very different cultures and historical experiences. It would be cultural condescension, or worse, to say that any people prefer dictatorship to democracy.

Who would voluntarily choose not to have the right to vote, decide to purchase government propaganda handouts instead of independent newspapers, prefer government- to worker-controlled unions, opt for land to be owned by the state instead of those who till it, want government repression of religious liberty, a single political party instead of a free choice, a rigid cultural orthodoxy instead of democratic tolerance and diversity?

Since 1917, the Soviet Union has given covert political training and assistance to Marxist Leninists in many countries. Of course, it also has promoted the use of violence and subversion by these same forces. . . .

It is time that we (in the United States) committed ourselves as a nation—in both the public and private sectors—to assisting democratic development. . . .

(W)e invite the Soviet Union to consider with us how the competition of ideas and values—which it is committed to support—can be conducted on a peaceful and reciprocal basis. For example, I am prepared to offer President Brezhnev an opportunity to speak to the American people on our television if he will allow me the same opportunity with the Soviet people. We also suggest that panels of our newsmen periodically appear on each other's television. . . .

Now, I don't wish to sound overly optimistic, yet the Soviet Union is not immune from the reality of what is going on in the world. It has happened in the past—a small ruling elite either mistakenly attempts to ease domestic unrest through greater repression and foreign adventure, or it chooses a wiser course. It begins to allow its people a voice in their own destiny. Even if this latter process is not realized soon, I believe the renewed strength of the democratic movement, complemented by a global campaign for freedom, will strengthen the prospects for arms control and a world at peace.

I have discussed on other occasions . . . the elements of Western policies toward the Soviet Union to safeguard our interests and protect the peace. What I am describing now is a plan and a hope for the long term—the march of freedom and democracy which will leave Marxism-Leninism on the ash heap of history as it has left other tyrannies which stifle the freedom and muzzle the self-expression of the people. . . .

Our military strength is a prerequisite to peace, but let it be clear we maintain the strength in the hope it will never be used, for the ultimate determinant in the struggle that's now going on in the world will not be bombs and rockets, but a test of wills and ideas, a trial of spiritual resolve, the values we hold, the beliefs we cherish, the ideals to which we are dedicated.

The British people know that, given strong leadership, time, and a little bit of hope, the forces of good ultimately rally and triumph over evil. Here among you is the cradle of self-government, the mother of parliaments. Here is the enduring greatness of the British contribution to mankind, the great civilized ideas: individual liberty, representative government, and the rule of law under God.

I've often wondered about the shyness of some of us in the West about standing for these ideals that have done so much to ease the plight of man and the hardships of our imperfect world.

This reluctance to use those vast resources at our command reminds me of the elderly lady whose home was bombed in the blitz. As the rescuers moved about, they found a bottle of brandy she'd stored behind the staircase, which was all that was left standing. And since she was barely conscious, one of the workers pulled the cork to give her a taste of it. She came around immediately and said, "Here now—there now, put it back. That's for emergencies." [*Laughter*]

Well, that emergency is upon us. Let us be shy no longer. . . . Let us tell the world that a new age is not only possible but probable.

During the dark days of the Second World War, when this island was incandescent with courage, Winston Churchill exclaimed about Britain's adversaries, "What kind of a people do they think we are?" Well, Britain's adversaries found out what extraordinary people the British are.

But all the democracies (of that time) paid a terrible price for allowing the dictators to underestimate us. We dare not make that mistake again.

So let us ask ourselves, "What kind of people do we think we are?" And let us answer, "Free people, worthy of freedom and determined not only to remain so but to help others gain their freedom as well."

Sir Winston led his people to great victory in war and then lost an election just as the fruits of victory were about to be enjoyed. But he left office honorably, and, as it turned out, temporarily, knowing that the liberty of his people was more important than the fate of any single leader. History recalls his greatness in ways no dictator will ever know. And he left us a message of hope for the future, as timely now as when he first uttered it, as opposition leader in the Commons nearly twenty-seven years ago, when he said, "When we look back on all the perils through which we have passed, and at the mighty foes that we have laid low, and all the dark and deadly designs that we have frustrated, why should we fear for our future? We have," he said, "come safely through the worst."

> The task I've set forth will long outlive our own generation, but together, we too have come through the worst. Let us now begin a major effort to secure the best—a crusade for freedom that will engage the faith and fortitude of the next generation. For the sake of peace and justice, let us move toward a world in which all people are at last free to determine their own destiny.
>
> Thank you.

The applause was mighty, thunderous. It was a beautiful moment in Western history, certainly one of the most stunning of the past century. A whole speech marked by bravery and truth, as rousing as any of those spoken by Churchill, and as important too. And it signaled the beginning of a massive shift: from the defensive crouch in which the Western democracies had long huddled into a tall-walking, truth-telling style of faithfulness that would, ultimately, move mountains.

Criticism of the speech of course was immediate, heavy, from all points of the globe. Wasn't such talk warmongering? Reagan thought no: No one wants war and no one is going to launch a missile because we in the West aren't evil and the Soviet leaders aren't stupid. Wasn't Reagan just "playing to his base" and "throwing red meat" to his ferocious supporters? Reagan thought that was silly: He was speaking to the world, not his constituency, which didn't need persuading. He was talking to those who did *not* share his views. But wasn't the speech insulting to the Russians? Reagan would smile at this: He would never insult the Russian people, he was only pointing out what they already knew, which was that their government was an insult to them, and to humanity too. And at any rate, candor is a compliment: It assumes the person receiving it is strong enough to take it, and think about it.

That was the first speech. The second was given at home in America, in Orlando, Florida, to the annual convention of the National Association of Evangelicals on March 8, 1983. This was the famous Evil Empire speech. Most of the speech is about issues America was struggling with at home, but in the final third of the speech Reagan turned to international relations:

> During my first press conference as president, in answer to a direct question, I pointed out that as good Marxist Leninists the Soviet leaders have openly and publicly declared that the only morality they recognize is that which will further their cause, which is world revolution. I think I should point out that I was only quoting Lenin, their guiding spirit, who said in 1920 that they repudiate all morality that proceeds from supernatural ideas—that's their name for religion—or ideas that are outside class conceptions. Morality is entirely subordinate to the interests of class war. And everything is moral that is necessary for the annihilation of the old, exploiting social order and for uniting the proletariat.
>
> Well, I think the refusal of many influential people to accept this elementary fact of Soviet doctrine illustrates a historical reluctance to see totalitarian powers for what they are. We saw this phenomenon in the 1930s. We see it too often today.
>
> This doesn't mean we should isolate ourselves and refuse to seek an understanding with [the Soviet Union]. I intend to do everything I can to persuade them of our peaceful intent, to remind them that it was the West that refused to use its nuclear monopoly in the forties and fifties for territorial gain and which now proposes a fifty percent cut in strategic ballistic missiles and the elimination of an entire class of land-based, intermediate-range nuclear missiles.
>
> At the same time, however, they must be made to understand we will never compromise our principles and standards. We will never give away our freedom. We will never abandon our belief in God. And we will never stop searching for a genuine peace. . . .
>
> A number of years ago, I heard a young father, a very prominent young man in the entertainment world, addressing a tremendous gathering in California. It was during the time of the cold war, and communism and our way of life were

very much on people's minds. And he was speaking to that subject. And suddenly, though, I heard him saying, "I love my little girls more than anything—" And I said to myself, "Oh no, don't. You can't—don't say that." But I had underestimated him. He went on, "I would rather see my little girls die now, still believing in God, than have them grow up under communism and one day die no longer believing in God."

There were thousands of young people in that audience. They came to their feet with shouts of joy. They had instantly recognized the profound truth in what he had said, with regard to the physical and the soul and what was truly important.

Yes, let us pray for the salvation of all of those who live in their totalitarian darkness—pray that they will discover the joy of knowing God. But until they do, let us be aware that while they preach the supremacy of the state, declare its omnipotence over individual man, and predict its eventual domination of all peoples on the earth, they are the locus of evil in the modern world.

It was C. S. Lewis who, in his unforgettable *Screwtape Letters,* wrote: "The greatest evil is not done now in those sordid 'dens of crime' that Dickens loved to paint. It is not even done in concentration camps and labor camps. In those we see its final result. But it is conceived and ordered (moved, seconded, carried and minuted) in clean, carpeted, warmed, and well lighted offices, by quiet men with white collars and cut fingernails and smooth-shaven cheeks who do not need to raise their voice. . . ."

Some would have us accept [the Soviets] at their word and accommodate ourselves to their aggressive impulses. But if history teaches anything, it teaches that simpleminded appeasement or wishful thinking about our adversaries is folly. It means the betrayal of our past, the squandering of our freedom.

So I urge you to speak out against those who would place the United States in a position of military and moral inferiority. You know, I've always believed that old Screwtape reserved his best efforts for those of you in the church. So, in your discussions of the nuclear freeze proposals, I urge you to beware

> the temptation of pride—the temptation of blithely declaring yourselves above it all and label both sides equally at fault, to ignore the facts of history and the aggressive impulses of an evil empire, to simply call the arms race a giant misunderstanding and thereby remove yourself from the struggle between right and wrong and good and evil.
>
> I ask you to resist the attempts of those who would have you withhold your support for our efforts, this administration's efforts, to keep America strong and free while we negotiate real and verifiable reductions in the world's nuclear arsenals and one day, with God's help, their total elimination.
>
> While America's military strength is important, let me add here that I've always maintained that the struggle now going on for the world will never be decided by bombs or rockets, by armies or military might. The real crisis we face today is a spiritual one; at root, it is a test of moral will and faith.

"The locus of evil in the modern world." Those are tough hard words and this time, even more than in the Westminster speech, it shocked people when Ronald Reagan said them. Not because it wasn't or couldn't possibly be true but because it wasn't the kind of thing that was *said,* and by a president.

Anatoly Dobrynin, the Soviet ambassador to Washington, complained. He told Al Haig, the secretary of state, that the Soviets were unhappy about the harsh things Reagan had said. He hinted that they were interested in reopening arms control talks. Haig told the president. The president said to tell Dobrynin that his words were meant to convey a message: The White House was under new management, and it was informed by a new realism toward the Russians, and unless they changed their ways there would be more.

Again Reagan thought honest words the only possible predicate for progress. It should be noted that these words, which made history, were essentially what he had been saying since the 1950s, since he first came to recognize what communism was and how its adherents operated.

He had remained consistent. The immature are always finding new truths, and the cynical are always discovering new philosophies to claim to believe in, but Reagan was neither immature nor cynical. And so his consistency, which would have been impressive in anybody, but which was startling in a politician.

Now I'll get back to Anatoly Shcharansky. When they passed word of the Evil Empire speech he was in Permanent Labor Camp 35, in the Urals. He had been arrested for treason by the Soviet government in the spring of 1977, during a government crackdown on human rights activists. He was tried on trumped-up charges and sentenced to thirteen years' imprisonment and hard labor. He was in a way a special man—a renowned scientist—but really he was just another victim of Soviet oppression who one day disappeared from the streets and who then was forced to live on reduced food rations, doing hard labor in isolation from the outside world.

I talked to him on March 10, 2001, at 4 P.M. my time and 11 P.M. his. He lives in Israel now, where he changed his name from Anatoly Shcharansky to Natan Sharansky. He called me in New York from a cell phone in his Jeep as he drove from Tel Aviv to Jerusalem on government business. For Natan Sharansky, formerly of the Russian gulag, was now deputy prime minister and minister of housing of the Israeli government. (Life is rich with such marvels but when you bump into one it can take your breath away.)

Sharansky told me of his time in prison in Russia. "We would overhear guards, we would overhear radio attacks on Reagan, we would hear that Reagan was attacked in *Pravda*." And these reports, meant to inflame the Russian people against the American president, instead encouraged and inspired the men of the gulag.

"I think the most important step in the cold war and the defeat of the Soviet empire was his words and his actions at the beginning of his presidency," Sharansky continued.

"There was fear in the West to deal with the Soviet Union. 'The Soviet empire is forever, whether we want to or not we will have to deal with it, and by the Soviet Union's rules.' But pragmatism led to our suffering! Reagan was one who understood the Soviet Union is [an] evil empire and we could change it. And he also believed that all the people of the world, Russians and Arabs and Jews, are as good for democracy as anyone. Not just Americans but everyone. And he acted in accord with it."

Sharansky was released from prison after heavy and unrelenting pressure from the Reagan administration, and after he left Russia he went to Israel, and then visited the United States. "I came to America," he told me, "and I was invited to the White House to meet President Reagan. And I told him that his speech about the Evil Empire was a great encourager for us. An American leader was calling a spade a spade—he understood the nature of the Soviet Union. I told Reagan, and he turned and said to his colleagues, 'Hear what he is saying, listen to him.' Shultz was there, McFarlane too, Poindexter, maybe Baker."

He continued, "President Reagan understood the nature of a totalitarian regime. He believed freedom is something that belongs to all the people, and if you encourage it and support it you can win. He had very healthy instincts about it. He was a fresh change after Nixon's attempts at détente and Carter, who talked well but couldn't link practical policy to his talk. When it came to action there was nothing—and then came Reagan, and Star Wars—Star Wars was a way of talking to the Soviet Union! And he linked the fate of dissidents to the policy of the United States of America."

What, ultimately, was the meaning of all of Reagan's speeches about communism? What exactly did they do apart from anger the Soviets and encourage those who opposed them?

They signaled a new era. They inaugurated something new. Now we would tell the truth. And why was that important? Because dictatorships cannot continue forever in an atmosphere of truth. Dictatorship requires the complicity, the acquiescence of a whole people in order to continue in power. The great novelist Alexander Solzhenitsyn wrote that it is only when people refuse to lie, with all the courage involved in that refusal, that dictators and dictatorships fall.

That was the amazing thing Ronald Reagan did when he looked at the Soviet Union. He refused to lie, and with his words the fall of the ugliest dictatorship of human history began. And nine months after he walked out of the White House, the Berlin Wall crashed to the ground. Though of course it didn't fall. It was pushed.

Tough Choices

Modern presidents usually begin their day with a briefing on the state of the world. Reagan's briefings, at the height of the cold war, tended to reveal or underscore areas of geopolitical opportunity or anxiety. Richard Reeves, in his recent history of the administration of President Kennedy, noted that the sheer range and scale of the issues Kennedy dealt with each day were, in retrospect, astounding. The eighties were like that too: So much was happening, so much popping, new problems arose on the backs of the old, new solutions created unanticipated consequences.

He was told the Soviet economy was in even worse shape than he knew—this was good. They were bankrupting themselves building arms—bad, better they should bankrupt themselves in other ways. Reagan had always believed the Soviet Communist elite had in a way simply taken the place of the aristocratic elite of the czars, but that by killing freedom as opposed to limiting it, they'd doomed themselves. Poland and the Eastern-bloc countries were falling apart. The empire could not hold.

Every administration since Harry Truman's had struggled to find the right balance toward the Soviet Union. Reagan wanted to change the equation; he wanted to break with the traditional American strategy of containment and move on to strategies aimed at forcing the Soviets back. Central and South America were the scene of Communist insurgencies in Nicaragua and El Salvador. How to fight without lending credence to the idea that America was as big a threat to Latin America as the Soviet Union? The people of these countries lived in poverty, 90 percent lived under dictatorships, and to some the Marxist idea could seem like liberation.

But Reagan decided that the West had already lost Cuba to communism and the free world—he still used that phrase—was not going to lose any more of Central America or the Caribbean.

The preliminary plan: Do everything possible to help these countries free themselves of poverty, set an economic example, give assistance, create an attitude that showed the Soviets that if they meant to take any more of this hemisphere, they would have to fight for it.

Reagan had been shot on March thirtieth and was home from the hospital on April eleventh. He was still getting X rays and blood tests but they were letting up on the antibiotics and his appetite came roaring back. Food tasted good again for the first time in weeks.

He read memos and reports, held meetings in the residence, watched the space shuttle *Columbia* return to Earth in triumph after its first voyage. He watched it on television in the Lincoln bedroom, where they'd set up his hospital-style bed.

He had a lot of time to think in his robe and pajamas. His mind went back again and again to the Soviets, and to some thoughts he'd had a few days before he was shot. He had been thinking about the policy of mutually assured destruction, MAD, or as he called it, "the well-named MAD." He understood why it existed, how it had come to be, and that it had in one essential way worked: The Soviets and the Americans had not unleashed their nuclear arsenals at each other because both knew the outcome would be a mutally assured destruction.

There was nothing he wanted more than to lessen the risk of nuclear war. This was something that those who knew him and those who followed him had understood about him for a long time, something his foes had never fully absorbed. He had been preoccupied for years with how to lessen the chance of nuclear war. He was appalled by MAD, understood that while it was probably the most stable means of dealing with an armed Soviet Union it was, like everything else in the world, open to the unknowable, to mistakes, accidents and ill fortune.

He thought that someone in the Kremlin must be able to understand, to see that keeping the United States and the Soviet Union standing like two cowboys, guns drawn, was a waste of energy, resources, creativity; it was exhausting, and dangerous. Someone in the

Kremlin must understand that they were bankrupting themselves and endangering their own personal power by spending on arms like this. But he didn't know if he'd ever meet that person.

How could he make it better, make deterrence saner? The traditional American answer had been more détente—more talks and summits and meetings and agreements that, in his view, tended to result in more freedom for the Soviets to pursue whatever policies of subversion and expansionism they wanted. He thought this was wrong, that it encouraged what it was meant to discourage and gave a legitimacy to the Soviet government that it did not deserve.

He respected communism in this way: He respected its intention to pursue its announced plans. No American president ever quoted Lenin as much and as often, or as seriously. Reagan took him seriously. Every Soviet leader since Lenin, up to and including the one now, Brezhnev, had declared the goal of the Soviet Union was to make the world Communist.

In the years after World War II, much American blood and treasure had gone to resisting Soviet expansionism in Turkey, Greece, Korea, Southeast Asia. We had acted as if we had a special responsibility, as the world's great democracy, to help bring freedom to others and to help protect them when their freedom was threatened. But Reagan felt that since at least the 1970s America had begun to abdicate her role. The Soviet Union had seen our new diffidence, our lack of sureness, our weakened commitment. And they had moved boldly forward, invading Afghanistan, using their surrogates to destabilize El Salvador, Angola, Ethiopia, Cambodia, trying to destroy and destabilize non-Communist governments.

They were threatening to invade Poland after the Solidarity movement began, making the same sounds they made before they invaded Hungary in 1956 and Czechoslovakia in 1968.

And so he decided on a new realism.

At his first news conference as president, Reagan had been asked whether we could trust the Soviet Union. He said the answer to that question could be found in the writings of the Soviet leaders, whose declared policy was that it was moral to lie and cheat in pursuit of advancing world communism. He said they had told us, without meaning to, that they could not in fact be trusted.

Reagan told the Soviets they were prolonging the nuclear arms race by continuing their policy of expansionism; that America would never allow herself to be outspent in terms of defense, never accept second place; that we would outspend them forever, and could too, because a free economy will always allow us the wealth to do it.

At the same time he communicated to them the fact that a nuclear standoff was futile and dangerous, that they had nothing to fear from us if they stepped back, that a lessening of tensions would be welcome.

He was still recuperating, still in the Lincoln bedroom in his pajamas, when he decided to write a personal letter to Leonid Brezhnev, the Soviet leader. He wrote the first draft on a pad of yellow legal paper, not sure he would send it but eager to get his thoughts down.

He had decided while convalescing something he hadn't told anyone, not his NSC adviser and not his secretary of state. He wanted to lift the Soviet grain embargo, which prohibited American farmers from selling grain to Russia. It had been imposed by Jimmy Carter in 1979, after the Soviets invaded Afghanistan. Reagan now decided to lift it to demonstrate to the Soviets his seriousness about improving relations. He also wanted to show America's allies that he was serious. In Germany and Western Europe the green movement for unilateral disarmament was taking hold; its members painted America not as a guarantor of peace but as an impediment to it.

Secretary of State Al Haig resisted lifting the embargo—we should wait, he said, until the Soviets took some action to earn it. Reagan understood, but explained that he wanted to take the initiative. Then he told Haig about the letter he was writing Brezhnev. Haig didn't want him to do it—he said the State Department could draft it. This gave Reagan pause—he said later that it was the first time he got a sense that Al Haig didn't want Ronald Reagan messing around in Ronald Reagan's foreign policy.

When Reagan's letter was done, Reagan showed it to Haig, who had the State Department revise it. Reagan received it back and revised their revisions. Finally he sent the letter he'd intended, along with a more official one outlining American views on Soviet arms building and expansionism.

The personal, handwritten letter Reagan ultimately sent Brezhnev was warm and imploring.

> Mr. President, in writing the attached letter I am reminded of our meeting in San Clemente a decade or so ago. I was Governor of California at the time and you were concluding a series of meetings with President Nixon. Those meetings had captured the imagination of all the world. Never had peace and good will among men seemed closer at hand.
>
> When we met I asked if you were aware that the hopes and aspirations of millions of people throughout the world were dependent on the decisions that would be reached in your meetings.
>
> You took my hand in both of yours and assured me that you were aware of that and that you were dedicated with all your heart and mind to fulfilling those hopes and dreams. . . .

Reagan said the people of the world are all the same in this: They want the dignity of having some control over their individual destiny.

> They want to work at the craft or trade of their own choosing and to be fairly rewarded. They want to raise their families in peace without harming anyone or suffering harm themselves. Governments exist for their convenience, not the other way around. . . .

He asked,

> Is it possible we have permitted ideology, political and economic philosophies, and governmental policies to keep us from considering the very real, everyday problems of peoples? Will the average Soviet family be better off or even aware that the

> Soviet Union has imposed a government of its own choice on the people of Afghanistan? Is life better for the people of Cuba because the Cuban military dictate who shall govern the people of Angola?

He said he knew that there were those in the Soviet Union who would argue that it was the United States that had territorial ambitions and imperialistic designs, that America was a threat to the Soviet Union. But this is not true, he said.

> When World War II ended, the United States had the only undamaged industrial power in the world. Our military might was at its peak—and we alone had the ultimate weapon; the nuclear weapon, with the unquestioned ability to deliver it anywhere in the world. If we had sought world domination then, who could have opposed us? But the United States followed a different course—one unique in all the history of mankind. We used our power and wealth to rebuild the war-ravaged economies of the world, including those nations who had been our enemies. . . .

He asked Brezhnev to join him in eliminating the obstacles to peace.

> It is in this spirit, in the spirit of helping the people of both our nations, that I have lifted the grain embargo. Perhaps this decision will contribute to creating the circumstances . . . which will assist us in fulfilling our joint obligation to find lasting peace.

The reply came just a few days later. It was ice cold. Brezhnev repudiated Reagan's points, blamed the United States for starting and perpetuating the cold war, and said it had no business telling the Soviets what they could or could not do anywhere in the world.

"So much for my first attempt at personal diplomacy," Reagan said.

Why did Reagan do this—write a personal letter from his sickbed to a man he didn't trust who headed a government that could not be trusted? And why so early in his presidency, when he was establishing that there's a new sheriff in town, and he meant to operate in a new way?

I think that, in part, the answer is this. When you're strong you can be "weak." When you know you are strong, you can trust yourself to make the first move, the first appeal, a request or a plea. Reagan trusted himself and his motives, and when you trust yourself like that, you can hold all options open.

But when you fear you are weak or fear the world thinks you are weak, you are more inclined to make a great show of being "strong," and never write a personal letter asking for peace.

And then something happened, something big. But the paradox is that no one understood at the time exactly how important it was.

It was a domestic matter—a looming union strike. And no one knew that how Ronald Reagan would handle it would be noticed by the world, and would have a profound impact on his relationship with the Soviet Union.

Even Reagan didn't know. He was just doing what he thought was right.

It had been a busy springtime in 1981 for the seventy-year-old president. He had promised during the campaign to be the first president to appoint a woman to the Supreme Court, and he'd begun the search even before a vacancy opened up. He met with Sandra Day O'Connor of the Arizona Court of Appeals on July first in the White House, found her forthright and solid and decided to appoint her.

Other things were happening. A Libyan terrorist had been implicated in a murder in Chicago, and Reagan closed down Muammar Qaddafi's embassy in Washington. The United States stepped up covert activities in Libya and found out exactly how the Soviets were supplying arms and aid to Qaddafi, which he used to help terrorist groups throughout the world. Reagan met with the NSC and authorized the Sixth Fleet to conduct maneuvers in the Gulf of Sidra, which Qaddafi had begun to insist was part of Libya, not international waters. He had ordered all foreign ships out. Reagan ordered U.S. ships in.

After he appointed O'Connor to the high court, Reagan had a meeting with Drew Lewis at Camp David. Lewis, his secretary of transportation, had bad news. The Professional Air Traffic Controllers Organization, PATCO, was threatening to go out on strike.

The controllers were the tough and hardy professionals who manned airport control towers and radar centers across the country. Their jobs were stressful, demanding, high stakes. They were federal government jobs and their contract was up. They decided to demand a huge pay increase.

Reagan agreed with their argument that the pressures of the jobs justified a pay hike, and he offered an 11 percent pay increase—substantial in a time of budget cuts. But PATCO was demanding a 100 percent increase. It would cost the taxpayers $700 million, and no way would Reagan accept anything even approaching that.

Reagan told Lewis to tell the union that under no circumstances would he accept an illegal strike, and under no circumstances would he negotiate a contract while a strike was on. He added this: You tell the leaders of PATCO that as a former union president I am the best friend they've ever had in the White House.

But Reagan's decision was not an easy one. Very few unions had supported him when he ran for president in 1980—but PATCO had. Very few union leaders had been friendly to him—but PATCO's had. And Reagan always had supported the rights of workingmen and -women to bargain collectively and protect their interests.

But no president, he thought, should ever tolerate an illegal strike by federal employees. These weren't workers moving against a business or industry; these were professionals who provided a vital government service. Moreover, there was a law forbidding federal employee strikes, and each member of the union had signed a sworn affidavit agreeing not to strike.

Reagan told Lewis he agreed with Calvin Coolidge: "There is no right to strike against the public safety by anybody, anywhere, at any time."

Talks resumed, fell apart, and a few weeks later 70 percent of the nation's seventeen thousand controllers walked out. The union's leaders thought Reagan was bluffing: They knew he wasn't going to fire them because if he did it would endanger the economy and inconvenience hundreds of thousands of passengers and products.

The strike was the first immediate national emergency Reagan faced. Naturally, friends and foes throughout the world looked to see what he would do.

Reagan not only refused to accept the strike—he also refused to resume negotiations. He summoned reporters to the Rose Garden and read to them a handwritten statement he'd drafted in his study the night before.

He said that if the strikers did not return to work within fourty-eight hours they would be fired, every one of them, and not rehired. The fourty-eight hours was meant to give the workers a chance to have second thoughts, but Drew Lewis told me that in retrospect he felt it was a mistake—because it didn't allow enough time. "We should have given them until Friday"—two days later—"so they'd know what it was to go home without a paycheck."

But the fourty-eight hours seemed a good way to forestall drastic action and give everyone a chance to cool off. And Reagan made clear what was coming if they didn't return. He told reporters about the measures that had been taken to make sure the nonstriking controllers and supervisory personnel could keep the skies open and operating safely with reduced flights.

What he did not tell reporters, and what has not been generally known until now, is that a strike by American air traffic controllers carried real national security implications. PATCO in effect controlled the skies, and American AWACS bombers that might on a moment's notice be ordered to head for Moscow were also in those skies every day. "American flight controllers controlled the air space over America, and if they went on strike we had no control of the skies," Drew Lewis told me in the spring of 2001. "So the issue was not only that it was an illegal strike and a demand for a one hundred percent [wage] increase, it was also that a strike had real national security implications—the AWACS couldn't have gone up."

I asked Lewis if the leaders of PATCO understood this. "I knew they had to know it. Because of national security we didn't mention it [in talks before the strike was called] but they had to know it. We knew they were savvy and knew of the implications." In fact, the union's leaders might have calculated that the national security implications were another reason Reagan would give in.

During the two days between Reagan's announcement and what would have to be the workers' final decision, there was a lot of behind-the-scenes action. "Once they turned down the contract," Lewis said, "what we did is, between the Federal Aviation Administration and the Defense Department and some private controllers, we put together an organization that could keep commercial traffic and government planes [including the AWACS] in the air."

"This hasn't come out, but the Soviets and others in the world understood the implications of the strike," Lewis told me.

"The French, the free world, they all understood that we would not accept a strike," he continued. "The French gave us trouble. Great Britain was with us. This was an international event! We had a problem with Canada—the flight controllers there shut down Gander in sympathy for the American union." Drew Lewis told them that if they didn't open Gander in two hours the United States would never ever land there again. "They had to open the airport. . . . They folded. The French did the same thing. So this was a worldwide shutdown because in terms of air traffic we run the world!"

There were some impressive moments. The administration could have arrested the union leadership but decided not to. And the Democrats in Congress could have opposed the president and used the labor struggle for partisan advantage, but didn't. In part this was due to the help of Senator Edward Kennedy and AFL-CIO President Lane Kirkland.

Lewis had called Kennedy, explained the administration's position, reviewed the facts of the case and asked for help. "I knew we'd look antiunion," Lewis said. "Kennedy listened and told me to call Lane Kirkland and see what he had to say. Lane Kirkland told me, 'I think the head of the union is off base, you're going to have a strike and there's nothing you can do about it, I have to support them but do what you're doing.' [Kirkland] called other union leaders—a lot of them thought [the United States] couldn't afford a strike. We called union professors at Harvard, economic guys. I called Ted Kennedy again—and he'd called the same people! Ted said, 'I heard the same thing, I'll help get you Democratic support'—meaning they groused but they didn't come out strong against us. They felt a hundred percent increase was too much, and eleven percent was reasonable."

That was a meaningful bipartisan moment, Kennedy's support and Kirkland's.

But there was some selfishness and stupidity too. Some of Ronald Reagan's friends and supporters were wealthy men, and many of them owned their own jets. One of them became so enraged that the strike was inconveniencing him that he called the secretary of transportation and told him he was going to get him fired.

Drew Lewis immediately called the Oval Office. "I said, 'Mr. President, you're going out to California soon and Justin Dart and all those guys have private planes and they're all raising Cain with me.' I said, 'I hope you don't cut my legs out from under me.'

"He said, 'I've never cut the legs out from anybody in my life. You let me worry about my friends, you worry about the strike.' "

"He was good as his word. I had a lot of flexibility because I knew the president would support me. And he was easy to work for because you knew where he was philosophically. The point I'm trying to make is if you had a rapport with Ronald Reagan and he trusted you, you got enough control and he'd count on you to do the job. The Great Communicator was a Great Delegator." (Years later the extent to which he delegated would cause him great trouble.)

When the two-day strike deadline passed, 30 percent of the PATCO members showed up for work; 70 percent stayed out.

And every one of them lost his job.

"We fired 11,400 traffic controllers," Drew Lewis told me. "That's a lot of families that were affected. And the union had supported us, and it was a good union. It was very sad. We were both upset about the firing. He was almost in tears that he was going to hurt these families."

It was a crucial moment.

First, it worked. The administration promised it would keep the skies open and in time full flight schedules would resume, and that's what happened. The controllers who returned plus the number who could be pulled from the ranks—all bureaucracies have built-in fat and featherbedding—plus the new controllers who were hired yielded a safe and fully functioning new air control system even more quickly than the administration had hoped. In fact, they had a few thousand more controllers than they needed.

Second, the PATCO decision set the pattern for wage negotiations for the next eight years throughout all levels of government, which turned out to have a real and positive impact on the controlling of inflation. The U.S. Post Office, whose half million members had been set to go on strike the following Saturday, was not struck. And the nation's mayors found that Reagan's action set a climate for municipal negotiations as well.

Third, foreign governments saw that the new president meant what he said and that he would take a hit in public opinion to make his point.

But fourth, and ultimately most important, the Soviet Union was watching. They saw how the American president dealt with a national security issue, saw that his rhetorical toughness could be matched by tough action. They absorbed this, and thought about it.

That's why George Shultz, Reagan's last and most effective secretary of state, said that the PATCO decision was the most important foreign policy decision Ronald Reagan ever made.

The tragedy was that a lot of good men and women lost their jobs. They had tough jobs and deserved a raise. But they misread Reagan.

Drew Lewis again: "They were a very decent bunch of guys, the flight controllers. Even Bob Poli [the union president] I told him, 'This is a mistake for the country, the union and you.' And he said 'Drew, if I gotta make a mistake I want to make it defending my union.' "

I tried to reach Bob Poli, but was unable to. He lost his job as head of the union after the strike, and PATCO itself collapsed a year later, bankrupt and dispirited. But—the law of unintended consequences—I've always thought Poli should be thanked for his role in the great PATCO drama of 1981, because if he hadn't made the wrong calculation about who Ronald Reagan was, the Soviets might not have made the right one.

"Expect the unexpected," the old *New York Times* columnist Harrison Salisbury said when asked what he'd learned from watching history up close. Another way to say it, as a friend did to me once, is: Life isn't static, it's dynamic. A painting of a room is static, nothing in the painting moves. But in a real room curtains blow, people walk in, people leave, a bedroom is turned into a den, the house is torn down and rebuilt or there's an earthquake . . . you just never know.

And that's how it was with the PATCO strike. Everyone knew it was important, but no one knew how important. And everyone knew it was a domestic crisis, but no one knew it was a foreign affairs triumph.

Comedy

"Comedy keeps the heart sweet," said Mark Twain in a philosophical mood. And it often comes from sweet hearts too.

Reagan liked anything that was funny that happened in life and would turn it into a story. He didn't care if it was off-color or innocent as long as it was amusing or witty or spoke to life as it is lived by human beings. He liked accents, brogues and patois and could do them all, had no political correctness and didn't mind if a joke was about sex, religion or war. He was one of those men who had an encyclopedic memory for jokes, but he was also possessed of a burbling brook of natural good humor and comic cleverness. If life wasn't funny enough on any given day, he'd goose it along until it was.

Years ago, thinking about his humor, I said it seemed to me that wit penetrates and humor envelopes, that wit seems a function of verbal intelligence while humor is imagination operating on good nature. I still think that, and think Reagan was a man of abundant humor with a great appreciation for comedy.

His humor was particularly male and of his generation, not only in its lack of political correctness and the volume of memorized jokes but also in a kind of pratfall quality, a physical gaiety. He made a speech once before the White House photographers' association and in the middle of a quiet, thoughtful passage on their impressive ability to get the picture even when surprising and shocking things are happening, he quickly, smoothly brought his thumbs to his ears, twirled his fingers, rolled his eyes and continued talking. It brought down the house. A photographer got the picture and the next day it was in all the papers. When your detractors' main criticism of you is that you're a bit of an idiot it doesn't really help to give them idiot pictures, but Reagan didn't mind.

On long rides home from summits in Europe or Asia on Air Force One, he'd walk along the aisles in the staff area, and when he saw a George Shultz or Paul Nitze sound asleep with his head back and his mouth hanging open he'd quietly lean down and pantomime, "George, please, America has been invaded!" He'd shake his head as George, still sleeping, would snore away.

I think he thought everyone was too serious. I think he realized today's dreadfully somber problem is next week's joke about the hell we went through last week, and he figured he'd just speed up the process. I think he was also fun all the time because the constant tragedies and injustices of life while painful were also by definition passing—everything changes, today is setback, tomorrow bounty. I used to wonder if he thought man doesn't deserve injustice but then man doesn't deserve flowers either, so what the heck, it all balances out.

I think there was something else, something he related to in others, something he referred to once in a speech when talking about John F. Kennedy. Reagan said there was a sense in JFK that life was a fast-moving train and you want to grab on and hold on and enjoy the feel of the wind in your hair—"Enjoy the ride, it's ungrateful not to." When I worked on that speech I was thinking not only of the subject of the speech but also of its giver.

One of his ways of dealing with criticism was not to get mad but to undermine his critics by agreeing with them. When they said he was lazy he didn't deny it, he said, "I know hard work never killed anyone, but I figure why take a chance?" When word spread early in the administration that a foreign affairs crisis had begun in the middle of the night and Ed Meese chose not to wake the president, there was a scandal. Reagan's response: "I've laid down the law to my staff, to everyone from now on about anything that happens: No matter what time it is, wake me—even if it's in the middle of a cabinet meeting." When it was said that he was stupid and controlled by his staff he'd have exchanges like this: During the PATCO strike Drew Lewis called him a few times a day to keep him up on events as they unfolded.

Sometimes Lewis needed the president to make statements that signaled certain things to union management or to America's allies. Reagan would say pleasantly, "Well, Drew, tell me what to say, and then tell me how to say it. And by the way, when you're done tell me what I said." Lewis would laugh and say, "I need you to tell the Democrats in Congress . . ."

When a crisis occurred and reporters asked the president's staff how hard he was working, Reagan would tell them to pass it on that he was really burning the midday oil. During the 1988 presidential campaign he heard one of the candidates say that "what we need is a president for the nineties" and Reagan told his friends he got all excited until he realized the guy hadn't said "We need a president *in* his nineties."

Some of Reagan's humor was just off-hand silliness. Robert Higdon remembers briefing the first lady on an upcoming political event in the late 1980s. Robert, though then a young man in his twenties, had known the Reagans for years, and they were particularly relaxed around him. So Robert happened to be in the presidential bedroom that afternoon, briefing the first lady as she lay in bed after a nap. Robert was seated on the edge of the bed, going over the schedule, and they were both laughing about something when the president walked in from the bathroom, where he'd been showering. He looked over, saw them together, stood there with a towel around his middle, dripping on the floor, and said, "That's just like you, Nancy. As soon as I turn my back you're in bed with another man." Then he spun around and walked huffily back into the bathroom as Nancy and Robert laughed some more.

Reagan had natural dignity so he didn't have to have false dignity. People gave him funny gifts and if they amused him they became his props. Someone gave him a Bozo the Clown wig, bald on top with wild red hair shooting out from the sides. He put it on in the Oval Office and somberly walked into a cabinet meeting. Everyone looked up and the laughter was explosive, and Reagan cracked up and did a little routine. He didn't mean for the White House photographer to catch it but he did. They destroyed the negatives, except for one, which is hidden in the Virginia home of a former aide who keeps it because it still makes him laugh.

He liked playfulness in others. Dave Fischer, in the early days of Reagan's presidency, usually rode in the limousine in front of the president's—the decoy limousine—when they were in a motorcade. One day someone gave Fischer one of those big Reagan masks, the kind they make of presidents at Halloween. Dave put it in his briefcase, and sometimes he'd wear it in the motorcade. He'd sit by the window and they'd go by a big crowd and he'd put it on. People would applaud and wave and then stop, get a good look and start to laugh. One day Reagan called Fischer into his compartment on Air Force One and said to Dave, "I think we ought to reconsider the configuration of the motorcade. A lot of people seem to think the car in front of mine has me in it and they get all excited. And the oddest thing is when it goes by I see them all starting to laugh."

Fisher reddened and told him what he was doing. Reagan laughed, waved his hand and told him to carry on.

Once, in 1981, the president and Mrs. Reagan gave a formal state dinner for the president of Venezuela, Luis Herrera Campins. They had asked Frank Sinatra to take charge of the entertainment. Sinatra, of course, was a veteran of such things—he'd put together JFK's inaugural gala and had helped the Reagans before. But this time Sinatra thought he'd do something different, jazz things up a little.

He asked Robert Goulet to be the evening's main entertainment. Goulet, the former Broadway star who played Vegas and other venues, was honored to be asked but had never sung at the White House and wasn't quite sure what kind of material he should do. He asked Sinatra what would be appropriate.

Sinatra told him these people at these formal parties have had enough with strings and cellists, let's swing, do your act. So Goulet did his act, singing a certain kind of sexy love song of the get-down variety and swinging his mike toward the Venezuelan president's wife and crooning to her. It was . . . a little cheesy, a little vulgar for a state dinner at the White House, but everyone was good-humored about it and applauded. Then, in his between-songs patter, Goulet told of touring recently in Lake Tahoe. The audience there was a bunch of stiffs, he said, but there was one gorgeous girl, a stunner standing in the back. Tall, statuesque, a real fox. So he pitched all his songs to her, and flirted. And it was only later, he now told the dinner guests, that he found out that the beautiful woman was the biggest transvestite in Tahoe. Then he joked that it all worked out, "He writes me every week!"

There was mildly embarrassed silence. Goulet then sang another song and left the stage, and Sinatra finished up. Soon President Reagan rose to thank everyone for coming. He thanked Sinatra for all his efforts arranging such a show, and then he said, "And thank you, Bob Goulet, not only for entertaining us with your wonderful voice but for remembering our night in Lake Tahoe."

The whole audience let out a gust of pent-up laughter and sidelong glances. It allowed everyone to acknowledge what had been said, and laugh at it, and the dinner went on and was a success.

There were stories he'd tell on himself. There is one he liked to tell of the big state dinner with Monsieur Mitterrand and his formidable wife. The French of course can be exasperating, but everything was fine and everyone looked beautiful, the gentlemen in white tie and tails and the ladies in long gowns. The Reagans and Mitterrands met at the stairs for the official photo. They were then to move into dinner. President Reagan gestured to Madame Mitterrand to walk forward with him, but she stood back. He gestured again—she stood stock still. He took her arm, tried to guide her, she would not move. Finally, he called over an interpreter. "Could you tell Madame we are supposed to walk together now to the dining room?" The interpreter speaks to her, and she speaks to him. The interpreter nods, turns to the president, clears his throat. "She wants you to know that you are standing on her dress." Reagan looked down, saw his foot on her hem, moved back as they laughed and walked on.

It is the early nineties and Reagan is talking with friends at breakfast on vacation, and the conversation turns to Ireland's bitter history, to the long war of the Orange and the Green. Naturally, this reminds him of a story.

A young priest came over from Ireland to New York. "His first day in New York he started out across Broadway against the light, and one of the those big New York cops, who was probably pretty much Irish himself, grabbed him and said 'What do you think you're doing?'

"And the priest said, 'I'm simply trying to get to the other side of the street.'

"Well, when he heard the brogue, the policeman then took him back to the curb and said, 'Now, you wait here.' He said, 'That red light up there—you can't cross when that's on. But when it turns green, that's for you to go.'

"The young Irish priest repeated, 'When the light is green it's for me.' And he's watching and waiting and the light turned orange for the several seconds that it does, and then turned green. And the priest started walking and got ten or fifteen feet out into the street, and he turned around to the policeman and said, 'They don't give those damn Protestants much time, do they!' "

Reagan sometimes used humor as a matter of courtesy. He knew people enjoyed laughing and he liked to give them little gifts—that's what his jokes were sometimes. Sometimes he used humor to make people who were nervous in his presence feel more confident. Sometimes he used it because he knew a gust of laughter gave people a chance to get their nervousness out. Sometimes he used it to get his own nervousness out, which is why he liked to begin his speeches with jokes.

Bill Bennett likes to tell the story of his own early days as secretary of education. Bennett was controversial. He'd been hired in part to get the agency into shape and in part because he shared Reagan's views. But when he articulated Reagan's views bluntly, he got into trouble.

"I was not a close Reagan friend or confidant. I didn't know him. I wasn't from California. . . . But when I got to the Department of Education I took seriously what the president said and what I said back. I said, 'I'll try to make sense in the department.'

"The first three weeks I was making all sorts of comments. And *The Washington Post* ran headlines that BENNETT FAVORS PARENTS OVER EDUCATION ESTABLISHMENT, BENNETT ATTACKS TEACHERS' UNIONS, BENNETT CALLS FOR MORE HOMEWORK.' You know, terribly controversial positions. . . .

"I was in a lot of trouble for attacking the teachers' unions for saying one thing I said which—I led the *CBS Evening News* my first day in office. We said we were going to cut some of the college scholarships because of the budget. I said, 'You know, we're not going to cut the grants for the poor kids but for the wealthier kids. They're going to have to give up grants and go on loans and some of them will have to give up loans.'

"But, you know, a lot of kids on college aid, they're down at the beach. They may have to practice stereo divestiture or two weeks at the beach divestiture—and the media went crazy. They went absolutely crazy. 'Insensitive, horrible person.'

"The kids didn't go crazy. I got tons of postcards from the beach. You know, from Fort Lauderdale, 'Hey, Bill, having a great time. Send a check, we're out of beer, we need another government check.' That sort of thing.

"Anyway, I was in very serious trouble. My wife, Elaine, and I flew out for a meeting on policy and on the way back we got the papers at Dallas Airport. And we got *The New York Times* and *The Washington Post* and two other papers. And there was an editorial in each one of them calling for Ronald Reagan to ask for my resignation, saying that I was outrageous, a bully. On and on.

"And I went home. There was a cabinet meeting the next week and I came in the cabinet room and there was a folder—three folders. One of the folders said, BENNETT. And I was sitting by myself and I thought some of my colleagues were inching their chairs a little away from me.

"And we finally got to the last item: Bennett. And the president—I was pretty isolated at this point and the president started to read aloud just the headlines. 'BENNETT, A DUNCE IN THE CLASSROOM,' 'BENNETT, THE JAMES WATT OF THE SECOND TERM,' 'BENNETT MUST BE FIRED.'

"And I was sinking farther and farther in my seat as the president read aloud. And my colleagues were drawing farther away. Reagan put the last clipping in and folded it up and he said, 'Now, that's Bill Bennett's first three weeks in office. What's wrong with the rest of you?'

"It was a great moment—it was an exhale moment too. . . . But it was also one of the kindest and most considerate things anybody ever did for me. . . . It was a moment I'll never forget, and it taught me what a leader can do, and what it can mean to the morale of people to have done that."

When the meeting was over, Bennett went to the president and said, "Boss, thank you. Thank you very, very much."

And Reagan told him, "You know, they like to criticize me for being in show business. But one thing you learn in show business, there's a difference between the critics and the box office. Don't worry about the critics, just keep doing your job."

Bennett later summed up Reagan this way: "He was a man in possession of his own soul."

There's another story Bennett tells, and it gets back to the slapstick Reagan—the one who, when his dog would growl and get barky, would pleasantly pet him and croon "Man's best friend" and then put his hands around the dog's throat and make believe for the Secret Service that he was strangling him.

The Department of Education had asked the president to tour some good public schools and meet the children. The president and Bill Bennett wound up taking a number of trips together.

Bennett: "One trip was to Columbia, Missouri, which had received three School of Excellence awards. We were driving in the presidential limousine, and Ronald Reagan was on that little thing, that microphone with the loud speaker on the side of the car. And he was saying hello to the crowds. And he said to the Secret Service, 'You know, I don't think this thing is working.' He said, 'I don't think people can hear me. Let's drive off to the side here, somewhere there aren't a lot of people, and try to see if we can hear it.'

"So they did what he told them. He said, 'Let me roll down the window, I want to stick my head out the window and see if I can hear myself.'

"They said, 'No sir, no, Mr. President, you can't do that."

"So he said, 'How about Bill? Can he do it?'

"Secret Service didn't care about me. Most people thought I was security anyway. Every job I've had I've been mistaken for my security. People come up to me and say, 'Where's the secretary?' I say, 'Over there, the guy with the silver hair.'

"Anyway, so Ronald Reagan had me out in the field there in Columbia, Missouri. I'm about a hundred yards from the car. He's saying, 'Hello? Hello? Bill, can you hear me? Go farther back.'

"Then, of course, he took off in the car."

There were, of course, the Russian jokes. They were, of course, not Russian jokes but Soviet jokes and he told them all over the country, and told them also to Mikhail Gorbachev, who was not always amused.

The Soviet jokes were ones that he'd been collecting most of his adult life. They were real jokes from within the Soviet Union—jokes the Russian people told themselves and that Reagan thought were a kind of barometer of how the average Russian felt about Soviet control. He also collected stories and jokes from the Warsaw Pact countries, the humor that was circulating behind the Iron Curtain.

"There's a story I told to General Secretary Gorbachev, and he laughed. An American and a Russian were arguing about their two countries, and the American said, 'Look, in my country I can walk into the Oval Office, I can pound the president's desk and say Mr. President, I don't like the way you're running our country!' and the Russian said, 'I can do that too.' The American is surprised. He said, 'You can?' The Russian said, 'Yes, I can march into the general secretary's office, I can pound on his desk and say, 'Mr. General Secretary, I don't like the way President Reagan's running his country!' "

"In the Soviet Union, if you want to buy an automobile there is a ten-year wait. And you go through quite a process when you're ready to buy, and you put up the money in advance. So there was a young fellow who'd finally made it, and he went through all the agencies you have to go to and signed all of the papers you have to go sign, and finally at the last agency where they put the final stamp on it, the man there said, 'Okay, we have everything, now come back in ten years.' And the young fellow said, 'Morning or afternoon?' And the man says, 'It's ten years from now—what difference does it make?' And the young fellow says, 'Well, the plumber's coming in the morning.' "

Everyone knows he liked jokes about his age. He liked to quote the old baseball player who once asked, "How old would you be if you didn't know how old you was?" For him it was thirty-nine, and every birthday after that was an anniversary of his thirty-ninth birthday. But he also liked to refer to his age.

At his first State of the Union address he quoted George Washington on the need for all presidents to report directly to the American people, and then he turned to the press and said it wasn't true, by the way, that he'd literally heard Washington say those words. He liked to say that when he played reporters in the movies, it was so long ago that he'd burst through the newsroom door and say, "Stop the chisels!" He said when he went to the doctor's for a checkup they didn't ask his age anymore, "they just carbon date me." He said he hoped he'd never need a transplant because "I've got parts they don't make anymore."

He liked to tell schoolchildren, "History's no easy subject. Even in my day it wasn't, and we had so much less of it to learn then." He'd get a sentimental look and say, "I can still remember my first Republican convention. . . . Abraham Lincoln giving a speech that sent shivers down my spine. . . ." Then he'd say it wasn't true he'd been there, back then he was a Democrat.

There's a Reagan story I used to tell when I spoke about him, and though I don't have a good memory for jokes I remember this one because it captured not only Reagan's sense of what it is to grow old but his merriness about it.

"There was an elderly couple who were getting ready for bed one night, and she said, 'Oh I am just so hungry for ice cream, and there isn't any in the house.'

"And he said, 'I'll get some.'

"And she said, 'You're a dear.' She said, 'Vanilla with chocolate sauce.' She said, 'Write it down, you'll forget it.'

"He said, 'I won't forget.'

"She said, 'With some whipped cream on top.'

"He said, 'Vanilla with chocolate sauce and whipped cream on top.'

"And she said, 'And a cherry.'

"He said, 'And a cherry on top.'

"'Well,' she said, 'please write it down, I know you'll forget.'

"He said, 'I won't forget. Vanilla with chocolate sauce, whipped cream and a cherry on top.'

"And he went out. By the time he got back she was already in bed, and he handed her the paper bag. She opened it and there was a ham sandwich. And she said, 'I told you to write it down—you forgot the mustard!'

He liked stories that illustrated human nature. He liked the one about the prosperous businessman who, every day, would pass an old woman selling pretzels on the street. And every day he'd rush by and put a quarter in her cup and never take a pretzel. He did this for years and finally one day he puts down his quarter and she takes him by the arm and looks at him. And he looked at her and said, "Ah, you probably want to know why every day I leave twenty-five cents down and never take a pretzel." And she said, "No, I just want to tell you that pretzels are thirty-five cents now."

He had partisan standbys for Republican crowds.

"I remember once there was a fellow who was running for office, and he was in a rural area that wasn't known to be Republican. And he stopped by a farm to do some campaigning. And when the farmer heard he was a Republican his jaw dropped and he said, 'Wait right here while I go get Ma, she's never seen a Republican before.' So he got her, brought her round. And the candidate looked around for a podium from which to give his speech, and the only thing he could find was a pile of that stuff that Bess Truman spent thirty-five years trying to get Harry to call fertilizer. So he got up on that mound, and they gathered in front and he gave his speech. And at the end of it the farmer said, 'That's the first time I ever heard a Republican speech!' And the candidate said, 'That's the first time I've ever given a Republican speech on a Democratic platform.' "

He liked to tell a joke about the Democratic politician making a big speech to a crowd, and he was heckled by a farmer. Politician said, "What is your party, sir?" The farmer said proudly, "I'm a Republican and my father was a Republican and my mother was a Republican." Politician knew he could get the best of him now and said, "Isn't it sad you can't think for yourself? What would you be if your father was a jackass and your mother was a jackass?" And the farmer shot back, "A Democrat!"

And he liked to tell audiences that he came from a Democratic family, they were all Democrats, and he'll never forget the time his uncle got a formal letter from the local Democratic Party thanking him for voting in every one of the past fifteen elections. "And he'd been dead fourteen years."

I'll end with a note of something I read about last summer that I still can't get out of my mind. It was a story that ran on the wires about a trucker who was hauling along a major freeway in Florida and suddenly a bird started flying along with him, right outside the window. He was going fast but the bird stayed with him, always right outside the window, and if he slowed down the bird slowed down. The bird stayed with him almost a hundred miles, the trucker later said. It seemed fanciful—how did that bird do that, and why, and what did it mean?—but I guess there were witnesses, because they made the wires and then news Web sites on the Internet.

But when I read the story it made me think of one Reagan told.

"A Realtor was out on a back road driving along, looking at some property. And all of a sudden beside him there's a chicken keeping pace with him. He was doing sixty miles an hour, and suddenly the chicken spurts on ahead of him. And it looked to him as if the chicken had three legs. And then the chicken turned and went down a side road near a barnyard and the driver turns and goes onto the barn road and he sees a farmer there and he asks him, he says, 'Did you see a chicken go by here?' Farmer says yeah. He says, 'Did he have three legs?' Farmer says yeah, 'I raise 'em that way, I breed 'em.' Guy says, 'You do? How come?' Farmer says, 'Well, I just love the drumstick and ma loves the drumstick and our son likes the drumstick too. We just got tired of fighting over it, so I started breeding three-legged chickens.' The guy says, 'Well—how do they taste?' Farmer says, 'I don't know, I haven't been able to catch any of them yet.' "

Rosty, Rush, Reagan

Not long after he was shot, President Reagan asked Democratic House Speaker Tip O'Neill if he could address a joint session of Congress. O'Neill graciously agreed. Reagan walked in a hero and gave a charming and pointed address about his proposed tax and spending cuts. At one point forty Democrats stood up to cheer, and Reagan felt a shiver go down his spine. He later joked it was almost worth getting shot for.

But he thought those Democrats had guts, and he thought their guts meant his program had a chance. Reagan and his aides worked to put together a coalition, calling into the Oval Office Democratic congressmen who'd never been in the White House. He got his budget cuts through the House by a landslide, with sixty-three Democratic votes. He compromised on the tax cut, giving up a 30 percent cut over three years for a 25 percent over three years, but there was a sweetener: The Congress agreed to lower the top income rate from 70 percent to 50 percent.

Probably the most important Democrat in those days, apart from Tip O'Neill, was Dan Rostenkowski of Illinois, the chairman of the House Ways and Means Committee, mention of which is always preceded by the words "the all-powerful."

Rostenkowski, a Chicago boy who'd served for two years with the infantry in Korea, was first elected to Congress in 1958 and had become head of Ways and Means in 1981, when Reagan became president.

I spoke to Rostenkowski in March of 2001. He had left the House in 1994 and does consulting and commentary now, and when he returned my call from his office outside Chicago he was slightly out of breath. He'd just returned from a long walk. "Doing my senior citizen exercises," he laughed. I always saw Rostenkowski as a tough and good-natured barrel of a man. He was known for his willingness to compromise and work with the other side, and in his Capitol Hill office he kept an eleven-foot pole, for the things he wouldn't touch with a ten-foot one. I suspected that twenty years after fighting Reagan in the Congress every day he'd be mellow and affectionate about him. But the mention of his old foe's name got Rostenkowski's partisan juices going, and he made me laugh as he came out swinging.

I asked him what it was like to go up against Reagan over the tax bill. He said it was tough. "He was so popular he could do anything he wanted to do. And he had the Boll Weevils [Southern Democrats who had begun to support Reagan]. The success of Ronald Reagan's administration, and I don't mean this uncomplimentary, but Ronald Reagan had tunnel vision about what he was going to do as president. He was going to build up defense and he was going to cut taxes. . . .

"But his popularity was overwhelming. In '81, I was credited with getting into a bidding war with the administration. I knew where we were going, and I tried to draw a line in the sand. Reagan wanted to empty the Treasury—emptying the Treasury was cutting taxes! The president would give the Dixiecrats more and more and more to be with him . . . and we came up with an alternative to his bill and he knocked our socks off because everyone wanted to get on the Reagan bandwagon.

"I don't say this uncomplimentary, but he was not a sophisticated member of the eastern seaboard intellectual fraternity. He was a sensible person that spoke to the ordinary man. They understood him. And he gave everyone the impression that he was the kind of guy that you could go into a coffee shop and sit next to him and talk to him. . . .

"He was very bold—the Evil Empire. And I'm not going to say that I agree with you and your contemporaries that he was one of the greatest presidents—but he was a good president. He brought the country back to terra firma."

Rostenkowski chuckled and told me that when Reagan tried to cut back funding on federal programs, he thought "there would be revolt in the streets!" He said that maybe Reagan was right on some of those cuts—"because there was no rioting."

I asked Rostenkowski how he viewed Reagan in comparison to other presidents he'd known and worked with. He said that he'd been in Congress for every president since Dwight Eisenhower. "You serve with Eisenhower, you're just a number. You serve with Jack Kennedy, you know him, you're important. With Reagan my importance was, I was working the politics of the House of Representatives. I was exposed to Nixon and I knew Jerry Ford very well. My relationships varied. With Ronald Reagan, I was chairman of the Ways and Means Committee, so I was on a first name basis with Ronald Reagan. I called him 'Mr. President'—he was old enough to be my father, for Christ's sake! His admirable quality was if he gave you his word you could sleep very well that night.

"The people who worked for him were in a protective state all the time. Nancy was protective too, and those around the president who didn't extremely show loyalty and protection, she'd go after them. But the fact of the matter is the president—I don't want this to read as if I don't respect Ronald Reagan, but the fact of the matter is I would sit down with Reagan and when I saw something complicated was true I'd try to explain it to him, and he'd say, 'If what you're saying is true, I'll support you.'

"And I'll never forget in the '86 tax reform act, when we were negotiating I said, 'Mr. President, I want you to understand something. If you're serious about this bill I'm gonna do things with this bill in the process of getting this together that you won't like—and that I won't like. But I'll use those things as bargaining tools with the members of the House and the conference with the Senate. I know the press will drive you crazy about things in the bill and ask you, and if you say 'If that's in the bill I'll kill the bill,' that kills any progress I can make. I'd like for you to say 'I gave my word to Dan Rostenkowski that I won't make any reservations about this bill until it's completed.' And then I can fashion a bill.

"And Ronald Reagan said, 'If you don't want me to say anything about the bill until it's over with, then I won't say anything.' He called Don Regan in. He said, 'Don, I want you to know I have an understanding with Danny that I won't talk about the bill until it's completed.'

"And Regan starts to say something and Reagan said, 'I want it.' And I said to Don Regan, 'I'm dealing with the president,' and the president said, 'That's right, you're dealing with me.'

"He never said one word about that bill until I passed it in the

House. What I cherished and admired was that when we shook hands he never left his commitment. No question about it, we operated with trust.

"We passed the bill, and Reagan called me and said, 'That piece of garbage!' "

Rostenkowski laughed. "I said to him, 'The bill is passed, now it's on Bob Dole's desk [in the Senate.]"

Rostenkowski meant: Now, Mr. President, you must go work it out with your Republicans, many of whom, in his view, were only giving lip service to reforming the tax code. (I think he was right.)

I laughed when Rostenkowski told this story because we both knew what is all too rarely said when tax reform is the subject. It is that members of Congress, and especially the Senate, do not want to reform and simplify the American tax system because they do not believe it is in their political interests to do so. As long as they can keep the system complicated, inscrutable and thousands of pages long, they can hold their ability to add or delete a specific tax break or tax hike over the heads of potential contributors in business, in PACs, in all sorts of organizations. Why do the makers of luxury boats give money to Congress? Because Congress has the power to levy a new tax on the buyers of luxury boats—that is, the customers of the boat makers. If the system was clean and easily understandable, Congress would lose all power to squeeze campaign money from contributors. (It is because of this that reforms such as the flat tax, which would reduce the entire tax code to a one-page system by which all citizens pay a straight 10 percent or 12 percent or 14 percent of their income in taxes, never receive much support in the Congress.)

Rostenkowski remembered the private Reagan for me. "I used to go up to the family quarters with [Congressman and Republican Whip Dick] Cheney and [Wyoming Republican Senator] Al Simpson, we used to tell stories. Reagan was the greatest storyteller.

"Reagan wasn't a technician. Jim Baker did the arm twisting, and he did a goddamn good job too."

And now, I said, it is twenty years later. A whole generation has passed since your great battles. When you look back at those days, and at the Reagan tax and budget cuts, were they ultimately a good thing? I wasn't sure what Rostenkowski would say, but he answered right away.

"Oh yeah. I got a lot of things from that tax bill—it took eight million people off the tax roles; it simplified the code from eleven brackets to three."

He said Republican members of Congress are often too narrow, too radical, "like Gingrich." But Republican presidents, he said, "represent all the people, and are pretty good.

"Ronald Reagan was almost paradoxical," he continued. "He wanted little government—but he's got almost every monument in the world named after him!"

"But we're gifted in this country. And I'll tell you how I think we're gifted. After the war, Truman took charge and did some miraculous things. Eisenhower came in and settled the country down, built highways. He's a general, he's thinking about roads. Jack Kennedy came in, he brought lofty ideals, he was big on commitment to education but didn't accomplish too much. But he gave us Camelot. After Jack Kennedy, Lyndon Johnson built the country—changed the social structure, gave people big breaks. I'm a little irritated sometimes with the blacks"—African Americans who in Rostenkowski's view don't seem to give Johnson sufficient credit for his efforts. "Nixon opened up China, a great president, he got carried away with Haldeman and Ehrlichman but he had great domestic programs, and if we'd adopted some of his social programs we'd be better off now. Jerry Ford, perfect guy at the perfect time. Regular ordinary person. He got the knock really of pardoning Dick Nixon but he came at a good time for us as president.

"Jimmy Carter—you know, although I served with him he never impressed me as president. But then he didn't know how to be president. He should have been a naval navigator and stayed there.

"Ronald Reagan brought dignity. He wore a lot of makeup but he lifted the American people and helped them understand the government was too big."

Bill Clinton, he said, was "fabulous." Except for "the thing with the girls." (Rostenkowski had reason for warm feelings about Clinton. A little more than a month before we spoke, Clinton had given him a presidential pardon. Rostenkowski had been indicted in 1994 on corruption charges, had pled guilty to mail fraud in 1996 and had served fifteen months in prison. Many of Clinton's final pardons were controversial, but Rostenkowski's did not engender big headlines or great opposition; I think people had a sense that he had paid his dues, and had served his country.)

I found Rostenkowski garrulous and funny, quite a charming guy with an edge. For him, Reagan was a fine guy too, had his good points and bad, was essentially a good president but was, always, an actor.

And Reagan *was* an actor. All of our great modern presidents have been actors—FDR with his plummy tones and the cigarette holder tilted jauntily upward, JFK with his lovely diffident humor and love of lofty rhetoric. In the modern media age, presidents have to act the part of president even as they are doing the job of president. It's not terrible. But the key, always, is to be an "actor" without being a "phony"—without being insincere, inauthentic, not your true self.

Reagan did this; so did JFK. Nixon never learned; he couldn't act, his oddness always came through. Nor did Carter, whose smallness seemed to come through. Johnson was too big and too vivid and didn't always seem truthful; the first Bush was awkward, didn't really know how to dance and made the mistake of thinking he didn't have to. Clinton could dance, and though he was a compelling figure and riveting, he was, by the end, seen even by his friends as more a gifted phony than a gifted actor.

Another thing presidents need, and this may sound odd, is imagination. You'd think this more a need of a Hollywood director than a political figure but leaders have to understand the flow of history and have imagination about it. . . .

Ronald Reagan recognized reality not as a thing to bow to but a thing that could be changed and shaped. You could make a new reality.

People say they know this, of course reality can be changed. And in a way most of us get up each morning and enter the day eager to move things forward, but in a way a lot of people are limited by their own lack of a sense of possibility and how history, from your own to that of your country, is mutable, changeable, can be bent and reshaped and refashioned.

It is considered realistic to think you have to work *around* reality. And there are very modern men and women who think the real thing is to change the *perception* of reality, for changing the perception changes the reality itself. (This is what spin is. It is why presidents in trouble, such as Richard Nixon and Bill Clinton, always go traveling. They go on international jaunts to the Mideast and Africa literally to change the scenery and thus literally to change what reporters will write, literally to change the perception of the citizens of America of what a fix the president was in. "Richard Nixon isn't drowning in a scandal called Watergate, he's waving at crowds in Cairo delirious at the sight of him." "Bill Clinton's reputation isn't cratering in the Starr Report, he's in South Africa gazing soulfully out of an old prison window with a hero named Nelson Mandela.")

But Ronald Reagan wanted to change reality itself—by changing the reigning rules. If the top tax rate was in the 90 percent range when Jack Kennedy was president, and Kennedy got it down to the 70 percent range, and as a result the economy got boosted, he, Reagan, would get the top rates down even further. Because it was practical and because it was more just.

He thought he could change reality in part because he had imagination—a rather robust imagination. He thought history with its big sweep was romantic and full of momentum and energy and great men doing great things. It takes imagination to see history this way and not as a flat line endlessly spooling out. To see it as multilayered, dynamic, rich with potential action.

Once his eyes brightened up as he told me about the economic report that had been done in the 1920s. They got the best economists in America to look at the country's current and future economy, to try to give a sense of what the future might hold. They studied everything—farm production, the stock market, the impact of new modes of transportation, medical breakthroughs.

But they left out one thing: the rise of the electronic media, the rise of radio, of national radio networks, which of course transformed the marketplace. Were the economists stupid? No. They just lacked imagination for what other people could invent and produce. They lacked the ability to imagine what other people could imagine.

Reagan thought people were smart. He thought they were creative. He thought this in part because in Hollywood he had seen the greatest creativity every day, and not only from actors and directors but from cinematographers, editors, stuntmen, writers and the producers who made artistic advances possible.

Reagan thought the genius of America was that it was the place where genius was allowed. You could be your weirdly uniquely creative self and be celebrated for it and make a lot of money at it and go on to do creative things with your money or responsible things or silly things, waste it at the track—it's all up to you, that's what freedom is in part, the freedom to be silly and irresponsible.

And to be creative.

And to imagine.

And so he never saw history as static, as sitting there like a dry and dusty plain. He saw it as something you could change.

He took to making speeches about peace while he wore a bulletproof vest. He was aware of the irony. But U.S. law enforcement and intelligence officials kept getting death threats, and reliable information about terrorists' tracking Reagan's moves, including one from Libya.

He was wearing the heavy vest when he made a speech at the National Press Club, which he later called the most important speech on foreign policy he'd made so far. It was his announcement of a plan to begin reducing the number and power of arms held by the Soviet Union and the United States.

He wouldn't talk about arms control, but arms reduction. His idea was to start by having both sides eliminate all the intermediate-range nuclear weapons in Europe. He asked the Soviets to discuss the possibility of cutting back both sides' stockpiles of long-range nuclear weapons to equal levels. Equal levels that could be verified.

And he said it would be good to stop calling such initiatives SALT talks—for strategic arms limitation talks—and instead call them START—for strategic arms reduction talks.

He felt that America could make its call for progress only from a position of strength. He felt he had to approach the Soviets "with a dove of peace in one hand" and "a sword in the other."

He thought this partially because from 1945 through the 1970s we had maintained a lead over the Soviets in nuclear weapons. But by the late 1970s the Soviets had caught up with and surpassed the United States in a number of areas. The Soviets were building arms hand over fist, and their nuclear forces outnumbered ours.

If the Russians would dismantle their SS-20 missiles and two shorter range missiles they had targeted at Western Europe, Reagan told the Russians America would scrap plans to install the Pershing II and cruise missiles in Europe. That way there would be zero INF weapons in Europe.

It came to be called the Zero Option.

Al Haig fought it in cabinet meetings. Caspar Weinberger supported it. Reagan thought both sides had good arguments and went to think about it. Normally he'd go for a ride to think it through, but he found himself having to make his decision while flying across the country in a unique and brand-new Boeing 747—the Doomsday plane, a jumbo jet with no windows, crammed inside with communications equipment. It seemed to him like a flying submarine. During an airborne briefing he was told that wherever he was, the Doomsday plane was never far away. During a major crisis he was to go to it to keep the government functioning in case of nuclear attack.

That is where he decided what to do.

He decided on the Zero Option.

And in the end he got it.

But he got it after many years and many difficulties, and many insults at home and rebuffs abroad.

—

All presidents feel insulted. All presidents *are* insulted. Reagan was more insulted than most.

They called him stupid. They called him warlike. They called him unsophisticated, lazy, a mere actor, a cornball blowhard who believes in a mythic America that never existed. Clark Clifford, the Democratic Party mandarin and adviser to every Democratic president since Harry Truman, told a Georgetown gathering at Pamela Harriman's house that Reagan was "an affable dunce." The putdown became famous. Tip O'Neill called Reagan's mind "an absolute and utter disgrace." He said Reagan worked only three to three and a half hours a day, and "It's sinful that this man is president of the United States." Andre Faulds of the British Labor Party called him "that incoherent cretin." Congressmen said that when they tried to talk about complex defense issues he only wanted to talk about movies like *War Games.* In 1984, the *Chicago Tribune* called Reagan ignorant and said "his air-headed rhetoric on the issues of foreign policy and arms control have reached the limits of tolerance and have become an embarrassment to the US and a danger to world peace." The famously measured journalist David Broder said the job of Reagan's staff is to water "the desert between Ronald Reagan's ears." Henry Kissinger told a group of scholars in 1986 that when you meet Reagan you wonder "How did it ever occur to anyone that he should be governor, much less president?" The columnist Jimmy Breslin called him senile and said that when America applauds Reagan they prove "that senility is a communicable disease." Breslin also called him "shockingly dumb." Eleanor Clift of *Newsweek* said that "greed in this country is associated with Ronald Reagan." Sarah McClendon, the White House reporter for *USA Today,* said at the end of his presidency that "it will take a hundred years to get the government back into place after Reagan. He hurt people: the disabled, women, nursing mothers, the homeless." Lesley Stahl of CBS News said a few days before the end of Reagan's second term, "I predict historians are going to be totally baffled by how the American people fell in love with this man." Jimmy Carter's forces in the 1980 presidential race portrayed him as a mad bomber. The great Hollywood director and actor John Huston called Reagan "a bore" with "a low order of intelligence," who is "inflated" and "egotistical." Huston did call him cunning, but said it was "not animal cunning, human cunning. Animal cunning is too fine an expression for him." And the affectionate author of this book wrote, in a moment of exasperation in 1989, that when you worked for Ronald Reagan and got really tired you had moments in which you felt that the war for Ronald Reagan's mind throughout his administrations was like "the trench warfare of World War I—never had so many fought so hard for such barren terrain."

I was all wrong.

We were wrong.

But Reagan could drive you crazy. He really made no show whatsoever of listening to arguments that he'd already dismissed as wrong; he had no desire to engage in White House battles; he greeted our well-stated urgencies with a philosophical shrug; and he told the same stories over and over. The first time you heard it, at a meeting in 1984, you'd laugh with delight and take his point. The second time, in 1985, you'd smile and nod. The third time you'd find yourself daydreaming and have to catch yourself at the end. The fourth time, in, say, 1988—the fourth time was one time too many.

And Nancy Reagan heard every one of them a hundred times. And listened every time, and laughed. You know what you deserve for that kind of patience and encouragement? A Medal of Freedom.

Reagan would hear the criticisms, putdowns and insults and shrug, and sometimes laugh. Sometimes he'd grimace slightly and shake his head.

I always thought criticism hurt him now and then, but never made an impression on him. He wasn't up nights thrashing around being angry. It didn't get to his core the way it got to Nixon's and LBJ's. Criticism didn't inspire him to take action to deflect or mollify or defy. He became expert at the shrug and the laugh, so much so that when he met with the press in the Rose Garden, as he walked away, he looked like he was shaking his leg as if to shake off a herd of wild puppies who were trying to bite his pants cuffs.

The reason he took criticism so well is that he had been trained in receiving it in Hollywood. Not as an actor in the reviews, though there was some of that, but when he went up against Communists and Communist sympathizers and the anti-anti-Communists of Hollywood. They had threatened his life and livelihood. What was being called an evil idiot compared to that?

Plus he thought he was right. When you believe you are right and know your motives are high you don't have to worry too much about criticism.

In March 2001, I met with Rush Limbaugh, a man I admire, and asked him about his views on Reagan. He was sitting in his Manhattan apartment with a beautiful view of Central Park glittering in the nighttime distance. He was wearing a gray sweater and gray slacks and his graying hair was softly combed back. He sat at a table where we were eating takeout Chinese on plates white and gleaming as monuments.

He leaned back and looked out the window for a moment.

Limbaugh, like Ronald Reagan, has spent most of his professional life as a controversial figure. He is a man who can literally stop traffic walking down the street, whose presence inspires shouted greetings, cheers and catcalls, whose autograph is sold for money, who is highly paid for a popular talk show with a huge and loyal following, whose political views have weight, whose name has come to signify either something you really like or something you don't.

I had thought to speak to Limbaugh because I had recently been thinking about how Ronald Reagan stayed alive politically between his failed 1976 campaign for the GOP presidential nomination and his successful 1980 campaign for the presidency. Reagan, to stay live politically, did a daily two-minute radio commentary, a twice-a-week newspaper column and traveled throughout the country making speeches. There was no conservative media infrastructure to help him—no Rush Limbaugh show, no cadre of popular conservative local radio talk show hosts, no Internet, no Fox News. All of that came after Reagan. Reagan didn't have it to help him get his views out there. He had to be his own "network."

But it was the similarities between Reagan and Limbaugh—the fact that they both, in effect, came to lead a movement, the fact that they were and are the focus of heavy opposition—that led me to ask Rush what he thought of when he thought of Reagan. And the answer had to do with what Limbaugh learned from him.

He told me, "Reagan helped me coalesce so much of what I believe. So many people have done that, but he is at the top of the list of people who helped me to understand why I believed what I believed instinctively. And the whole concept of not punishing achievement, of rewarding it, came from Reagan.

"The notion of going about your controversial existence with good cheer came from Reagan. Smiling and laughing, not letting your enemies bother you at all, at least that anybody knows. I studied Reagan's response because he was hated, he was vilified.

"The Clinton people talk about how vicious the Clinton haters were but we've forgotten—Reagan was *despised*. They accused him of stealing cans of pork and beans from the homeless in Washington, and going home and opening the cans and eating it and feeling happy and good! And of course nothing like that was ever the truth, and yet he never responded to it—never.

"I studied it constantly. I wondered how, with all that being said about him, it never took. He won two landslides.

"And so I've been interested in everybody who was around him that was involved in the image creation, the Deavers and so forth. And what I finally figured out was there was no image creation. There was no image. There was just genuine Ronald Reagan, and that's what cut through all the noise.

"I remember one occasion in Washington. It was the ABC building in Washington across from the Mayflower, and it was being dedicated. And the head of ABC asked Reagan to come and dedicate it. And it's supposed to be a ceremonial event, but Sam Donaldson's there and starts asking questions of this type." He meant of a critical and aggressive type.

"And the ABC people are sort of cringing. And no one really apologized to Reagan but he didn't take offense at it, he just said, 'Oh, that's just Sam.' I mean—as though he didn't take it seriously, that he didn't really mean it. He forgave them! 'Oh they don't mean that,' 'Oh, it's just Sam.' He never took it personally."

I said that he never gave them the tribute of his resentment. Limbaugh agreed, thought that was part of Reagan's strength.

Later I remembered that I thought when I worked for Reagan that some immovably innocent part of him couldn't wholly believe and absorb antipathy.

I also always thought this: A lot of people have a way of projecting their own flaws, their own sins, onto others. They see in others the transgressions they themselves routinely commit. If you are envious by nature you are more likely to attribute the dislike of another person to their envy of you.

A lot of Reagan's critics, not all by any means but many, seemed to have a kind of talent for hatred, a well-honed ability to disparage. Reagan himself didn't have those things—he wasn't a hater and found it hard to see hatred and enmity in others.

And Reagan also knew that, as Orson Welles once put it, "it's the business of the American people to take the mickey out of the president." It's their job. It's our tradition. They did it to Washington, they did it to Lincoln, they'd do it to Truman and to Reagan. It keeps the president from being too confident, or rather from letting his confidence turn into arrogance. You don't want an arrogant president. It's not good for the country's health.

So if they misunderstand you, just keep trying to help them understand, make your speeches and statements clear as clean water. And if they continue to criticize, remember it's their job. "Oh, that's just Sam."

Strong Women

There's something I've always wanted to say about Reagan that I'm not sure ever fully got said about him. Reagan's entire political career, from 1964 through 1989, was concurrent with two great societal movements that had a great impact on our country and how our countrymen and -women see one another, deal with one another and live with one another. The first was the great civil rights movement of the modern era and the second was the great feminist movement that began in the 1960s. I have spoken of Reagan's feelings regarding race—he thought everyone equal pure and simple, equal in the eyes of God and equal therefore by necessity under man's laws. He did not believe in racial preferences, did not believe in quotas or what has come to be institutionalized as affirmative action and thought it necessary that no one be given special treatment on account of his race or religion. In this he felt he was consistent with the thinking not only of his parents and the good liberals of the 1940s and 1950s, but also of Martin Luther King, Jr., himself: We must be judged not by the color of our skin but the content of our character.

As for women, I think there is some misunderstanding about Reagan's views. He was seen by the National Organization for Women and by *Ms.* magazine and by what could be called the women's leftist establishment as a hopeless throwback to an age when Dad was home puffing his pipe in an easy chair after a hard day's work and Mom was tending to the house and children, as women do and should. He was a throwback to the *Father Knows Best* days, when men were in charge and women said, "Yes, dear." He was sexist, limited in his ability to see the rich potential of women, bound down by the assumptions of traditional gender roles.

One way feminists knew this was by something that seemed to irritate them no end, Nancy Reagan's tendency to look up at her husband, as he spoke in public, with complete admiration. "The gaze," they called it. Why would she look at him like that if she weren't either just back from Surrendered Wife school or utterly under his thumb or at least unconsciously supportive of the subservience of women? And she never even wore pants. She was a girly girl who liked to talk about clothing and jewelry just as the age of the guy-y girls was dawning.

But it was all more complicated than that, and Reagan's attitudes toward women have been misunderstood, in part because he didn't talk much about those attitudes—because when he did he was consistently and perhaps deliberately misunderstood.

But Reagan was the first president of the past century who had worked with women every day of his adult life as not only his equals but very often his superiors. He came out of a home run by a woman and went to work in an industry where women held positions of authority and respect. He knew they were smart and capable of wielding power, capable of leadership and capable of changing the landscape because every day he went to work with them in Hollywood.

So all of his adult life Ronald Reagan worked with and respected tough women. Hollywood had always been a comparatively progressive community in this sense. You couldn't work in a little universe with Bette Davis and Olivia de Havilland and Ida Lupino and think women were less strong, less tough and less intelligent than men. The powerful press that covered the industry was dominated by two women, Hedda Hopper and Louella Parsons. The people who ran Hollywood society, the social arbiters of the town whose social decisions had a sharp impact on professional decisions, were women—among them Irene Selznick and her sister Edie Goetz. The studio heads were tough men but all of them were married to and ran their studios with the help of tough women.

In some ways, there was a division of labor that was not fully equal. Women stars and women writers, women artists and designers were all equal to men. But women weren't often chosen to direct movies, and they weren't chosen to produce them.

But the point is, Ronald Reagan grew to manhood in a town dominated in many ways by strong and talented women. And that is why, when he met strong and talented women in politics, he did not patronize them as some other men of his generation and party (and the other party too) did. He didn't think Margaret Thatcher was an oddity, he thought she was a future prime minister who'd knock you over the head with her purse if you didn't see things her way. When he met with Jeane Kirkpatrick before he won the presidency in 1980 and heard her observations on the difference between totalitarian societies and dictatorships, he decided on the spot to include her in his administration—not because she was a woman but because her attitudes toward the Soviets were as blunt and tough as his. Ann McLaughlin, Margaret Tutwiler, Anne Higgins, Roz Ridgway, Becky Norton Dunlop, Liddy Dole—all were accomplished women in significant positions in his White House, not tokens but tough guys.

And there were, of course, the women he married. Jane Wyman was as ambitious and hard-working as he, and a superior artist; Nancy Davis was also ambitious and hard-working and the most influential voice in his life, the first he heard in the morning and the last at night.

But Reagan was not a supporter of the Equal Rights Amendment, was never impressed by what he saw as the party line of the feminist groups and always opposed quotas and codified affirmative action. There were a number of reasons, including this: Even though he thought women were the equal of men, he did not think they *were* men. Reagan thought men and women were different. He thought women were better than men, their superiors. Early in his administration he was asked about his position on women and he said that he honestly thought that without them "men would still be walking around in hair suits." Without women, men would not have evolved so quickly and fully; they'd still be cavemen. He was astonished at the outcry that followed. Didn't women know they were better? But the basic argument of modern feminism seemed, in those days, to come down to this: Women are not better and not worse, they are the same.

Reagan didn't think so. He thought they were better, capable of the toughness of men, equal in brain power with men but possessed of a natural desire to continue humanity, to civilize humanity, with a special tenderness and wisdom. He didn't think they were men. And he was grateful they weren't.

Anne Higgins, a wonderful big strong blond woman with short hair and a direct manner, was director of correspondence and special assistant to the president during the eight years of Ronald Reagan's presidency. She was not as a rule treated as a person of great importance within the White House, partly because she didn't claim importance and in part because her importance was not easily recognized. She wasn't at the key meetings, wasn't cc'd on important memos. She stayed in her office and worked.

But she was a woman of real influence because the president trusted her to do something that was important to him, and to do it with a sense of balance, discretion and fun. Anne Higgins was the woman who, every day, received the tens of thousands of pieces of mail sent to Ronald Reagan. Anne Higgins and her assistants read them, and it was Anne who decided which would go to the president. He had asked her to isolate a dozen or so each day and send them through. From them he got a sense of what the public was thinking, how it was responding to his ideas and programs. The letters gave him an opportunity to write back, to learn more, to acknowledge or just say hello, to be funny. (And, of course, he was. The bombing of Qaddafi's headquarters happened around the same time as the popularity of the Sylvester Stallone movie *Rambo,* and when he got letters congratulating him on the success of the mission he signed them "Ronbo.")

I asked Anne last spring what it was like reading the letters that went to him and the letters he wrote back, and she told me what she had learned about him through reading them.

She told me that "the biggest thing was his love for his parents. He would write about them all the time, to people he knew and to strangers who'd lost someone. 'When my mother died I thought I would never smile again, but after a while you will smile.' He always talked about the lessons his parents taught him. The first was that bigotry is a terrible thing. It was part of what they talked about, unusual for his day."

I asked how she decided which letters to send to him.

"I always knew what letters he was going to answer and who he was going to send money to. He saw on TV a Save the Children ad, and the next day he wanted to adopt a child. He'd send money each month. He understood pain. He was very sad about things that happened to people. You could see it when he and Mrs. R visited the sick. When we told him about a family that adopted fourteen handicapped kids he met with them, he called them and spoke to every one of the fourteen children, including the baby who was born without a brain stem. At the end of it all he invited them to Washington. They came in vans and were wheeled over to the Oval and he spent half the morning with them. . . . He called me after they left asking for their address so he could send a check.

"He gave a lot of contributions to people that wouldn't show up on his tax returns because they were individual charity and he wouldn't claim them. A woman in a wheelchair wrote him about her son. She wanted the president to know that even though he was a teenager he took the garbage out and fixed dinner and took care of her and she just wanted the president to know there were some wonderful kids out there. So he wrote her and sent a check for a hundred dollars. She called a week later—the bank wouldn't cash the check because it was worth so much. I told the president. So he said, 'Tell her to keep it' and then had his accountant send another check without his name on it. . . .

"He sent a lot of personal checks. People wouldn't cash them, so his checkbook was always out of balance.

"You know what else I saw?" she continued. "He never lost a friend. His friends followed him for life from Dixon, from Eureka, from the Rock River. We were still getting letters from people he saved [when he was a life guard]. He must have saved half of Illinois! They all stayed in touch with him and he'd answer all their letters.

"The Hollywood people, like George Murphy [the former movie star and U.S. senator from California]. He stayed friendly with the makeup people and stuntmen from Hollywood and old broken-down actors. He had some real penpals, William F. Buckley, for instance.

"Once we got a letter from a guy who years ago had a little restaurant somewhere in California. A family came into the restaurant. And a Hollywood crew was shooting there in the desert, and Reagan was there, and he noticed the family and told the guy who had the restaurant, 'I never saw a better group of kids in my life, better behaved.' When the father went to pay the bill the restaurant guy told him Reagan had paid it and left. So the restaurant guy always wrote to him and Reagan wrote back."

Sometimes people would hear from the president and be surprised when he didn't limit himself to one letter.

"There was a woman—she wrote a beautiful letter to the president," said Anne. "She told him about saying good-bye to her son when he joined the army. She says, 'There were his Nike shoes and his shorts and his socks.' And she said please Mr. President take care of my son, please be good to him. And he wrote and said 'I will do my best to keep your son safe.' A month later her wrote her again—'Dear Mrs. what it was, I haven't heard from you, how is your son, please let me know and keep me posted. . . .'

"People sensed something in Reagan. They thought that he was their friend, they felt close to him and he thought they cared about him."

I asked what he did with letters telling him off. She said she forwarded them too.

•"When they wrote negative letters he would call them up and if they said mean things he'd call and talk to them about their criticism. . . .

"We had a meeting in the cabinet room every January twenty second, and all the right to life leaders were there, and as the meeting was ending he said, 'Wait a minute, we haven't asked about whether the baby feels pain during an abortion, we have to talk about it.' So they did. The next year Bernie Nathanson did the film *The Silent Scream,* with the baby kicking away from the needle—he did that because of Reagan. The old lifesaver at it again. . . .

"He was just a great man. We were lucky he was there. I think God put him there for that specific time in history to do what he had to do."

I wrote once that Reagan was utterly egalitarian, never thought he was stooping to the people he wrote to, and I also thought he was possessed of an intuitive sense of the purpose of royalty, the need for people to flee the normal petty tyrants of their lives, the boss, the difficult spouse or child or parent, and tell their story to "the king," and be heard. And I still think I was right but I don't really know, or sense, that he thought about this at all. It was all instinctive. He realized that people pour their hearts out to presidents and in a modern, highly technological society with a quarter billion people it was important that they know that they have at least a chance to make it through to the top guy. That is why he answered letters from citizens with the same kind of care and respect that he gave to letters from world leaders, from popes and prime ministers. That moment, when you treat the lonely mother like a great leader, is the Great Democratic Moment, the one in your office, alone, that silently expresses who we are.

And that is why, when Anne Higgins sent in letters from people who included Polaroids and snapshots of their kids and their neighbors and parents, he wouldn't look at them and throw them away. He'd look and mention them in his reply and then put the picture in his pocket. They'd wind up in lamp-table drawers in the residence, and the staff would keep them and put them aside thinking they must be important, the president wouldn't want them misplaced.

It was Anne Higgins, and later a principal in the story I'm about to tell, who told me a few years ago of the story of Mrs. Green. I told it in my speech to the University of Texas at Austin, when I was asked to speak on Reagan's character, and since then it's been repeated a lot, and I'm often asked to retell it.

Frances Green was an eighty-three-year-old woman who lived by herself in a rough neighborhood in Daly City, California. She supported herself on Social Security and had very little money. But for eight years she'd been sending either a dollar a year or a dollar a month to the Republican National Committee. That was her party, and she loved it. And she loved Ronald Reagan.

One day Frances Green received in the mail a letter from the Republican National Committee. It was nice—thick, cream-colored stationery, black script—and it thanked her for her regular contributions to the Republican Party. It invited her to come to the White House to meet President Reagan. Unfortunately, she didn't notice the little RSVP notation.

Frances Green was thrilled. She'd been invited to the White House to meet the president of the United States. So she took every cent she had and she took a four-day train trip across America. She couldn't afford a sleeper, so she slept sitting up in coach. And she got to Washington and got herself a small room in a bad hotel and she showed up at the appointed time at the White House gate—a little old lady with white hair, white powder all over her face, an old white suit that was now yellow with age, white shoes, white stockings and an old hat with netting. She stood on line waiting to get in. There was an executive with the Ford Motor Company standing behind her, and he noticed her, this extraordinary-looking old woman all by herself who looked like Mary Pickford.

She gets to the marine guard at the gate and gives her name. He goes down the list, and says, brusquely, "Your name isn't here, you're not cleared in."

"Oh," she said, "I was invited."

But he wouldn't let her in. She was heartbroken, wordless with woe. But the Ford executive was watching and listening to the whole thing, and he took her aside and got her story. He told her, "Stay here."

She stayed at the gate, he was cleared into the White House, he couldn't find anyone to help him, he went back outside to Mrs. Green and she's standing there looking through the gate at the White House. He said to her, "Can you stay in Washington a day or two?" She said yes, she planned to. He said, "Good. Go back to your hotel and meet me here at nine in the morning on Tuesday."

She was still heartbroken but she left, in the Ford executive's car. And he went in again and found Anne Higgins, and Anne went to President Reagan's secretary, Kathy Osborne, who went to the president. Reagan said, please bring her in here when she comes back.

Tuesday morning arrives. But as luck had it, it was a heavy news day, with a lot going on. Ed Meese had just resigned, and there was a military action going on overseas. The Ford executive knew the president wouldn't be able to meet Mrs. Green, but at least he knew he would be able to give her a tour of the White House and show her everything and make it special for her.

So the Ford executive met Mrs. Green at the gate, and they were both cleared in, no problem, and he gave her a wonderful tour. At the end, because you never know, he walked her by the Oval Office for a moment. Maybe she could get a glimpse of the president through the door.

So they're standing outside the Oval Office. The National Security Council comes out, generals come out. The Ford executive peered in. Reagan gestured to him. Frances Green walked into the Oval Office.

"This," I said in the speech about Reagan's character, "is why Reagan is Reagan. He knows Mrs. Green is a little old lady all by herself in the world, she's no one, with nothing to give him, and Reagan is behind his desk and he rises and calls out, 'Frances!' He says, 'Those darn computers, they fouled up again! If I'd known you were coming I would have come out there to get you myself.' "

He asked her to sit down and they talked about California and he gave her a lot of time, and if you say on a day like that it was time wasted, there are a lot of people who'd say, Oh no it wasn't. No it wasn't.

He had a big heart, a kind of liquid heart that flowed out to others.

Big Trouble

Ronald Reagan had the last hard presidency—up until right now. George Bush the Elder, who followed Reagan, presided over the end of Soviet communism, the reunification of Germany, a hundred-hour war in the Gulf and a mild recession. Bill Clinton had Bosnia, the bombing of the federal building in Oklahoma City and the long boom. The second President Bush, however, has been handed by history a great and crucial challange: the terrorist threat and the beginning of the long war. He is having, and will continue to have, the first truly hard presidency since Reagan.

Reagan was immersed in crises from the moment he entered the White House. Some were of his own "making"—the kind that come from attempting to change your country's (and the world's) attitudes on a host of issues. Some were simply his from the time he walked into the presidency, because history gave them to him. Among these were dealing with the last, most dangerous days of Soviet communism, Communist aggression in Latin America, tax battles, budget battles, philosophical battles, the shooting down of a Korean airliner that was carrying an American congressman and hundreds of others in international airspace, the Philippines and the fall of Marcos, the Falklands war, arms control disruptions, continuations, failures and victories; China, the Beirut hostage crisis, the *Challenger* explosion, the war in Lebanon, the invasion of Grenada, the assassination of Egyptian President Anwar Sadat, the murder of the American ambassador to Pakistan and the president of Pakistan when their plane was blown up in midair; the terrorist bombing of the American embassy in Beirut, the truck bombing of the American marine barracks in Beirut, which killed 241 men, NATO tensions, the threatened coming apart of the Western alliance, Brezhnev, Andropov and Gorbachev, the hijacking to Beirut of a TWA 727 loaded with American tourists and their rescue, economic recession, the spread of state-sponsored and rogue-group international terrorism, the rise of the Green and antinuclear parties of Western Europe, the crisis over the placing of Pershing missiles in Western Europe, struggles with Japan over American imports and the making of the long boom, the highest economy in all of American history, which continues to echo through our country to this day.

There were personal crises also: the shooting and its aftermath, two cancer surgeries, two invokings of the Twenty-fifth Amendment temporarily passing the power of the presidency to Vice President Bush while Reagan was in surgery, Nancy Reagan's breast cancer and surgery.

Crisis after crisis. But Reagan had, during his second administration, two crises that were particularly painful for him. From the remove of fifteen years, it seems to me that the first crisis seemed to change everything but didn't while the second crisis didn't seem to change everything but did.

The first damaged Reagan, and his handling of it was not successful. The second cemented his high place in history, and this one he handled with a kind of brilliant honesty.

The first was the Iran-contra scandal. This is the story as we tend to remember it:

The Reagan administration was caught breaking the law after it sold some military weapons to self-proclaimed representatives of Iran, which had for almost a decade been amusing itself trying to torment the Great Satan, the United States, and had succeeded in helping tear down the presidency of Jimmy Carter. Iran was now at war with Iraq. The Reagan administration allowed the provision of the weapons to Iranian contacts on the promise that a handful of American hostages being held by pro-Iranian terrorists in Beirut would be freed. This was an arms for hostages deal—a break with U.S. and administration policy not to barter with terrorists because it would, obviously, only encourage the taking of more hostages. To make it worse, when the story of the arms deal came out, President Reagan denied it. To make it worse than that, the Iran initiative was revealed in time to be an almost bizarre operation in which American operatives had put their trust in conmen, and communicated with them through what seemed childish cloak-and-dagger methods, with inscriptions in bibles and cakes baked like keys. And to make it all just a little bit worse, the profits from the arms deal were apparently put in a secret bank account to finance the pro-democracy freedom fighters in Nicaragua. This too was against the law.

It all looked "nutty," as George Shultz, the secretary of state who fought against it from the day he first heard of it, later said.

How could all this have happened? And how could it have happened in a well-run and highly professional organization like the Reagan White House?

In July 1985, Ronald Reagan was in Bethesda Naval Hospital recovering from surgery for colon cancer. National Security Council chief, Bud McFarlane, went to him and told him of what might be a break in the ongoing Beirut hostage situation. Since the early 1980s the pro-Iranian terrorist group the Hezbollah—"the party of God"—had been holding and torturing American hostages taken from the streets of Beirut. Among them was a CIA station chief, William Buckley, whom they apparently tortured without mercy. Reagan had met with families of some of the hostages in the White House and had been told what was being done to Buckley. It made him angry, and it was one of the greatest frustrations of his presidency. With all the hardware in the world, with a first-rate intelligence system and gifted personnel and spy-in-the-sky satellites, we couldn't find where the hostages were held. The Hezbollah moved them around at random, at night, from the cities to the mountains to the desert. Whenever the United States would get a fix on where they were, Reagan couldn't move because of the potential loss of innocent civilian life or the likelihood of retaliation against hostages.

In the hospital, McFarlane told the president that Israeli contacts had given him some interesting information. There were moderate and politically connected Iranians who wanted to establish a quiet channel to the United States in hopes of encouraging the forging of new relations between America and Iran. The ayatollah was sick and near death; subtle jockeying to take his place as head of the Iranian government had begun. The situation was fluid; this might be a good time to take a chance and make a move. McFarlane asked the president if he could meet with the moderate Iranians. Reagan said yes. Soon

McFarlane reported that the Israelis had told him that, to show their sincerity, the Iranian moderates were offering to persuade the Hezbollah to free the American hostages they were holding.

This wasn't the first time an intriguing possibility on getting the hostages out was floated; none had ever worked. But Reagan thought this one seemed worth a try.

Talks between McFarlane and the Israelis and Iranians began. Ronald Reagan later wrote, "The Israelis said the Iranians wanted us to permit Israel to sell a small number of TOW antitank missiles to the moderate Iranians; they said that this would enhance their prestige with the Iranians and demonstrate that they actually had connections with high officials of the United States government."

This was the first mention of weapons. Reagan could have shut the initiative down at this point, but didn't. Instead he listened.

Israel had the TOW missiles; the Israelis asked for permission to ship some of them to the Iranian moderates, who would pay for them. The United States would replenish the Israeli stock. Reagan again: "As Bud outlined the plan, the transaction was to be solely between Israel and the Iranian moderates and would not involve our country, although we would have to waive for Israel our policy prohibiting any transfer of American-made weapons to Iran."

Reagan says he turned the deal down at this point. He couldn't condone trade with countries that support and sponsor terrorism. But Israel pushed for the deal; their intelligence agency, the Mossad, which Reagan and American intelligence tended to hold in high regard, said the Iranian moderates were the real thing—that they had in fact stood up to terrorism in the past, at some cost. This impressed Reagan. So did the information that the Israeli prime minister, Shimon Peres, supported the deal and was close to the Israelis who were advocating it.

Now Reagan agreed. "The truth is, once we had information from Israel that we could trust the people in Iran, I didn't have to think thirty seconds about saying yes to their proposal."

He felt he was agreeing to what was in effect the action of another government, Israel. And it was only a one-shipment deal. But Reagan insisted that the moderate faction from Iran use all its influence to get the U.S. hostages out.

They said they would.

So Reagan agreed.

The shipment of TOW missiles was made. And soon an American hostage, Benjamin Weir, was released from his Beirut imprisonment.

Reagan waited for the next six hostages. The White House was told the terrorists holding them were slowing things up but don't worry, the hostages are coming.

Instead the Mideast blew up again. In early October, Israel bombed Yasir Arafat's PLO headquarters in Tunis, killing a number of people and enraging the Palestinians. Palestinian radicals promised to take revenge. Three days later, the terrorist group the Islamic Jihad announced it had killed CIA officer William Buckley. (He may have died before then and may in fact have died not because of the torture but of natural causes—a fellow hostage, Father Lawrence Jenco, said later that he believed this to be so.) Three days after the Islamic Jihad announcement about Buckley, four armed Palestinians hijacked the Italian cruise ship *Achille Lauro* in the Mediterranean.

Reagan's attention turned to rescuing the fifty American tourists on the Italian ship. The *Achille Lauro* terrorists announced they would soon begin killing Americans. Then they killed a sixty-nine-year-old American named Leon Klinghoffer, who was helpless and wheelchair-bound when they shot him and threw him into the sea.

The terrorists then made sail for Egypt, where they surrendered to Egyptian officials. The hijackers were turned over to the PLO, who were thought to have taken them out of Egypt. Then Reagan learned that they were still in Egypt, and that an Egyptian airliner was going to take them to Tunisia.

Reagan ordered U.S. fighter planes to intercept the Egyptian airliner and force it down at a U.S. base in the Mediterranean. Four navy F-14's from the USS *Saratoga* intercepted the Boeing 737 and forced it down in Sicily, where navy SEALs rushed to the airstrip to arrest the terrorists and bring them to America for trial. But the Italian government refused extradition and took custody of the terrorists themselves.

Still, they had been caught and would be tried and jailed. Reagan was pleased. A few months later, in December 1985, Bud McFarlane resigned, pleading exhaustion, and his deputy, John Poindexter, was made NSC chief.

Poindexter talked to Reagan about the hostage release plan. It had not yielded any results since the previous October, but Reagan remained hopeful—in spite of strong and growing opposition to the initiative within the administration from Secretary of State George Shultz and Defense Secretary Caspar Weinberger. When Shultz learned of it he made a strong case to Reagan that this might not technically be an arms-for-hostages deal, but it would certainly *look* like one when it leaked. And such things always leak.

But Reagan was undeterred. In his second memoir he quotes the argument he made to Shultz. " 'Look,' I said, 'we all agree we can't pay ransom to the Hizballah to get the hostages. But we are not dealing with the Hizballah, we are not doing a thing for them. We are trying to help some people who are looking forward to becoming the next government of Iran, and they are getting the weapons in return for saying that they are going to try to use their influence to free our hostages. It's the same thing as if one of my children was kidnapped and there was a demand for ransom; sure, I don't believe in ransom because it leads to more kidnapping. But if I find out that there's somebody who has access to the kidnapper and can get my child back without doing anything for the kidnapper, I'd sure do that. And it would be perfectly fitting for me to reward that individual if he got my child back. That's not paying ransom to the kidnappers.' "

He had a point. And he was motivated both by hope and compassion. But Shultz was right: When this thing blew, it was going to get some ugly on everybody.

McFarlane was called in to meet with Israeli and Iranian agents once again, but no hostage release followed. By December 10, Reagan realized that at least one of the Iranian go-betweens, the arms merchant Manucher Ghorbanifar, was "a dubious character." And McFarlane himself had qualms and said he no longer supported the initiative. The plan, the president now wrote in his diary, was "a no-go."

Two days later, on December 12, 250 American soldiers on their way home from a U.S. peacekeeping mission in the Sinai were killed when their plane crashed after stopping to refuel in Newfoundland. Just after Christmas, Palestinian terrorists attacked the Rome and Vienna airports, killing twenty people, including five Americans. The act was traced to the government of Libya. Reagan was certain America must do something about Qaddafi and his endless encouragement and support of terrorism. "We all feel we must do something, yet there are problems, including 1,000 Americans living and working in the mad clown's country," Reagan wrote in his diary as the New Year began.

In January 1986, the president broke relations with Libya and ordered Americans in Libya home.

At the same time John Poindexter and his NSC staff were asking for another shipment of TOW missiles to the Iranian-Israeli connection, to be followed by direct negotiations with moderate members of the Iranian government. Reagan had already decided against the initiative—but now CIA Director William Casey weighed in: People involved in this kind of thing tend to be shady characters, but maybe we should take a chance that these shady characters can deliver. They did get one hostage out.

Reagan then agreed that "warts and all" the Iranian moderates were America's best hope for the release of the hostages. Shultz and Weinberger once again argued fiercely against the decision. Reagan in his own words: "I just put my foot down."

He said that if it failed or leaked, he'd take the heat.

Relations with the Iranian moderates continued. But throughout February no hostages were released. Once again Reagan could have and should have pulled the plug. He didn't.

His attention had moved again to Qaddafi, who had declared all of the Gulf of Sidra to no longer be international waters but Libyan territory. Reagan ordered the Sixth Fleet into the Gulf; Qaddafi fired missiles at American planes and sent Libyan ships to track the fleet. The fleet sank the Libyan ships and U.S. warplanes knocked out radar installations. Libyan agents bombed a West Berlin disco popular with American servicemen and -women. More than two hundred people were injured, including fifty servicemen. United States intelligence learned of more plans for more terrorism aimed at Americans. Reagan now asked his Joint Chiefs for the best plan to stop or deter Qaddafi. He was concerned about harming civilians in a strike on Libyan soil but felt sure a strike was necessary. In April they settled on a target: Qaddafi's headquarters in Tripoli, which included the intelligence center for his terrorism campaigns. It was hit, hard, on April 14, 1986. Qaddafi survived the attack, but his terror infrastructure was badly damaged. He took revenge by paying ransom to the Hezbollah for one of the American hostages and murdered him in cold blood.

Shultz and Weinberger continued to fight the Iran initiative. Shultz went to Chief of Staff Don Regan and warned that the whole proposition was "crazy," that the president must "end this matter once and for all," that if it continued the president would be "gravely damaged." Regan seemed to agree with Shultz and said he would speak to the president.

But once in motion, the initiative continued, in spite of the fact that it had yielded little. In late May, Bud McFarlane returned to make a secret journey to Iran and met with Israeli agents and Iranian representatives. He was told that if he made the journey, the four surviving hostages—Associated Press reporter Terry Anderson, the Catholic relief worker Father Lawrence Jenco, Thomas Sutherland and David Jacobsen—would be freed. McFarlane went, met, heard absurd demands for the release of the hostages, left without them.

But two months later, seemingly from out of nowhere, the Catholic priest, Father Lawrence Jenco, was released. This made Reagan think that "the moderates in Teheran had demonstrated a second time that they could deliver." Now Bill Casey and the NSC staff pushed for a U.S. shipment of spare TOW missile parts to the Iranian military as a demonstration of good will and to keep our Iranian contacts from losing face.

Reagan authorized the shipment.

George Shultz now told the president he wanted to resign because he felt the NSC, CIA and Defense were undercutting him. Reagan told him he couldn't be replaced, he was invaluable, to please hang on. Scultz agreed.

When Father Jenco was released he went to Rome, where he met with the pope. Then he went to Washington, where he surprised President Reagan with an utter lack of bitterness or anger toward those who had imprisoned him for almost two years. (Reagan wondered if he didn't have Stockholm syndrome—the tendency of those held against their will to come to identify and sympathize with their captors.) Father Jenco showed Reagan two letters, one a copy of the letter he had written to the pope at the request of the terrorists. "It was essentially a condemnation of the West by Shiite Muslims for 'exploiting the female body,' " the president remembered. The other letter was from Father Jenco to Reagan himself. Phrased with dignity and delicacy, it nonetheless relayed a blunt demand from the Hezbollah: the remaining hostages would not be released until seventeen Shiite Muslims held in Kuwait on criminal charges were freed. One of the captors told Father Jenco that they had killed William Buckley because he was, in their words, "an evil man." They pleaded the Palestinian cause, asked for an adjustment in American policy toward the Mideast, that attention be given to "millions of poor Arabs in the Middle East who have legitimate human needs and rights that are denied them."

Father Jenco ended the letter, movingly, with "May the God of Abraham, Isaac and Jacob, of Jesus, of Mohammed, our God, answer our prayers, for the release of our fellow Americans . . . still held hostage somewhere."

What followed Father Jenco's release, however, was not encouraging. Three more hostages were taken from the streets of Beirut, this time by a *new* terrorist group.

It is perhaps at this point that many of us, hearing this story retold, will remember the famous old cliché about the Middle East that was often told in the Reagan era. A scorpion is drowning as he attempts to cross a river and sees a frog. "Please my friend frog," he says, "please help me to the other side of the river." And the frog says yes, and gives the scorpion safe passage on his back. As they approach the shore and safety the scorpion gives the frog a deadly sting and the frog, in his death throes, asks, "Scorpion, why did you do that?" And the Scorpion says, "Because this is the Mideast."

But Reagan didn't—wouldn't—give up. A new channel was opened to individuals in the Iranian government; a nephew of Hashemi Rafsanjani, the speaker of the Iranian House, was one of them. He was secretly brought to America, did not meet the president but asked for signed photographs and gifts, including an inscribed Bible. Amazingly, he was given these things, apparently by John Poindexter.

When Shultz learned of it he remembered an old phrase Bernard Kalb, then of the State Department, used to say when he wanted to communicate someone had been gullible or naïve. "Is that what they told you, Missy?" Shultz felt that the president was being deceived and misled by his staff. He decided, he later wrote, "I must fight for the president by fighting against members of his own staff."

But again, Reagan's attention turned to other pressing matters.

An American journalist, Nicholas Daniloff, had been arrested in Moscow on trumped-up espionage charges. A second summit with Mikhail Gorbachev was coming up, and the president's most important domestic initiative, an overhaul of the tax system, was struggling its way through Congress.

Suddenly another hostage, David Jacobsen, was released. To protect the new initiative with Iran, the president said nothing about Jacobsen and awaited the return of the last two remaining original hostages.

It was at that point that a Beirut newspaper published a story saying Bud McFarlane had gone to Teheran and America was trading arms for hostages.

That's when the whole story blew, and it blew as high as a scandal can. Ultimately there were calls for the president's impeachment, congressional hearings, investigations and subpoenas, testimony and grand juries. All hope of bringing back the final two hostages, Terry Anderson and Thomas Sutherland, faded. "It was one of the most unpleasant experiences of my presidency . . . hoping it would not happen, then accepting the reality that the other hostages weren't going to be coming home," Reagan said. He met with the press and gave a national address trying to explain the history of the hostage initiative and his part in it, but it did no good. In his memoirs he quoted Lincoln: " 'If it turns out right, the criticism will not matter. If it turns out wrong, ten angels swearing I was right will make no difference.' "

Reagan later said he was wrong, should have listened to Shultz and Weinberger, who had been wiser than he. Still, to Reagan it was true that we were not trading arms for hostages; we never dealt with the ayatollah, never dealt with the kidnappers. To his opponents, to the media, to many members of his own party, we were getting TOW missiles to bad guys who'd lean on bad guys to free Americans held captive by terrorists. In other words, we were trading arms for hostages.

This is how George Shultz later summed up the entire drama. "The U.S. government had violated its own policies on antiterrorism and against arms sales to Iran, was buying our own citizens' freedom in a manner that would only encourage the taking of others, was working through disreputable international go-betweens, was circumventing our constitutional system of governance, was misleading the American people—all in the guise of furthering some purported regional political transformation, or to obtain in actuality a hostage release. And somehow, by dressing up this arms-for-hostages scheme and disguising its worst aspects, first McFarlane, then Poindexter, apparently with the strong collaboration of Bill Casey, had sold it to a president all too ready to accept it, given his humanitarian urge to free American hostages."

Shultz then and later laid it at Reagan's feet. And Reagan, rather than rearing up defensively, listened, disagreed with some of it and urged Shultz to continue in the administration and keep working with him.

In an emotional meeting near the end of the initiative, George Shultz asked the president to fire John Poindexter. He was certain Poindexter had misled the president about the weapons shipments. Now the president wondered "if there were things about the Iranian initiative I didn't know about." He turned to Attorney General Ed Meese, his old and trusted friend and aide, and told him about Shultz's comments. Meese said he thought there were indications Shultz was right. Reagan asked him to conduct an immediate review to find and go over all the facts.

A few days later Meese reported that over the weekend one of Meese's assistants had found a memo indicating that Lt. Colonel Oliver North of the NSC had diverted part of the money the Iranians had paid for the weapons . . . to support the freedom fighters of Nicaragua. And Poindexter apparently had known.

Reagan said that he hadn't known of it. He later said that when he learned of it he felt compassion for Poindexter and North, felt that they were trying to do the right thing and protecting him by not telling him. But he changed his mind when he learned of the shredding of NSC documents that followed the discovery of the memo and the full dimensions of what had been done.

Reagan knew the story now would not only continue to explode, but would come crashing down around him. And it did.

Meese went public with his findings at a news conference, the president briefed congressional leaders, Poindexter resigned, North was fired, the president made a national address to tell the American people the history of what had happened and asked for a full investigation to determine exactly how it happened. Two congressional committees launched investigations and called hearings.

It was a good way to handle things—hide nothing, tell your story and take your hits. Reagan waived executive privilege so Poindexter and North could testify. Reagan called for an independent counsel to determine if laws had been broken. There were calls for the president to pardon Poindexter and North, but he wouldn't, saying the law must take its course.

But criticism of Reagan, of his aides, of his management style, of the entire scheme continued, from intelligent people on the left and right. Pat Moynihan called it "the worst handling of an intelligence problem in our history." Barry Goldwater echoed him: It was "one of the major mistakes the United States has ever made in foreign policy."

It is interesting what finally, essentially, ended the Iran-contra initiative. It wasn't really the daily revelations of the story, but it did happen on TV.

George Shultz, who felt his warnings were still not being fully and completely heard in the White House and NSC, was invited on *Face the Nation,* with Lesley Stahl. Shultz knew what the subject would be.

Stahl asked him, "Will there be any more arms shipments to Iran, either directly by the United States or through any third parties?"

"It's certainly against our policy," Shultz replied.

"That's not an answer," Stahl shot back. "Why don't you answer the question directly? I'll ask it again. Will there be any more arms shipments to Iran, either directly by the United States or through any third parties?"

Shultz: "Under the circumstances of Iran's war with Iraq, its pursuit of terrorism, its association with those holding our hostages, I would certainly say, as far as I'm concerned, no."

That was the kind of answer a professional like Lesley Stahl could drive a truck through. She hit the gas.

"Do you have the authority to speak for the entire administration?" she asked.

"No," Shultz said, looking her straight in the eye. Stahl, amazed by their exchange but out of time, went straight to commercial and the show was over.

When you read the transcript of the interview its subtext quickly becomes clear. At one point Stahl referred to her persistence in pursuing her line of questioning. "I don't want to badger you," she said. And Shultz immediately replied, "No, you can badger me."

He later told me he had not planned to say what he'd said—he couldn't have, he didn't know Stahl's questions in advance. But it's clear he wanted his cards on the table. He wanted either to be given full authority as secretary of state or to leave. And being the sophisticate he was, he knew that in one sense he couldn't lose. If he won, he won, and he could redirect U.S. policy. If he lost—if he was fired for embarrassing the president or not supporting the administration—he was losing a job that would no longer be worth having in an administration that was about to drown in a scandal it couldn't get out of.

He won. The full Iranian portfolio was given over to him and the State Department. And that, ultimately, is how the whole Iran initiative died. He killed it.

There were calls for Shultz's resignation. Reagan was angered by this, because Shultz had done nothing wrong. There were calls for the firing of Bill Casey, but Casey was dying of a brain tumor and Reagan wouldn't do it. (Later everyone involved wondered if Casey's illness had affected his judgment throughout the initiative and its aftermath.) There were calls for Don Regan's head, and Reagan resisted this too. When his children Ron and Maureen urged him to show more anger toward the people involved in the scandal, he told them he wouldn't fire people just to save his own neck.

Reagan brought in Frank Carlucci, and a Lt. General named Colin Powell, to tighten and righten the ship at NSC. He gave George Shultz full authority over all future dealings with Iran. And ultimately he dumped his chief of staff, Don Regan—not, the president later insisted, because of Iran-contra but because Regan's ego had grown too large and he'd come to think of himself as "a kind of 'deputy president.' "

I don't doubt Reagan thought that. In fact, now gone from the White House, having left in 1986, I shared his views. But looking back I think Regan's firing was a needed—but cruel—sacrifice to the media and political gods. Someone had to be thrown into the volcano. And Regan was irascible, imperious and all in all quite a package. But he had not been for Iran-contra and had not vigorously supported it.

Those are all facts. Here are some truths. One is that I think Reagan's goose was cooked from the moment he heard of the torture of

William Buckley, from the moment he met with relatives of all the other hostages. Buckley was a patriot, a good man who would die for his country and now could not be rescued by it. The others were innocents, Americans imprisoned and abused.

It all gnawed at Reagan. And everyone around him knew it. I do not doubt that McFarlane, Poindexter and North, whatever their personal or professional flaws or misjudgments, thought they were following the president's desires if not his directives. He wanted to save the hostages. And everyone knew he wanted to help the prodemocracy anti-Communist guerrillas in Nicaragua.

Drew Lewis had called Reagan the Great Delegator. But six years into his presidency, the Great Delegator was delegating not to a solid first string of Reagan veterans but to a second string that understood him less well. The Baker-Deaver-Meese triumvirate that had run the first administration was gone from the Oval Office, Baker to be secretary of the treasury, Deaver into private consulting, Meese heading the Justice Department. Deaver and Meese had worked with Ronald Reagan since the beginning of his political career in California; they knew him, knew how to run the office around him, knew what he needed. And Baker, who had emerged as the most important hand in the first administration, was a smart and experienced player who knew how to survive and how to lend his survival skills to others.

In their place came a crew that didn't work as well with Reagan or have the same insights and knowledge; they winged it and crashed.

The secret with Reagan wasn't much of a secret. He would tell his aides what he wanted done—a reduced and simplified tax code, for instance. He sent them off to do it. He didn't want to be bothered with details of strategy and tactics; he wanted the men and women he hired to create the strategy, decide on tactics and then tell him, completely. Then he would sign off or question this part of a plan or that.

But his famous lack of interest in details was not a lack of interest in facts. He wanted to be told everything and was kept informed by his first administration. But by the end, I think he was dealing with aides who interpreted his lack of interest in the nitty gritty with a lack of interest in knowing what was going on.

That was a mistake. And when Reagan understood what had happened, he no longer felt the respect and affection for them that he had in the past.

The men around Reagan in the second administration knew how important the hostages were to him. They knew that it was their charge to be as creative as possible in coming up with ideas to get them out—as long as every action and idea was within the law, both literally and technically, both in terms of reality and the appearance of reality.

They failed here. And in failing, they dealt a bad blow to the president they wished both to serve and honor.

It was tragic. Everyone involved paid a high price. The men who had broken the law were fined, lost their jobs and were thoroughly humiliated. The opposition party had, finally, what they had never had before: a Reagan defeat on which they could capitalize. The media had a field day, with Ben Bradlee, the editor of *The Washington Post,* being quoted as saying it was the most fun he'd had since Watergate.

But no one was as damaged as Ronald Reagan and his administration. A full housecleaning followed, a new chief of staff, the respected Hill Senate veteran Howard Baker, called in to set things right again. Things stabilized, and in time the president, who had for once lost his sunny disposition and given in to the blues, started to come back.

In the end, it seemed to emerge that some of the moderate Iranians McFarlane and North had been dealing with were probably in fact connected to the Ayatollah Khomeini in a scheme to get weapons through a sting operation that had the delicious side benefit of humiliating another American president.

In the end, the Democrats of Congress, eager to capitalize on the seeming wildness of the actions taken by Lt. Colonel North, held public and televised hearings to grill him. Instead he grilled them back, made a spirited defense of himself, his colleagues and his president, and the Democrats retreated in some disarray. North went on to run for the Senate in Virginia, lost and now has a radio show.

In the end, the prodemocracy freedom fighters, the contras of Nicaragua, held on and triumphed: The Communist Sandinista government fell, and democratic elections were held.

In the end, it became clear that for all the misjudgments and foolishness of the Iran initiative, none of Reagan's men was motivated by low motives—by a desire for money or the desire for partisan gain; their lowest motive seems to have been a desire for the applause that follows a triumph against the odds. They wanted to get the hostages back. Good reasons for bad actions, but bad actions nonetheless.

Bud McFarlane, feeling disgraced, fooled and abandoned, attempted suicide, survived and became a consultant, writer and speaker. Don Regan wrote a bitter book, George Shultz a triumphant one.

And in the end, there was one thing about Iran-contra that was different from every setback Ronald Reagan had ever suffered. It was this: It wasn't a lucky defeat. All his previous losses—his failure to get a big job with Montgomery Ward, the end of his first marriage to a woman who wasn't eager for and likely not suited to the political life; the end of his movie career, which sent him to television and the GE assembly lines; the loss of the 1976 campaign, which seemed at the time a career ender but was in fact a president maker—all of those losses, for all their hurt, had been blessings. Iran-contra wasn't. It contained no hidden gifts, was no lucky loss, was bad from beginning to end.

It should also probably be said that it was during this crisis that Nancy Reagan once again came to the fore, helping to raise her husband's spirits, getting people in to support him and make him laugh, taking hold of the White House mess—Don Regan didn't leave and Colin Powell didn't come in without her urging—and reaching out to her friends in the media for understanding. She quietly helped get things back on an even keel, and helped turn her husband's concentration and concern away from the scandal and on to a new and simmering crisis that both Reagans saw as rich with opportunity.

I have thought some about the different temperaments of those involved in the Iran initiative. It seems to me that if you were daring, bold, fancied yourself unbound by conventions, and were essentially romantic about history, you just might think that Reagan and Poindexter and North were right.

They were doing what they could to free innocent hostages; sometimes you have to cross the devil's bridge to get across rough waters.

If you were shrewd, tough, knowing and not at all romantic about the flow of history, you'd be with Shultz and Weinberger. Because they knew this: Devils don't let you take their bridge for free.

If you thought yourself savvy you just might go down the North/Poindexter path. If you actually were savvy you'd go down Shultz's.

Reagan was romantic, and this time paid dearly for it.

Big Triumph

This is about the second crisis I spoke of, the one that didn't seem at the time to be as earthshaking as it proved to be.

But before you read it I want you to go out, if it's daytime, and just look up into the sky. Maybe it's blue and clear and has some clouds and is just there, like the sky is. Now in your mind put things into the sky. Because that's what Reagan's imagination did, or rather that's what his understanding of history did. Reagan could see all that placid everyday beauty and then look just around its corner and see: the big terrible thing.

Jump with me now to the Oval Office in December of 1988. I am listening to the president as we discuss his farewell address, which I've returned to the White House to work with him on. It is within weeks of the end of his era, and he is telling me how, in his view, history had changed in some terrible ways in our century, particularly military history. It was in this century as never before that women and children and the old, civilians and innocents had been deliberately targeted for destruction in war. Even more terrible, he said, was that man had never developed a weapon that he had not used.

We both knew what weapon he was talking about. He spoke of Hiroshima and the agony there. And I knew what he was suggesting: We are wrong, so wrong, to think that these nuclear weapons at our fingertips will never be used again after those terrible days decades ago in Japan.

He returned to the thought that preoccupied him. Women and children and innocents had always died in wars, but what a terrible thing it was that now, in the nuclear age, civilians were not just "collateral damage," they were the target. That was the point of nuclear weapons, not that they'd take out a military headquarters but that they'd take out a city, a country. . . .

Now jump to a meeting Ronald Reagan had almost exactly eight years before, at the very beginning of his presidency. At that time he met with the Joint Chiefs of Staff, the heads of the services within the American military, and told them a variation of what he told me. Maybe he said exactly what he told me, but what he records in his memoirs is this. He told the Joint Chiefs that man has never developed a weapon for which he did not ultimately develop a means of protection. I want you to develop a way of protecting us from incoming nuclear weapons, he said. He asked if it was not possible to devise some sort of missile defense. They huddled, conferred and said yes, we think it may be possible. He asked them to go ahead, to consider every possibility and follow every lead to see if they couldn't make our country safe, at least from nuclear warheads launched by missile.

Thus was born SDI—the Strategic Defense Initiative. The press, when Reagan made a speech announcing it as a high priority, immediately gave it a movie name: Star Wars. Some of them did that because their attitude toward the idea was derisive, and they wanted to communicate how silly it was. It was as silly as George Lucas's *Star Wars,* a highly entertaining and utterly fantastic piece of fiction. But funny things can happen when you bestow a negative nickname—it can come to stand for something positive in ways you wouldn't guess. I realized this when I spoke to a thirty-year-old sailor on the USS *Reagan,* who told me of hearing about what he still called Star Wars when he was a kid. It made him want to be part of it, to join the great adventure. And now here he was on the newest aircraft carrier in the American arsenal.

The writer and political figure Clare Boothe Luce wrote Reagan and asked him not to call it SDI or Star Wars but the Space Shield—a shield against incoming horror. President George W. Bush, who still backs the initiative and has vowed to push it forward, sometimes calls it High Frontier.

In talking about it I'm going to call it what Reagan called it and what a lot of people still call it—SDI.

If there's any chance you're still outside, imagine again what Reagan imagined. Now this was a sunny-natured man, but he understood how history works. Are there a hundred thousand nuclear weapons out there? Then sooner or later one is going to be used, for the first time since 1945. And then someone else will use one in turn, and someone else will use two . . .

There are a number of ways to deliver a nuclear weapon and damage a nation, or even kill it. A "suitcase nuke" can be put on a barge and floated up the East River to take out Manhattan. Ultimately, only our intelligence abilities and our ability to act decisively on what we've learned can stop that. But bigger nuclear weapons—stronger, more potent, more killing—are more likely to be delivered through the launch of a missile that travels through the atmosphere and reaches its target.

We still don't have anything to protect us from that. So a quarter century after Ronald Reagan started worrying, there is still something to worry about.

I'll tell you when his worries first came to a head.

On July 31, 1979, after Reagan left the California governorship, he did something he'd long wanted to do. He went to the headquarters of NORAD (North American Aerospace Defense Command), the U.S. military's nuclear command center, in Cheyenne Mountain, near Colorado Springs. He got a VIP tour of the cavernous, multistoried center with all its gizmos—the satellite readouts; the busy brass; the blinking lights; the secure lines to the president, to the Joint Chiefs and top commanders; the nuclear launch system. All of it whirring, bipping and bopping in its impressive way. Reagan was shown around by the commander, a four-star air force general named James Hill. There were briefings about radar and force size. But at the end of the tour Reagan remained concerned. He and his aide, Marty Anderson, talked to the general about what would happen if the Soviets launched a missile right at this center. Without missing a beat the general said, "It would blow us away."

The general explained that they would know within seconds if the Soviets launched a missile, but that the reality was this: If a missile is going toward an American city, NORAD would have about fifteen minutes left to . . . tell people.

When Reagan left the meeting he was, as Marty Anderson who was one of his party later told me, "Pensive, disturbed by what he'd heard."

Reagan mused aloud on the plane to Los Angeles. "We have spent all that money and have all that equipment, and there is nothing we can do to prevent a nuclear missile from hitting us."

He thought about it as he prepared for his next presidential run; he got the Republican platform in 1980 to support research for a protective missile system. And as soon as he won the presidency he called in the Joint Chiefs, who now worked for him, and asked them to get going. On February 11, 1983, the Joint Chiefs went to President Reagan and, as Marty Anderson put it, "recommended to him that the United States abandon its complete dependence on the old doctrine of mutually assured destruction and move ahead with the research and development of a missile defense system."

On March 23, 1983, Reagan addressed the nation and told them of his dream.

I've mentioned Reagan's thinking on the nuclear doctrine of MAD (mutually assured destruction). It had worked for a long time: The Soviets hadn't bombed us and we hadn't bombed them because both sides knew that the first to send a missile would soon receive one. Fine—as long as it works. But, as Reagan said, "That's not the kind of thing that makes you sleep better at night." He thought it was like "having two westerners standing in a saloon aiming their guns at each other's head—permanently." It was clear to him: "There had to be a better way."

One of the first reports he received from the Pentagon when he became president was quite sobering. He said he would never forget it. It said that at least 150 million Americans would die in a nuclear war with the Soviet Union—"even if we 'won.' "

He was deeply concerned, and remained so. He saw in SDI the possible beginning of a solution.

You might think the world, on hearing of his plan, would say, "The possibility of a defense against nuclear weapons? The possibility of shooting down a missile carrying a warhead before it can hit the ground and kill millions of innocent people? What a relief that would be, good luck!"

But of course that is not how the world, or rather those who spoke most loudly in the world—the press, the leaders of other nations, the Soviet Union, the opposition party, columnists and chatterers of all sorts—saw it.

They said, first, that inventing a space shield was impossible. Reagan answered that since every weapon ever developed had inspired a defense, history suggested it was possible to create one here. He thought the ingenuity and original thinking that spark free societies could likely produce something helpful. He said that at the very least it was worth a try: It might save millions, tens of millions of lives.

They said, then, that it would be too expensive. Reagan said, it may well be expensive but then it just might be worth a lot of money to keep tens of millions of people from dying.

Then they said it wasn't necessary—that after all, MAD has worked so far, and we have a lot of treaties with a lot of countries outlawing the use of nuclear weapons. Yes, Reagan said, but treaties get broken. In 1925 we all signed treaties outlawing the use of poison gas, but poison gas has still probably or will probably be used again some day. (Saddam Hussein may have used it in the Gulf War.)

Then they said it would be destabilizing—after all, if America is building a nuclear defense, then Soviet generals will probably feel it necessary to push the Soviet premier to move now and attack America before the defense exists. Reagan said no, if they tried to attack us they know we'd still attack them—MAD would still work.

But more important, Reagan said, SDI would be inherently *stabilizing* in a world at the mercy of MAD. Because if America succeeded in building a nuclear defense, then we would share it with—literally *give* it to—every country in the world. With the Soviets, with the Eastern bloc, with every nation on God's globe. That way we'd all sleep better at night.

Critics said it was a mere bargaining chip, a chip dreamed up by Reagan to get what he really wanted: a cut in the number of Soviet nuclear weapons. Reagan said, How could it be a bargaining chip? I'm *giving* them the chip, I'm trying to create a global defense that will make nuclear missiles less of a threat to everyone.

And they said, finally, that if SDI was such a good idea, then everyone in the Pentagon, every captain in the navy and member of the defense establishment would be for it—and that was not so. But Reagan thought he knew why: Bureaucracies don't always like hearing about expensive new initiatives that just might make their own piece of the defense-spending pie smaller. Every service always has legitimate needs that aren't met, and the chief of every service finds his reputation rests in part on his ability to jigger the bureaucracy so his boys get what they need.

The Soviets were furious about the idea, and their opposition was loud, consistent, implacable, impervious to argument. Why? Essentially for one reason: It threatened their power and status. The Soviet Union was a superpower, was as important to the world as the United States in terms of influence, was treated with respect and fear . . . because they had nuclear missiles that could undo the world. Their economy couldn't compete with the world—their economy was a state-controlled failure. Their form of government, totalitarian dictatorship, wasn't going to spread successfully in the long term in a world where people increasingly wanted to be free. Even in the eighties, thoughtful people recognized that Marxist Leninism was at the very least an inhibitor of creativity and progress, at worst the incubator for a reign of criminals.

And anyway, a number of the Soviet Union's best scientists and most brilliant minds were in prison cells in the gulag. Instead of collaborating with other geniuses in laboratories and creating breakthroughs, they were doing hard labor and living in solitary.

The Soviets had one thing going for them: the ability to frighten the world with their missiles. And if they lost that ability, they would suffer a setback from which they might never recover as a world power.

Which they well knew.

There was another reason for the passion of the Soviets' resistance. In a way the Russian leaders were more believing in American brilliance and ingenuity, had more faith in our ability to make scientific breakthroughs, than we ourselves did. *They knew SDI might work*. That's why the Soviets themselves were working tirelessly and devoting great resources to developing their own SDI system. They didn't want America to beat them.

Reagan was opposed by the intelligentsia of his own country, and the Soviets, and the countries they controlled, and our more nervous allies, some of whom (the French, for instance) seemed to hate anything that might change their lives even when it would make their lives better.

So what Reagan did was what he always did. He used his voice. He used his power, tried every way to push it through. He spoke about SDI and tried to unravel the complexities in which its enemies each day wrapped it.

He also told the Soviets, and the world, that he not only wanted to hold serious arms control discussions, but he also wanted the Soviets and the United States talking about arms *reductions,* not only arms limitation. He actually wanted to cut the number of weapons in each country's sitting arsenal.

There was for many years no real movement. The Soviets went through four leaders in the time Reagan was president, Brezhnev, Andropov, Chernenko and finally Gorbachev. They would come to the bargaining table, they would leave the bargaining table, they would return to the bargaining table and filibuster.

Reagan knew that there were two ways to make the Soviets get serious about arms reduction no matter who their leader was. It was not through pleas; it was not through warm words; it was not to go Jimmy Carter's route and tell the Soviet premier that they shared the same hopes and dreams; it was not through trying to get the international media to lean on the Soviets.

There was only one way to do it, through strength. He would rebuild American defenses, rebuild the navy, make our armed forces the most effective and powerful in the world, and only that would bring the Soviets to the bargaining table. Because only at the bargaining table could the Soviets stop our rebuilding, by getting us to agree to stop and cut back.

Reagan did not see his buildup as provocative; every military expert in the world knew what he knew: The Soviets, in the late 1970s and early 1980s were engaged in the biggest arms buildup in history, which left Reagan, in his words, "amazed at its scale, cost, and breadth. . . ." The number of new long-range missiles alone was "staggering."

Ultimately, Reagan's strategy worked. A key moment: In 1983, the Soviets put a stock of SS-20 nuclear missiles in the Warsaw Pact countries aimed directly at our allies in Western Europe. Reagan said that if they did not take them down he, with the full agreement of NATO, would send American Pershing II and cruise missiles to Western Europe and have them put up and aimed at the Soviet Union. The Soviets refused to back down and walked out of ongoing arms negotiations. The peace movement of the West exploded throughout Western Europe, and in the United States too. Reagan was called a warmonger and took a clobbering in the press; there were anti-American demonstrations across Europe. Reagan stood firm, installed the Pershings and announced he would unhappily accept the end of arms reduction talks.

The Soviets blinked. They returned to the bargaining table.

All of this was part of an ongoing crisis that, near the end of the Reagan era, came to a head.

In March 1985, General Secretary Chernenko of the Soviet Union died, and Mikhail Gorbachev was chosen by the Politburo to succeed him. When Reagan and Shultz heard the news they moved quickly: Shultz would go to Chernenko's funeral and meet Gorbachev and give him a letter from the American president inviting Gorbachev to the United States.

In the Kremlin after the funeral, the young Gorbachev lectured the American delegation on international relations, first from note cards and then without them. He was fluid, articulate, insistent. He mouthed the old party line—America is the aggressor, the Soviet Union is not expansionist—but Shultz was nonetheless struck by his vigor and cleverness. "We have no territorial claims against the United States," Gorbachev said, "not even with respect to Alaska, or Russian Hill in San Francisco!" He said the Soviet Union was serious about ongoing arms negotiations in Geneva, but added, interestingly, "any new breakthroughs resulting from the scientific and technological revolution . . . could set in motion irreversible and uncontrollable processes." He was referring to SDI of course, and though the wordiness of his statement lessened its drama his message was clear: Build SDI and we can't be responsible for what will follow. An obvious threat.

Vice President George Bush, the leader of the American delegation, answered, rebutting Gorbachev point by point. Then George Shultz joined in: "Ronald Reagan believes that this is a very special moment in the history of mankind. You are starting your term . . . [he] is starting his second term as president. . . . President Reagan is ready to work with you. . . ." Gorbachev agreed it was "a unique moment" and said he would seriously consider the invitation to come to America.

When the meeting was over, Shultz told the press this was a different kind of Soviet leader. But still he remembered Soviet Foreign Minister Andrei Gromyko's description: "Gorbachev has a nice smile, but he has iron teeth."

Soon Gorbachev agreed to a meeting, and both leaders met, not in the United States but in Geneva. This is the famous meeting in which Reagan, November 19, 1985, bounded out of Fleur d'Eau, a twenty-room château near Lake Geneva, in the bitter cold in a handsome suit, no overcoat, and smilingly greeted the shorter, stockier Gorbachev bundled in overcoat and muffler and brown fedora. A small and essentially meaningless moment that produced a picture that famously suggested: Reagan has already won. (Reagan had been acting on instinct; he heard Gorbachev's car was coming and went to greet him. He was surprised by the reaction to "the meet," and the next time he appeared in public with Gorbachev he deliberately wore an overcoat.)

I was in Geneva at the time as a member of the president's party. What I remember was the excitement we all felt—a new day, new potential, a Soviet leader who wasn't old and doddering but young and quick, who seemed to have what no Soviet leader had ever had with the exception of Khrushchev: charm and humor. And he didn't look like he was going to fall over dead at any minute.

The American press wasn't sure the American president was up to it, but we were more than confident because we knew him. He was hopeful and skeptical, just like his own self, only maybe more so. Certainly we knew he was fine when he came back from his first meeting with Gorbachev and put his arm behind his head as if it had been broken in many pieces and pleasantly told his aides it had all gone fine.

But at the Reagan-Gorbachev summit in Geneva, chatty and close and informal as it was, SDI came up over and over again. It was clearly a major problem for Gorbachev, a major challenge. Reagan had already written him saying that a missile defense system "can provide the means of moving to the total abolition of nuclear weapons." But he knew SDI was also what brought the Soviets to the bargaining table, and he knew from Gorbachev's comments to U.S. diplomats that SDI was his major preoccupation.

When the Reagan-Gorbachev summit began, the wiliness of the latter immediately became clear. Weeks before, Gorbachev had met with George Shultz in the Kremlin and been aggressive, tough, uncompromising. Shultz had expected nothing less and was not surprised. But soon after he returned to Washington he was contacted by the Soviet embassy. Gorbachev, Shultz was told, felt he had perhaps come on too strong and wanted the Americans to know he didn't intend to be like that with Mr. Reagan.

But as soon as Reagan and Gorbachev sat down, Gorbachev came on strong—aggressive, tough, uncompromising.

Reagan was not surprised and not deterred. He kept in his mind the old titans of Hollywood who had taught him how to negotiate. You'll probably not get all you want . . . you'll probably get more if you don't issue ultimatums . . . don't back your adversary into a corner or embarrass him, humiliate him . . . sometimes the easiest way to break through a log jam is to get the two top guys alone together . . .

They made some progress alone, and in a later session they went head to head on SDI. Gorbachev suggested Reagan was lying when he said he would share it with the Soviets. He said SDI was a cover for its real purpose: It was an offensive system meant to give America the ability to strike the Soviet Union first. Reagan said no, we will share it and the world will see that we share it—and this way we will keep a nuclear holocaust from ever happening. And it's better, Reagan said, than a continuation of the arms race, "and I have to tell you that if it's an arms race, you must know it's an arms race you can't win, because we're not going to allow you to maintain this superiority over us."

But they had gentler moments. Reagan liked Gorbachev almost immediately, liked his quickness and humor. And he gave the Soviet leader something that I always thought of as Reagan's truthful malarkey. At one point they retreated together to a cozy pool house with a fire going. "What a unique position we are in," Reagan told him. "Here we are, two men born in obscure rural hamlets in the middle of our respective countries, each of us poor and from humble beginnings. And now we are the leaders of our countries, and now together we can forestall a World War III, and don't we owe this to mankind . . ."

It was all true of course but I'm sure that in Reagan's mind the violins were swelling, and he was hoping Gorbachev heard the music.

It was a good beginning. When it was over Reagan went home and addressed Congress and got such an ovation he thought, "I haven't gotten such a reception since I was shot."

A remarkable series of letters between Gorbachev and Reagan followed. They had a new tone, not as formal and bureaucratic and belligerent as such letters from Soviet premiers to presidents in the past. Reagan wrote first, addressing again all of Gorbachev's qualms on SDI. Gorbachev had said in Geneva that the development of SDI would lead, inexorably, as unanticipated scientific breakthroughs followed one on another, to the placement not of defensive but of *offensive* nuclear weapons in space.

Reagan sought to reassure him. ". . . I can understand, as you explained so eloquently," Reagan wrote, "that there are matters that cannot be taken on faith. Both of us must cope with what the other side is doing and judge these implications for the security of our own country. I do not ask you to take my assurances on faith. However, the truth is that the United States has no intention of using its strategic defense program to gain any advantage and there is no development under way to create space based weapons."

But Reagan wanted to find a deeper way to relieve Gorbachev's anxieties. So he offered to have an SDI meeting between Soviet and American representatives and scientists, in order to identify what areas of the program might be construed as threatening. "Should we not attempt to define what sort of systems have that potential and then try to find verifiable ways to prevent their development?"

Gorbachev replied by letter:

"You have said, Mr. President, that the U.S. has no intention of using the SDI program for achieving military superiority. I am sure that you personally could not have any such intention." But intentions are only intentions: "The 'space shield' is needed only by the side which is preparing for a first (preemptive) strike." SDI, he insisted, was essentially an offensive weapon. The USSR "cannot and will not accept" American development of SDI.

The letters continued and now, in January 1986, Gorbachev made public his latest letter to Reagan, telling the world about it even before Reagan had received it. It was stunning, and even if only propaganda it excited the world. The Soviet Union would do away with all its intermediate force nuclear weapons in Europe, it would agree to a moratorium on nuclear testing and it would consider the elimination of all nuclear weapons by both sides by the end of the century . . . in return for only one thing. That the United States stop "the development, testing and deployment of space-strike weapons." Which was how Gorbachev now referred to SDI.

Reagan knew it was a public relations move, but so what? It was a good one; after all, he wanted nuclear weapons eliminated too. But naturally he saw several roadblocks. One was how to get an honest and verifiable deal, something that had been very hard to get from the Soviets in the past. Next was what to do about long-range nuclear weapons, of which the Soviets had a clear and overwhelming majority. Another was that nuclear weapons were spreading among other countries—and an SDI could save millions of American lives if a Qaddafi, say, that good friend of the Soviets, got his hands on nuclear missiles. (In speechwriting we called this problem Nuts with Nukes, which is what a lot of people came to call it in-house.) The fourth roadblock: SDI was, still, the most promising means of ending the threat of nuclear horror and millions of deaths.

Reagan wrote a long reply, agreeing on this point and disagreeing on that; he followed up with a seven-page handwritten letter concerning verification, the spread of terrorism, and deterrence. He also proposed a broad cutback in nonnuclear forces in Europe.

At the same time, Reagan was getting more reports that the Soviet economy was cratering day by day. They couldn't afford a huge new arms race. Reagan saw this as the moment of maximum opportunity: Hold your ground, stand firm, and we'll get arms reductions.

But everything almost fell apart when the Soviets, in the summer of 1986, seized and arrested an American journalist, Nicholas Daniloff, in Moscow. They made their move in apparent retaliation for the arrest of a real Soviet spy, Gennadi Zakharov, in the United States. The Soviets said they'd swap—Reagan said no. Gorbachev refused to believe Reagan when he said Daniloff was just a reporter, not a spy. Reagan got "mad as hell." After weeks of tension Reagan threatened to kick out the Soviet KGB contingent at the UN, and lost his temper with the Soviet foreign minister in the Oval Office. Reagan wrote in his diary, "I gave him a little run down on the difference between our two systems and told him they couldn't understand the importance we place on the individual because they don't have any such feeling. I enjoyed being angry."

Now Gorbachev moved for a new meeting with Reagan. Reagan refused until Daniloff was freed. The Soviets freed him.

The next day the United States announced the Soviet spy had been found guilty of espionage, and would be deported to the Soviet Union . . . in return for the freedom of the dissident Yuri Orlov.

And by the way, the announcement said, there would be another meeting between Reagan and Gorbachev, this time in Iceland, in the city of Reykjavik.

This, now, was the crisis, the great crisis that occurred over what Reagan later called one of the angriest days of his presidency.

Reagan and Gorbachev met in Reykjavik in a waterfront home facing the Atlantic Ocean. (Like Geneva, where they could look out at the great lake; it was as if the summit planners decided, consciously or unconsciously, that it might be useful to get entrenched adversaries talking near what is, literally, a fluid environment.)

Now the two leaders knew each other, now they were old pen pals and now Reagan came on strong. Gorbachev wanted only to talk about arms, but Reagan wanted to speak first of the Soviet Union's disheartening actions in the world: the continuing invasion of Afghanistan, continuing Communist attempts at subversion in the third world, harsh human rights crackdowns, its refusal to allow the reuniting of separated families, the plight of thousands of Jews forbidden to leave the Soviet Union and abused within it.

No progress on those fronts. But when they turned to arms limitation, things turned breathtaking.

Gorbachev accepted Reagan's zero-zero option to eliminate nuclear missiles in Europe, but amazingly he also agreed to eliminate *all* ballistic missiles by 1996, ten years hence. Then they agreed to cut and eventually do away with other nuclear delivery systems—including bombers. Even more amazing, Gorbachev said he would go along with verification procedures that were serious, sophisticated and had been fully established by both sides.

But Reagan had a reservation, which he explained. The tactical battlefield nuclear weapons that were now in Western Europe were NATO's only real deterrent against an invasion by the Soviet bloc countries, which had much larger and stronger conventional forces—armies, tanks.

Gorbachev stunned Reagan by saying he understood, and he would seriously reduce the Warsaw Pact forces.

This was something the United States had dreamed of but never expected. No previous Soviet leader had ever come close to such an idea or such an offer.

They were in their second day of meetings now and Reagan, for once actually thrilled, his hopes rising by the minute, ignored, with Gorbachev, the clock and its previously agreed-upon noon deadline. They plowed on.

As the sky darkened in the late afternoon, Reagan felt something momentous in the history of man had occurred. He later said he felt they had negotiated "the most massive weapons reductions cut in history."

It was all decided.

Then Gorbachev smiled his warm smile and said, "This all depends of course on you giving up SDI."

Reagan couldn't believe his ears. Earlier in their meetings, Reagan had brought up SDI himself: He proposed that both sides cut their weapons by 50 percent right away, and as soon as they were done, the Soviets would come to our SDI testing and development areas, and if it looked like SDI would work the Soviets could take SDI with them, and go home and finish their—and our—final 50 percent of the cuts. Then both sides would, at the same moment, deploy SDI together.

Gorbachev hadn't objected to the idea. In fact, earlier in the meeting, when Gorbachev had criticized SDI, Reagan had told him Look, we will abide by the existing ABM treaty and not deploy SDI for a decade, don't worry.

And now, at the very end of their talks, Gorbachev yanked them back to square one. Back to where they'd been when they first started talking, when Reagan had sent his first letter, when Chernenko died.

Reagan's spirits fell, and he was clearly angry. Look, he said, I have told you again and again that SDI is not a bargaining chip, it will never be a bargaining chip, it can make the world safe. "There is no way we are going to give up research to find a defense against nuclear missiles," he said. Reagan knew through intelligence that the Soviets were working on their own system; SDI was insurance that the Soviets would keep their commitments at Reykjavik. And he had promised the American people and the world he wouldn't give up on this.

He challenged Gorbachev: "If you are willing to abolish nuclear weapons, why are you so anxious to get rid of a defense system against nuclear weapons?" He said he knew of the Soviet SDI initiative and knew America was ahead, and had to wonder if the Soviets weren't trying to stop us in our tracks. He repeated his offer to give the Soviet Union and the world an SDI system to make us all safe. That way, if "another Hitler" came along we would be safe from his nuclear weapons. "Who knows what kind of madman might come along when you and I are gone?" And finally, he argued, Gorbachev had to understand that offering SDI to the Soviets and to the entire world was not altruistic, not dreamy. The world being what it is, when America finally has an SDI system, other countries will wonder if they should attack before our system is deployed. But if they know they will immediately get SDI too, that they will immediately be protected too, they will not attack. It was a hard-headed offer, not a sweet one, he said.

Gorbachev said nothing as the interpreter busily repeated Reagan's words. He only smiled. He wouldn't budge.

Finally, Reagan understood what had happened. Gorbachev had yanked him over to Iceland to kill SDI once and for all. He'd called him there to offer Reagan the moon, and make SDI disappear forever.

Reagan sat back and pursed his lips. "The meeting is over," he announced. And he and George Shultz got up and left.

Gorbachev followed him out to his car, now wheedling and jocular. "I don't know what I could have done," he said. Reagan wasn't buying.

"You could have said yes," he said, his delivery short, his face haggard.

Gorbachev had misread Reagan. He thought Reagan sentimental—and Reagan was, in certain circumstances. He thought Reagan made much of personal relations and warmth—and Reagan did, in many circumstances. He thought Reagan believed in God and thought God would guide them; and Gorbachev thought all the unexpected riches he offered would make Reagan think: God must be here. Well, Reagan thought God was everywhere, always. But he thought devils were too. Gorbachev thought Reagan's vanity would make him accept a deal that the world would greet with the best reviews of his life. But Reagan was tougher than he was vain, and he was most of all a patriot. He knew Reagan was old, almost seventy-six now, and tired. And he was. But even old lions are still lions.

What followed is what Reagan said would follow that heartbreaking night on the journey home to Washington. He wrote of his anger and disappointment, but he said the Soviets would return to the bargaining table.

And his wife, Nancy, as crestfallen as he, held him hard and soothed him and told him it was going to be all right.

"Oh it was a heartbreaker," she told me. "He knew he had done the right thing, and he had. And that was the turning point. But it was a heartbreaker. He had called me at the White House and said everything was going fine in the afternoon. But when I saw them come out of that building on television and saw his face I knew now that everything was not fine."

She watched it on the news, back in the White House. She told him to persevere, she encouraged him, told him he'd made too much progress to let it all go away, that it would all turn out right.

It was a hard cold year for U.S.-Soviet relations after Reykjavik, but Reagan kept talking to Gorbachev through diplomatic contacts. And then he spoke to Gorbachev directly on June 12, 1987, even though Gorbachev wasn't, strictly speaking, there. But he heard the words Reagan said when he made a speech standing just a few yards from the Berlin Wall, which had come to symbolize for the world the nonfreedom and nonkindness of communism:

> We welcome change and open-ness, for we believe that freedom and security go together, that the advance of human liberty can only strengthen the cause of world peace. This is one sign the Soviets can make that would be unmistakable, that would advance dramatically the cause of freedom and peace.
>
> General Secretary Gorbachev, if you seek peace, if you seek prosperity for the Soviet Union and Eastern Europe, if you seek liberalization: Come here to this gate! Mr. Gorbachev, open this gate! Mr. Gorbachev, tear down this wall!

What a moment. Reagan found that as he stood near the wall and looked at it an anger welled within him, and he was certain it was reflected on his face. (I recently looked at a tape of the speech and realized it was true, his anger showed.)

Four months later Gorbachev asked for another summit. Reagan agreed. It would be in Washington, in December 1987. Gorbachev bristled as the talks began—America has fewer human rights than the Soviet Union, he said, and you should talk about the wall, you police your border with Mexico!

Now it was Reagan's turn to smile. Equating the Berlin Wall with America's borders was absurd, and both knew it.

Gorbachev dropped SDI. He knew, finally, that Reagan would not budge on it.

They came to final agreement on a treaty banning all intermediate-range nuclear weapons, with compliance agreements both sides could accept. Reagan said his whole approach was marked by the old Russian saying "Doverjai, no proverjai—trust but verify." Reagan had been saying that in public for a long time and Gorbachev chided him: "You repeat that at every meeting."

Reagan smiled his sweet smile. "I like it," he said.

Reagan had everything to gain—everything in the eyes of the world—if he had accepted the Reykjavik deal. He would have had the applause and respect of his foes, the thanks of a relieved world that would read headlines the next morning that said BREAKTHROUGH! He would have been celebrated by history, known the pleasure of having given the world a gift of extraordinary and undreamed-of progress. Nothing but win all around him.

But he wouldn't do it. Because he didn't think it was right.

And because he didn't do it, the Soviet Union finally fell, crushed by a hundred forces but most immediately by its inability to keep up with the United States. The only thing that would have saved them was a cave-in on SDI. That way, the old status quo could continue.

And so the wall fell and Soviet communism fell and the expansionist threat fell, and every globe maker who made the globes for every schoolroom and office in the world had to redraw all the lines.

What a crisis that day was. What a tragedy it seemed. What a triumph it was.

One thing interested Reagan. When he made his great Tear Down This Wall speech he didn't know how very soon the wall would fall, and literally a six-ton piece of it would be shipped to America to be installed at . . . the Reagan Library. Where people touch it. Where I have touched it.

George Bush the Elder didn't view SDI with the same hungry imagination Reagan brought to it, and in any case during his four-year presidency the mood in America turned to cutting our defense spending. Bill Clinton never supported SDI, and let the initiative languish. He probably would have killed it if such a decision would not have opened him to serious criticism from defense and foreign policy experts.

George W. Bush, however, is pushing SDI once again. The new president seemed to signal his support by choosing as his new head of the Joint Chiefs an air force general whose main area of expertise is space technology. Bush reiterated his support for SDI in his first full news conference after 9/11, saying we need it "now more than ever."

Surely the recent attacks on America underscore the importance of first-rate intelligence, of preparedness, of the continuing possibility that "conventional" weapons will and can be used against the United States. And surely the recent attack suggests that America may well face nuclear, chemical and biological challenges in the near future.

But it is always tempting, in a land where most all of us feel free to be armchair generals, to, as they used to say, "fight the last war." We just took a bad hit. We likely have some hard hits coming. There is much to be done and protected against. But nuclear weapons delivered by missiles continue to be a real threat too—and a more serious one every day.

It is interesting that Israel, a hardy little country that does not enjoy being surprised by history, successfully launched, on August 27, 2001, an Arrow-2 interceptor from an air base south of Tel Aviv. In the latest test of its own missile defense system the Arrow-2 hit—and took down—a target scud-class missile that had been launched over the Mediterranean.

From the wires the next day: "As a result, Israeli officials say, Israel now has a missile defense system capable of intercepting the most advanced ballistic missiles developed in the Middle East."

Way to go.

And those who believe the events of September 11 prove a missile defense is not needed are, simply, dreaming. The events of September 11 prove that SDI is needed—because they prove that history is full of surprises, shocks and unexpected turns.

Dubya Was Watching

In the recent presidential election of 2000, most of the candidates who put themselves forward associated themselves in one way or another with a Reagan policy or the Reagan style. Steve Forbes was the continuance of Reaganesque economic theory, John McCain the exemplar of Reaganesque courage. As for the Democrats, Vice President Al Gore is said to have studied tapes of Reagan talking and making speeches, which perhaps led to his decision to attempt to, in a way, *become* Reagan. In his first debate with his adversary, Republican nominee George Bush, Gore cocked his head like Reagan, moved his shoulders like him and was heavily made up in what appeared to be an attempt to look like him, even to the point of rouged cheekbones that recalled the heightened color Reagan sometimes had during public appearances. It was all a miscalculation—the Reagan mannerisms seemed strange on the sharper, more aggressive Gore, and the makeup, though it did put you in mind of Reagan, made you think of how Reagan would look if he had been a large orange crayon.

Still, the attempt itself was a compliment, a bow to the fact that there is a kind of general agreement in America that he was the last great man. (Until, of course, the next great man, or woman.)

George W. Bush did not attempt to imitate Reagan in his manner or announce in specific ways that his policies were Reaganesque. But he liked it a lot when others compared him to Reagan. In fact, he surprised me in the spring of 2001 when I talked to him for this book in twice comparing himself to Reagan, something I don't think he's ever done in a public forum. He told me he thought Reagan would be proud of how he had handled his first trip to Europe as president, which he had approached as "the humble leader of a great nation." And he told me that he thought his approach to the new president of Russia was essentially "Reaganesque."

Bush pointed out that he is a very different man from Reagan, with a different background, experience and history. But he told me he had watched Reagan closely for eight years while his father, George H. W. Bush, was Reagan's vice president.

One of the things I think the new president is most confident about in terms of his personal talents is his ability to read people, to, after meeting them and talking with them, come away with a sense of who they are inside, how they think and where they fit in the scheme of things. And so his read on Reagan, especially since he'd watched him over the years, was interesting to me.

So: It is June 2001 and for the first time in nine years I walk into the Oval Office to see a president, George W. Bush, fifty-five years of age. In two days he will have been president of the United States for exactly five months. I have not seen him since I saw him speak in New York in the early autumn of 2000, before the hard-fought election aftermath. He was standing behind his desk—the same one Ronald Reagan used—when I entered, and as he came forward and offered his hand I was so startled I think my head reared back a little. I had walked into this office and seen Ronald Reagan at his desk, and George Bush the Elder too. And here was his son, a virtual contemporary of mine, a man who had not seemed to me, thirteen years before when I used to see him every once in a while in the halls of his father's 1988 presidential campaign, as especially gifted or full of promise.

And now here he was, his hair grown grayer than when I'd last seen him, his face lined from the sun. With his hair grayer he reminded me more of his father, and yet this is odd because his father never went gray. But Bush seems to move his face more like his father now.

He stands comically straight, which makes us laugh. We shake hands and he gives me a peck on the cheek. The one long conversation I have had with him was in the spring of 2000, when I was invited, as just about every conservative writer or thinker in the land had eventually been, down to Austin to meet with the Texas governor and presidential hopeful. He and his staff seemed smart, talented, some of them intense and some already a little tired, but all up to the job, and when I left I felt certain that Bush would win the presidency. Asked, politely, if I had any advice for him I said yes, stand up straight. Bush had a businessman's slouch, a regular guy's posture. "You mean to be the leader of a great nation, the United States; you will be its president and you must stand tall." His staff had been telling him that for months, he told me. I told him: You must listen to them. And he did.

He does now. He's also working out and running and looks fit in a blue pinstripe suit, a white shirt and a blue patterned tie. He was full of talk, garrulous even, which surprised me. He normally speaks in quick short bursts, like his father, but today he can't tell me enough. He had just returned a day and a half before from his first trip to Europe as president. His eyes seemed red and I wondered if he was still catching up from jet lag but he said no, he'd had nine hours of sleep the night before.

Bush has had a unique education for a president: He watched two presidencies for twelve years, as son of a vice president and then son of a president. I wanted him to reflect on Reagan for me, tell me what he had observed of him and learned from him.

It was a sunny day, the Oval Office bright. "That's the door John John used to use," he says as he gestures toward the little door on the front of his desk. He points out his paintings—"A Charge to Keep" and a painting of the Alamo. A Lincoln bust has been moved in but will soon be replaced by one of Winston Churchill coming from England. This is Reagan's rug, soon to be replaced with his own. Bush had looked at pictures of the Oval Offices of each of the modern presidents and had noted that only two had been decorated with dark colors, deep blues, Nixon's and Clinton's. He wants his Oval Office bright, like Reagan's and his father's. "I wanted to make sure my Oval

Office was sunny, very open, kind of an open feel. Like Texas."

I asked him how and when he first met Ronald Reagan and was surprised to hear that it was thirty-three years ago, in 1968, when young Bush was twenty-two years old and working as the travel aide, or "body man," for a candidate for the U.S. Senate from Florida, Ed Gurney. Bush had just graduated from Yale and gone on to basic training in the air force in July and August. He was going to be a pilot in the Texas Air Guard, trained by the air force, and he had two months between pilot training and basic training. A friend of his was running the Gurney campaign, and asked Bush to come in and help.

"My job was to travel with Ed Gurney. We had a rally in Jacksonville, Florida, and Governor Ronald Reagan came over to campaign for Gurney. I met him. He was a larger-than-life person. He dominates the room. And clearly when you're in Ronald Reagan's presence you're in the presence of a person of stature. But—the thing that happens is there are people of stature who turn out to be disappointing. Ronald Reagan's the kind of person who turned out to be comforting. Because he was a genuinely nice man. And I could tell that as a twenty-two-year-old travel aide. I shook his hand. Like everyone else I was in awe."

I asked when he saw Reagan next, and smiled when he told me because it was such a perfect cliché of modern political life. George W. Bush next met Ronald Reagan during the balloon drop at the 1980 GOP convention. The Reagan and Bush families had gathered onstage to wave at the delegates as the confetti and balloons fell. "I didn't have much of a conversation with him." Bush smiled. He saw Reagan next on Inauguration Day in 1981.

But by then he had sized Reagan up.

"There was no question that he was a warm man. Just—the vibes, I mean my instincts told me he was a very welcoming kind of person."

I asked Bush if he had watched Ronald Reagan closely in the ensuing years, and he said he had.

"I watched him a lot. Yeah, I did. I admired him. I admired his leadership style. I think he was a great president, I do. Look, obviously I love my dad, but . . . I do think Ronald Reagan was one of the great presidents, and for a lot of reasons. One is his—he was able to change the mood of the country."

He gestures to his right, to the wall on which hangs an oil portrait of Abraham Lincoln. "I put the picture of Lincoln on the wall because the job of president is to unite the nation. And this guy [Lincoln] had the toughest job of all. But that's the job of the president. We'll argue about tax cuts and the size of tax cuts and the timing of tax cuts and military decisions. And there's a lot of debate and a lot of politics.

"But if you really think about it, a president's job is to define the spirit of the nation. And to help define the soul. And Ronald Reagan knew that. . . . And he brought a nation that had kind of fallen into malaise out of its so-called malaise by the pure strength of his leadership.

"And he defined a vision and he carried out a vision, he defined a philosophy and he stuck by a philosophy. And plus his disposition was such that he brightened America and its hopes.

"And I think he was a great, great president for that. He understood the job of the president. There's a lot of people . . . who don't understand that very well. First of all, presidents are never accurately judged by short-term history. It's a compilation of history, and how you end up—you know, your accomplishments in the long run, in a big perspective. And . . . I can assure you that Ronald Reagan's are more evident than most because he defined a moment.

"We could have drifted toward European-style socialism and central planning and no faith in the American system—no faith is too harsh, but little faith. And he changed that. He—it was his remarkable presidency."

I asked Bush who he thought was the last such president before Reagan.

"I'd say Franklin Roosevelt. He was a president able to be a mood setter and change a philosophy. He followed years of Republican presidents and he moved in and really changed the whole philosophical concept of the presidency. And so he was definitely kind of a cultural shift—not so much a cultural shift but a shift in how government functions. . . .

"There's another thing—an interesting president, Harry Truman. Had to deal with a lot of the tough issues. He was a problem solver. And you know, they say a presidency is defined by the crises you inherit. But the other part of the presidency is whether or not you are able to define what America should be about. Those are the two aspects. And Ronald Reagan was able to deal with both. He had a crisis—an economic crisis and a crisis of the spirit in the sense that Americans were doubting, beginning to doubt, their greatness. And he saw both. He dealt with the cold war, he dealt with the Russians and just as important he stood on a philosophy."

I asked Bush if he had the sense Reagan really knew him. He was frank.

"No. I never had the feeling—it was hard for me to tell whether or not he was interested or not interested. The president—I was thinking recently about catching myself, I mean I walk into a room where there are twenty people standing around, and I try to be polite to all twenty. But generally if there is something on my mind . . . occasionally I find myself thinking, 'There's some young aide over there probably wanting for me to chitchat and I didn't bother to do so.' And I don't think a president means to stiff anybody, I just—I'm much more of a gregarious person than Reagan was in the sense that I'm more of a hand shaker and like to talk to people. But I can understand why [Reagan] would not have talked to me, and I don't ascribe anything [to it.]"

I ask what he might ask Reagan if he could talk to him now.

He said, "I'd ask for his advice on the defense budget."

Then he changed tack. "I'd probably ask his advice, describe what I saw and ask his advice on Putin."

Bush had recently met with the new Russian president for the first time.

"It was a big moment. It was good. I have pretty good instincts, and I found a man who realizes his future lies with the West, not the East, that we share common security concerns, primarily Islamic fundamentalism. . . . On the other hand, he doesn't want to be diminished by America. And I said some very positive things about him [in a news conference after their meeting] precisely to set up a relationship that—

I just didn't complete the Reagan sentence. Reagan said 'Trust and verify.' My attitude was, I said 'Trust.' Sophisticates surely understand that once you lie, you know, that trust isn't forever, trust is something you must earn. But when I looked at Putin I felt he was shooting straight with me."

I asked if he had plans to keep up a personal relationship with Putin and he said yes, he had invited him to come to his ranch in Texas. Bush suggested that part of diplomacy is knowing what the person on the other side of the table is facing at home. He said he felt Putin was "battling with a kind of an anti-American bureaucracy" that was "a hangover" from the cold war.

"He probably thinks I'm dealing with a bunch of hard-liners here about him too. And the best way for me to welcome him to the West and to encourage him to make the right choices in terms of the rule of law and transparency and defense measures is to break down any barriers that he may have.

"I told him . . . 'You know, if you look at me and think I'm trying to pull one over on you and trying to weaken Russia, then we don't have much to talk about. We can go through the diplomatic niceties.' I said, 'Mr. Putin, you've got to look at me and decide whether I am hostile or not hostile, whether or not I want to diminish Russia or whether I want Russia as a friend and ally with whom we can trade and keep the peace. And if you think other than—if you think negative, then this is going to be an interesting conversation for us but short-lived, and we'll go out and play like we had a good conversation.'

"And he thought that was interesting. Then he started talking about Russian history. A *lot* about Russian history. About how 'We gave up this and gave up that—' I didn't argue with him. I felt like saying, 'Wait a minute, you didn't give up anything, the people actually demanded freedom and you didn't have any choice.' But—he viewed it as giving up, and he put it in the context of debt.' Putin argued the Russian government had sacrificed a great deal in the transition to democracy and had incurred a huge financial debt.

Bush said he told Putin it was clear he loved history. Putin replied, "Yes, I love history." Bush continued, remembering their conversation.

"I said, 'You know it's interesting, I do too. I like history a lot.' And Putin said, 'Oh yes, you were a history major, the film they showed me reminded me of that.'"

Russian intelligence had made a videotaped biography of Bush for Putin, just as American intelligence had made a Putin biography for Bush. Bush continued:

"I said, 'You know, sometimes when you study history you get stuck in the past.' I said, 'President Putin, you and I have a chance to make history. The reason one should love history is to determine how to make good history. And this meeting could be the beginning of making some fabulous history. We're young. Why do you want to stay stuck? These aren't the Nixon-Brezhnev conversations! Why do you want to stay stuck in that kind of attitude?'

"It really took him aback. I said to him, 'Why aren't we thinking about how to fashion something different, so when [historians] think about the Bush-Putin meeting and the Bush-Putin relationship they think about positive things? It's negative to think about blowing each other up! That's not a positive thought, that's a cold war thought. That's a thought from when we were enemies with each other.'"

Putin, Bush said, responded positively.

Bush leaned forward now and told me a story known only to those in the room during his talks with Putin. He thought the story not only interesting but indicative of a certain potential. In the weeks before he met with Putin, Bush had read a book consisting of a long interview the Russian president had given. In it, Putin had spoken at some length of his mother. Bush told me:

"He talks about his mother giving him a Christian cross that he had had blessed, I believe, in Jerusalem."

He decided, he said, to mention this to Putin.

"I said to him, 'You know, I found that story very interesting.' I said, 'You see, President Putin, I think you judge a person on something other than just politics. I think it's important for me and for you to look for the depth of a person's soul and character.' And I said, 'I was touched by the fact your mother gave you the cross.'"

Bush, at this point in our interview, was leaning forward in his chair and gesturing. He said that Putin told him a story in return. He had taken to wearing the cross his mother had given him, and one day had put it down in a house he was visiting. And the house, he said, had burned down.

Bush continues: "Putin said to me, 'The thing I was most worried about was I lost my cross that my mother had given me. And a worker came.' He wanted to tell the worker, 'Go find the cross—I lost my cross.' The worker came over."

Here, Bush said, Putin gestured toward Bush as he acted out the story. The worker walked up to Putin and put out his hand and opened it up. And the cross was there.

Putin told Bush, "It was as if something meant for me to have the cross." Bush felt, at their meeting, that Putin "basically seemed he was saying there was a higher power."

Bush again: "I said, 'Mr. Putin, President Putin, that's what it's all about—that's the *story* of the cross.' "

Bush was clearly moved by what he was telling me, and as he leaned forward in the telling of it he put his hand forward and opened it as the worker had to Putin.

Bush felt it was a special moment between them, one rich with meaning.

I thought later, after I had left the White House, that Bush, as a believer who feels he has been born again in Christ, would likely have interpreted what happened between them with great simplicity: God is here, is operating through us, wants good for the world, performs miracles.

There is no knowing what Putin thought of the exchange about the cross; the former KGB chief has not spoken of it publicly, and Bush never spoke of it until our interview in June. When I wrote of it for a piece in *The Wall Street Journal* I called the White House to let them know, and they asked me not to use it, that the president was speaking for my book when he told the story, and not for immediate publication.

After their meeting, Bush and Putin had met with the press; it was here that Bush had said he felt he could trust Putin. His comments had been roundly criticized at home in the United States, and now, in our talk, the president let off some steam.

"I've been noticing some of these guys popping off, saying Bush shouldn't have used the word 'trust.' But if you're trying to redefine a relationship and somebody asks you, 'Can you trust the guy?' imagine what it'd have been like if I'd have stood up in front of the *world,* which is where I *was,* and said, 'No, I don't think so!' Or, 'You know, perhaps.' Or, 'It's yet to be proven.' To me, my attitude is—and this is Reaganesque, in a sense—I trust him until he proves otherwise. But why say 'proves otherwise'? I mean, that to me goes without saying."

Bush told me that he believes Putin wants a relationship with the West. Bush had told him that Russia's problem is "China in the long run," not America. Bush told Putin, "You're European, Mr. President. You have no enemies in NATO, NATO has been good for you, not bad. NATO doesn't create any problems for you." And in this part of their meeting, Bush felt Putin had "almost hinted that he wanted to be in NATO." Bush did not push him on the idea but listened, and later said it was an interesting idea, that part of him thought "Why not?" but that he thought it required more thought.

There are obvious differences between Reagan and Bush. Reagan would not have made it a point to tell a visiting journalist that he had spoken with strength to Europe's leaders. On the other hand, the story of Putin and Bush and the cross, and the meaning of the cross—that could have come right out of the transcripts of a Reagan-Gorbachev summit. That kind of unembarrassed love of his faith was right up Reagan's alley. It was interesting to me that Bush was not shy to show it.

Reagan never would have—or I don't think he would have—based much policy on looking into a Russian leader's eyes; he didn't really think it was his job to look into the window of the soul and report on what he thought was there. But part of the reason for

Reagan's ultimate progress with Gorbachev was, indeed, that he thought Gorbachev was something new in the Soviet leadership—bright and quick, charming and unpredictable. He thought he "got" Gorbachev in the way Bush seemed to think he "got" Putin.

Since we spoke, and as the galleys of this book are being edited, the events of September 11, 2001 have unfolded. I find myself thinking of the Bush I talked to in our interview and what has happened to him since. He has given the greatest speech of his life in his address to the joint session of Congress—a speech in which Bush referred to prayer like someone who had been praying, and who delivered the speech in a way that suggested he knew he was the focus of much prayerful support.

Before that night many in the punditocracy, including me, had wondered if he could quite fill the screen as Reagan and Clinton had; some of us wondered too if Bush would in his presidency prove or disprove the idea that a modern president must be a riveting presence. Those questions seem old now, and off the point.

Events have made Bush riveting; history sometimes does this. And Bush has shown himself to be history's equal; presidents sometimes do this too. As this is written, President Putin of Russia appears to be offering unprecedented support to the United States in its current struggle. Mr. Bush seems to have read him right; maybe Putin read Bush right too; maybe this is the beginning of a beautiful relationship.

Since September 11, Bush has put me in mind over and over—I find in fact that in the first draft of this book he had put me in mind—of Harry Truman, whom Bush had brought up in our interview. Truman had followed a charismatic leader, had seemed too plain and uninteresting to fill a president's shoes and was, his first few years in office at least, a bland public speaker, an uninspiring man. But this plain, uninteresting, colorless man had managed to do pretty much everything right. He rallied his war-tired nation to rebuild Europe, to support the Marshall Plan, to stop Soviet communism in

Greece, to wage a war to stop it in Korea. He was a leader. He just didn't seem at the time, early on, to be one. I think in Bush we have a Truman. And my hunch is: Bush thinks so too.

The Old Man of St. Cloud Road

In November 1988, Vice President George H. W. Bush, now and always to be known as Bush the Elder, was elected president of the United States, and Ronald Reagan's two terms were, effectively, over.

I had left the White House two years before, but came back to work with him on his farewell address. I remember sitting in his office, in the muted silence of that rounded room, and hearing the old grandfather clock *tick-tock,* and asking him questions about what he wanted to include, what he wanted to say. He told me stories of what it was like to be with Gorbachev, what it was like, at the very last summit, to be in Moscow and go with Nancy out into the streets to meet the people. You would think a president leaving office after eight dense and action-filled years would be preoccupied with his farewell, but Reagan didn't seem to be. He had no interest in his own personal legacy, had little vanity in that area and felt no need, I later realized, to attempt to "spin" history. He thought the facts of the eight years were clear, and a modest summation would suffice.

There were times when I tried to draw him out, to get him to speak of things that were part of his story in an unusual way; I hoped he would share surprising yarns or observations. I wanted this for two reasons: to learn more about him and his times and to add the freshness of unknown information to his remarks. But he didn't want to be surprising. He just wanted to sum things up and put them in context, and he wanted to do it in the way he always had, with the same imagery and references. And of course he was right.

The one time I got him going, though, was on an old Hollywood story. When I had begun working for Reagan, in 1984, I used to watch him from across the Rose Garden, or as he walked from the White House to the Old Executive Office Building, or as he bounded into the East Room for a luncheon. And what always struck me was his friendly grace, his enjoyment of the moment and of other people and his intuitive understanding of the presidential style. No one is ever trained to be president, and usually a president either walks in getting it or he doesn't. Some learn the role along the way, some never do. Reagan always comported himself as if he got it so easily, so effortlessly, that he didn't even notice that he had it.

I'd long wondered if his presidential style had been affected by a memory of a famous movie of his young manhood, *Yankee Doodle Dandy,* starring his friend Jimmy Cagney. Cagney played George M. Cohan—it was a biopic, as *Variety* used to say, of the great song and dance man's life. Cohan had been a piece of Broadway work, a stage star and producer and writer of songs such as "Give My Regards to Broadway" and patriotic ballads such as "You're a Grand Ol' Flag."

Cagney played it for everything it was worth. And in one scene at the end, Cagney-as-Cohan is called in to meet President Franklin Roosevelt. It is the beginning of World War II, and Cagney-Cohan was honored but perplexed to be invited to the White House. He meets with the president in his office. The actor playing FDR growls sunnily about how Cohan and his family have enriched the American theatrical tradition, and how Cohan himself has added to our patriotic heritage through his songs. The president gives him a medal, like the Medal of Freedom, on behalf of a grateful nation.

Cagney-Cohan is overwhelmed. He says the words with which his show business family had often responded to curtain calls: "My mother thanks you, my father thanks you, my sister thanks you and I assure you, I thank you."

It's a beautiful scene, not least because the actor playing the president is so . . . warmly presidential, dignified and yet accessible, appreciative and yet not carried away.

When that scene ended, an even better one commenced. Cagney-Cohan leaves the White House residence by walking down the great staircase that leads to the rooms downstairs, the East Room and such. At first he walks down the stairs but then his step quickens, and just before he reaches the bottom, he is doing an old Vaudeville-type buck and wing. The music swells, he leaves the White House and on impulse joins a parade outside. The band is playing one of his America-loving songs.

It was all great. And when I would see Reagan he often reminded me of the man who played FDR in that movie.

So at one of our final meetings I asked Reagan if he remembered the movie *Yankee Doodle Dandy,* and his eyes brightened and he said yes. I asked him if it had meant something to him, and he said yes. I asked him if it had made a real impression, and he said yes again.

"Why, Mr. President?" I asked.

And he said, "Because nobody knew Jimmy Cagney could dance. No one imagined him as a dancer, that was the surprise. Up till then in the movies, you know, he'd played convicts and criminals and so forth." But Cagney, he said, had been a hoofer.

It was so . . . Reagan. I'm out there in movieland drawing parallels and he's into the practicalities of the situation, of show business. *Nobody knew Jimmy Cagney could dance.*

It was something to sit in that Oval Office late on a January evening as he gave his last speech to the nation. It was a first for me; I'd worked on speeches for him but never been there in the Oval Office when he gave one. And now I was there as he said good-bye to the nation.

I was fascinated at the cameras and crew; Reagan seemed confident but also tired, and I had a moment of concern when, moments before he was to go on the networks live, just after he'd given the text in his hands a final quick review and tested the TelePrompTer, he bowed his head and closed his eyes. He didn't open them for a few moments and I looked at Mari Maseng, his communications director, and asked, "What is he doing?"

"He's praying," she said.

Then he opened his eyes and lifted his head, winked at us, cleared his throat, fixed on the TelePrompTer, and began.

> *My fellow Americans,*
>
> *This is the thirty-fourth time I'll speak to you from the Oval Office, and the last. We've been together eight years now, and soon it will be time for me to go. . . .*
>
> *One of the things about the presidency is that you're always somewhat apart. You spend a lot of time going by too fast in a car some-*

one else is driving, and seeing the people through tinted glass—the parents holding up a child, and the wave you saw too late and couldn't return. And so many times I wanted to stop and reach out from behind the glass, and connect. Well, maybe I can do a little of that tonight. . . .

He said that he had a favorite view from a window upstairs in the residence, a view past the Washington and Jefferson monuments, to the Potomac River and on to the busy shore of Virginia. It was the view Lincoln had "when he watched the smoke rising from the battle of Bull Run." But he sees "more prosaic things"—"the morning traffic as people make their way to work, now and then a sailboat on the river . . ." And he realized that the image that came to his mind when he thought about the meaning of the past eight years was a nautical one: "a small story about a big ship and a refugee and a sailor."

It was back in the early eighties, at the height of the boat people. And the sailor was hard at work on the carrier Midway, *which was patrolling the South China Sea. The sailor, like most American servicemen, was young, smart, fiercely observant. The crew spied on the horizon a leaky little boat. And crammed inside were refugees from Indochina hoping to get to America. The Midway sent a small launch to bring them to the ship and safety. As the refugees made their way through the choppy seas, one spied the sailor on deck and stood up and called out to him. He yelled, "Hello, American sailor. Hello, freedom man."*

A small moment with a big meaning, a moment the sailor, who wrote it in a letter, couldn't get out of his mind. And when I saw it, neither could I. Because that's what it was to be an American in the 1980s. We stood, again, for freedom. I know we always have, but in the past few years the world again, and in a way we ourselves, rediscovered it.

He said he saw two great triumphs—the economic boom with its nineteen million new jobs, "the American miracle"—the end of the long recession and high inflation and interest rates. And the recovery of America's morale through the reapplication of American values and virtues to its foreign policy.

But he said it was not his gifts that produced this.

> *. . . in all of that time I won a nickname, the "Great Communicator." But I never thought it was my style or the words I used that made a difference: It was the content. I wasn't a great communicator, but I communicated great things, and they didn't spring full bloom from my brow, they came from the heart of a great nation—from our experience, our wisdom and our belief in the principles that have guided us for two centuries. They called it the Reagan revolution. Well, I'll accept that, but for me it always seemed like the Great Rediscovery—a rediscovery of our values and our common sense.*

He spoke of the breakthroughs with the Soviet Union, of the arms reductions agreements, of their withdrawal from Afghanistan.

> *The lesson of all this was, of course, that because we're a great nation our challenges seem complex. It will always be that way. But as long as we remember our first principles and believe in ourselves, the future will always be ours. And something else we learned: Once you begin a great movement, there's no telling where it will end. We meant to change a nation, and instead we changed a world.*

He spoke of some personal things—the great decision in the middle of his life to go into politics, which he hadn't intended as a boy or young man. And the reason for it: to return our country to constitutional principles that he felt we were losing, to stop that loss, to bring the principles of "We the people" back to our governance.

And then the end:

> *I've spoken of the shining city all my political life, but I don't know if I ever quite communicated what I saw when I said it. But in*

my mind it was a tall proud city built on rocks stronger than oceans, wind swept, God blessed and teeming with people of all kinds living in harmony and peace, a city with free ports that hummed with commerce and creativity, and if there had to be city walls the walls had doors and the doors were open to anyone with the will and the heart to get here. . . .

And how stands the city on this winter night? More prosperous, more secure and happier than it was eight years ago. But more than that; after two hundred years, two centuries, she still stands strong and true on the granite ridge, and her glow has held steady no matter what storm. And she's still a beacon, still a magnet for all who must have freedom, for all the pilgrims from all the lost places who are hurtling through the darkness, toward home.

We've done our part. And as I walk into the city streets, a final word to the men and women of the Reagan revolution, the men and women across America who for eight years did the work that brought America back. My friends: We did it. We weren't just marking time, we made a difference. We made the city stronger, we made the city freer, and we left her in good hands.

All in all, not bad. Not bad at all.

And so, good-bye. God bless you, and God bless the United States of America.

And so it ended. The long journey that began in Tampico in the rental apartment over the bank . . . or, if you prefer, the journey that began on a night in 1964 when Ronald Reagan stated his political principles in support of Barry Goldwater . . . or if you'd rather, the journey that began that day in August 1976 when, defeated and finished by Ford, he knew he'd come back and take the leadership of the country . . . was over.

And he was right: He had not only changed the country but also the world. The American economic boom had given birth to a technological boom that was spreading around the globe, and more and more countries were moving toward freedom and democracy. And not, as Reagan would say and as he truly felt, because of him but because the ideas of the founders, whose centuries-old ideas had lost none of their power with the passing of time.

That night, as soon as he signed off and was off the air, we applauded him, the dozen of us in the Oval Office. He shook my hand, thanked me for my help and the next day he called me at my home in Virginia; we talked, and he was patient as I asked him to say a few words to my son, aged seven months, so that I could tell him one day that he'd spoken to Ronald Reagan. I don't know what the president said but my boy liked hearing the sounds, and when I took the phone away his arms shot out as if to say, "Not so fast, lady."

I didn't see him again for nine years, and so much by then had changed, of course. I had written him in the interim. Once, in 1993, frustrated that Reagan's historical standing was not considered high, as it is now, but low, I wrote and asked him some questions. I wanted to know if he worried about his standing with historians, and he replied, "I'm not the sort to lose sleep over what a few revisionists say about my record. I'm more than willing to submit my actions to the judgment of time. Let history decide; it usually does."

I asked him how he viewed his leadership. He replied, "I never thought of myself as a great man, just a man commited to great ideas. I've always believed that individuals should take priority over the state. History has taught me that this is what sets America apart—not to remake the world in our image, but to inspire people everywhere with a sense of their own boundless possibilities. There's no question I am an idealist, which is another way of saying I am an American."

He said with some pride, "I've never hesitated to challenge or question the prevailing wisdom. Whether that meant condemning communism to the ash heap of history or insisting that mankind did not have to live under the cloud of a nuclear holocaust."

He added that he had gotten through his presidency only with the help of prayer. "I've prayed a lot throughout my life. Abraham Lincoln once said that he could never have fulfilled his duties as president for even fifteen minutes without God's help. I felt the same way."

Finally, I asked him what he thought his legacy was. He wrote a single sentence. "He tried to expand the frontiers of freedom, in a world at peace with itself."

I saw Reagan in the winter of 1998, when I was asked to speak at a symposium at the Reagan Library, which had been built in Simi Valley, California, where many years before the early moviemakers of Hollywood had shot the first westerns.

I told the library people that I would bring my eleven-year-old son, and I'd like him to meet the old man. They couldn't guarantee it: The news that Reagan had Alzheimer's had been made public almost five years before, and he didn't come to his Century City office now unless he was feeling well, and he wasn't always feeling well.

I took my chances. My son had recently begun to see Reagan as more than a family rumor, more than a picture on the wall of a guy Mom had worked with once. PBS, as part of its series on the American presidency, had recently devoted two hours to Reagan; my son had watched, and suddenly it all came together for him. "He brought down the Berlin Wall," he told me, impressed. And I'd asked if he'd like to meet him.

And they did meet. I waited each day for the call and it didn't come, and on our last day in California I called the Century City office and asked if he was in and was told yes, but he'd just arrived and was leaving soon. I said, "We're only ten minutes away, we'll go outside and wait for him on a bench." And Joanne Drake, who ran his office, was surprised and said, "Oh no, come on over, we'll make it happen."

So we went to the top of a skyscraper and waited in an office with an American flag and a big table and a big window; we were up so high you could see the ocean.

And then Reagan came in. And the sight of him took my breath away. The old brown suit, the one we always made fun of—he was wearing it, with a brown striped grandpa tie. He walked toward us and it was the old stride, his shoulders straight, his hands cupped at his sides. But he was smaller—it was the same Reagan but smaller, and I realized the suit had been altered, he couldn't work out anymore, he had lost mass. His hair seemed thicker, with wiry gray hairs, and wavier, because it was longer. And he wore glasses. Grandpa kind of glasses.

We shook hands. I introduced myself. I told him that we had worked together years back in Washington. I introduced my son, told him he was an admirer. My son looked up at Reagan as if he were looking at Gwyneth Paltrow, with shyness and adoration. Reagan said, "Nice to see you," complimented my son on his hat, a baseball cap, looked at me and said, "Good to see you."

And then—

I had planned to tell Reagan that I wanted to thank him for all he'd done for our country, and I meant to be specific and detailed, lay it all out. But I looked in his eyes and realized: That's what his life is now, hearing things he doesn't understand from strangers and trying to come up with the right response, trying to say the right thing when they say these words that no longer make sense . . .

So I just looked at him, and then I think an angel whispered in my ear because I remembered the thing everyone understands, old people and little babies and everyone in between. I took his hand and said, "Mr. President, I just came here to tell you that I love you. I want you to know that we love you very much."

And his eyes flickered and he smiled and nodded his head in the old way and said in his old soft voice, "Oh, thank you! Thank you. Thanks." And he nodded again.

And we stood there happily holding hands. Soon the head of his Secret Service detail came in, and Joanne Drake told him he had a dentist appointment and they'd take him, and he became perplexed and seemed anxious. "With them?" he said, pointing at the detail. "Yes, sir," she said. "You know them."

"We'll take you there, Mr. President," the head of the detail said, softly, and they left in a scrum of suits. . . .

And that's the last I saw him. Now I understood the story George Shultz had told me a year or two before. He had gone to see the president at his home; Nancy had invited him. When Shultz arrived, the president was in his bedroom. Shultz sat in the living room and caught up with Nancy, and suddenly through a glassed wall he could see Reagan crossing the grass outside with his nurse. He saw Shultz, and he said something to the nurse, who said something back. Later Shultz asked what had passed between them, and the nurse told him the president had said, "Who is that man? I think he was very famous once."

Everyone always asks if Reagan showed signs of Alzheimer's disease when he was president. I never saw any, but I wasn't always with him.

The last time I worked with him, in December 1988, he made it clear what he wanted in the speech through his comments and edits, and made it quite clear what he didn't want too. I saw letters that he was writing in those days and they had the same touch, the same style and humor, the same detail when detail was required. I thought he was tired by the end of his presidency, but he was seventy-eight years old and had earned his fatigue.

When I was working on this book I went to his friends and colleagues from the old days and asked them if they had seen the signs. To Dave Fischer I pressed the point—no signs of confusion, forgetfulness, anxiety at new situations, confusing the past and the present? "No," he said, "no signs of Alzheimer's. I never saw a change in Ronald Reagan, I just didn't. Ronald Reagan always told the same kind of stories in the White House that he told when he was running for president back in the seventies. But he told new stories too. I never saw any sign whatsoever, and I'd tell you if I did." I believed him.

I've asked other people too who were around and they said they didn't see a change. Mike Deaver saw it the way Fischer did, and told me; so did Mike Deaver and Ed Meese and Reagan's last chief of staff, Ken Duberstein. And I know them well enough that if they had something to say off the record or not for attribution they would have said it.

I continued asking during the spring and summer of 2001, talked to more people who'd been in the White House, and what was striking about their unanimity on this point was that some of them were precisely the people who would have enjoyed saying, "He was showing signs in '87, I had to help him through."

Nancy Reagan knew there was trouble for the first time in the early nineties, when they had been out of the White House for three or four years. He had a speech in another city and they stayed at a big hotel. He walked into their room with her and thanked everyone for carrying their bags. And then, alone with his wife, he stood and looked around the room for a few moments and turned to her and said, "I'm afraid I don't know where I am."

That began the doctor visits, which culminated in the Mayo Clinic.

Marion Jorgensen knew there was trouble when something similar happened at around the same time, in 1992 or 1993. "Ronnie and Nancy were coming up to the house. They used to come up for early dinner, about six-thirty. And they'd been there hundreds of times. And Ron came in and walked in and saw me . . . and then he walked to the window and looked out . . . and then he looked at me again and said, 'This place is familiar to me, I think I've been here before.' "

He had celebrated his election to the governorship of California there. He had celebrated his election to the presidency of the United States there.

For Charlie Wick it was also a time he had the Reagans to dinner, along with a number of others. They were all having a drink before dinner was served, chatting and telling stories. Suddenly Reagan looked at him and said impatiently, "Jeez, when are we going to eat?" Wick was taken aback; it seemed rude, and never, ever in the forty years he had known him had he ever seen Ronald Reagan do or say anything rude.

There was also the dinner for Mrs. Thatcher. Again, a few years out of the White House, and Reagan stood up and introduced her. And then she spoke. And when she was done he stood up again and began to introduce her. And she rose, and made a joke of it, and it all ended in laughter but she knew: Something is very wrong.

For me it was a speech in Washington in 1992. Reagan was speaking, and I hadn't set eyes on him since 1989. He looked fine on the stage, high coloring on his cheeks, the same smile, same look. He began with jokes and it was the ol' old man. He was reading the speech from cards, as he had for more than half a century, and I could see them as he turned them on the podium. I was sitting with my friend Peter Rusthoven, a lawyer in Reagan's White House counsel's office. We were listening, and suddenly I realized the president was repeating a card. He was reading the same card twice. I turned to Peter at the exact moment he turned to me. We said nothing and knew: Something is wrong.

In August 1993, at his yearly physical at the Mayo Clinic, they found out what it was. He was diagnosed with Alzheimer's disease. "I didn't know what it meant," Nancy later told me. It was explained to her, and she thought of her husband's family. "I realized, oh of course—his mother had it. And Moon too."

When he went home he wrote the famous letter telling people he was sick, and what his sickness was. He wrote it at the table in the library in the house on St. Cloud Road. Years later, Nancy Reagan's eyes filled as she told me of it. "He wanted to write it," she said. "We'd always been very public about the things that were happening to us, and he thought it was right."

It did not take him long. "He just sat down and wrote it, in one draft," she said. "He gave it to me and I read it and I thought, good." He was alone when he wrote it, and when he gave it to her in the next room she was with Fred Ryan, a former White House aide who now helped run his office.

When I read the published letter I realized he'd written it himself because it had the roundness, the ease and fluidity of his letters. It was candid, like him, but modest too: He didn't tell you anything you didn't have to know, didn't burden you with Too Much Information.

His close friends say that, in retrospect, they can see now that there was an incident that seemed to make his illness more pronounced, that was perhaps the moment when it all began to progress at greater speed. A year or so before the visit to the Mayo Clinic the Reagans went on vacation, to the ranch of their close friends Bill and Betty Wilson, in Mexico. The president went riding on a handsome white stallion. It was a small riding party. Marion Jorgensen was there. "Horses," she said, "can be a bit nutty when they get together." They were all riding along a trail when some teenagers came riding by at full gallop. The horses in the Reagan party became excited, got competitive. As the kids galloped by, Reagan's horse reared, and reared again so high, so straight up, that Marion feared his horse would fall over and Reagan be crushed by it. The horse reared again and then bucked and Reagan flew off, landing hard on gravel and rocks.

Marion was at first relieved he'd fallen off and hadn't been crushed. But Reagan didn't move. There was blood. They wrapped him in a horse blanket, called a helicopter, got Nancy from the house and she got in the helicopter with him. Reagan was still unconscious. He was taken to a hospital, where they found a concussion.

But amazingly enough, before the day was over, the helicopter returned to the Wilsons' ranch, and both Reagans were in it. He laughed and said he didn't have to stay in the hospital, it was no big deal, a little lump on the noggin'.

But the fall from the horse was followed by an operation, and everyone close to Reagan now agrees, looking back, that the blow to his head and the concussion and operation seemed to accelerate the growing illness within him. He just wasn't the same after that.

And so he is sick now, quite severely sick, and old, going on ninety-one, as you read this. He has just surpassed John Adams as the oldest ever of the former presidents. Even his closest friends don't see him anymore. Nancy doesn't want them to, wants them to remember him as he was. Only Nancy and the children and the caretakers, the nurses, the Secret Service agents see him.

He doesn't know that his daughter Maureen died, doesn't know Jane Wyman and Nancy Reagan were united, together, at her funeral, walked together and spoke together like old allies in a forgotten struggle. He would have appreciated too what was communicated about his first child by the warmth and intelligence of the speakers at her funeral.

He doesn't know he was president, doesn't know he was a great man. He knows the frustrations, anxiety and fluctuating emotions of those with Alzheimer's, spends more time sleeping than he did, can't get around on his own, still loves his cornflakes in the morning and his sweets at night, his vanilla ice cream. Sometimes he seems to know those around him, but more and more often not. For some time he became animated at the sight of his son Ron, became excited when he entered the room. But now, mostly, he's lost in the sickness that robs you of all solace, because you don't know anymore what solace is.

Nancy Reagan gets lonely, doesn't talk about it much, doesn't talk about his condition except to say, "It's hard," or "Well, you know." She is with him every day, with a nurse, but she misses him. He was her best and closest friend, the love of her life for more than half a century, and he is no longer available to her.

I asked her recently to tell me about a day in her life with the president. She said, "Well, I get up in the morning . . ." And she looked away and looked back at me. "This is a progressive disease. It doesn't stay the same, so your days don't stay the same. We're older now. It's a time when you look forward to sharing memories."

She continued, "I can't tell you the number of times I'll turn to him and I'll start to say 'Honey, remember when—.' And then I stop. And sometimes I think of something and I long to have his opinion on things. It's very hard and it's very lonely. Your friends are wonderful but nobody knows what this is like until they've lived it. People call on the phone and they're so nice but you don't want to unload your grief, people don't want that and it's understandable."

She stays close to her friends on the phone, sees them at lunch or small gatherings. She used to sometimes take short trips to see friends farther away, but doesn't anymore.

Mostly she's there with him, and if you want to see her you go to Bel Air, or to the Reagan Library a little more than an hour away, where when speakers come she is in the front row, applauding and cheering on those who speak of her husband and the meaning of his life.

"She is protecting his dignity," said his old protector, Jerry Parr. "And if there ever was a disease that can take away your dignity it's Alzheimer's. Like ALS [Lou Gehrig's disease] it can remove your strength, your ability to walk and talk and eat and bathe yourself, but it has an added layer of terror in that it also takes your ability to reason, to comfort yourself, to remember, to feel secure in the hands of those you know and love; and in its place it puts anxiety, confusion, defensive anger."

So that's what it's like for him now, and for her. It isn't easy. But as she says when you ask her about it, "You just put one foot in front of the other and do what you have to do." She has no illusions. "There is no ending to this, it isn't going to get better, it's going to get worse." It got a little worse last year, when he stepped out of bed and slipped and broke his hip. There was an operation, he healed—Nancy said he's still so strong and healed so well that you can't see the incision mark from the operation anymore. Now they must sleep in separate rooms. "We had slept in the same bed for forty-nine years," she told me last spring. "This is the first time that we haven't. . . . He'd always sort of reach out to touch me, to make sure that I was there." Her great fear is that her husband might be forced some day by circumstances to go where people with Alzheimer's often go, to a home, to one that specializes in their treatment. "No, no," she said. "I would hate to do that, I would just hate to. I hope the day never, ever comes."

So that is how it is now for Ronald Reagan, the old man of St. Cloud Road. The world drives by his house, and he hears the sound of a car going by, the sound of the birds in the garden, the ring of the phone. His life is quiet. He was a great man once and doesn't know it, was a hero too, a man who changed the world for the better by being who he was. He started out with little, and rose very far. And the great thing with him was not his personality or charm, celebrated though they were and are, but his character.

He had courage. He always tried to do what he thought was right. And when doing what was right demanded from him great effort or patience or tenacity, or made him the focus of unending attacks and criticism, he summoned from within the patience and the tenacity and the courage to face it all. To face it down. And when his great work was finished he left, and went peacefully home.

These are among the things that made him not an ordinary man, but a most extraordinary man indeed.

You may wonder, as I have, what he would think and then say about the epic struggle we have so recently faced. I do not know, of course, but I can guess. He would tell us, first, to know in our hearts that we will prevail, and triumph. He would remind us that we have faced terrible challenges before, and sometimes been anxious, but always pulled through. He might remember for us that the snow of Valley Forge was streaked with blood, the blood of America's cold and starving fighting force—and yet we are a nation. And there was the day at first Bull Run, when the Union was surprised to learn that the fight would not be easy—and yet we are a nation. And that terrible day in December of 1941, when our fleet was lost and our continent exposed—and yet we are a nation.

We have a way of pulling through and pushing on, and the blood of the men and women who have gotten us through our rocky past beats within us still. It is our patrimony, and our inspiration. And whether you are tenth generation or recently arrived it's your blood too, because we are a brotherhood of belief, a family. And we have a history.

He might note the recent proliferation of American flags. He'd like that. And I think he might use modern technology—the Internet—to give our children a lesson that will hold them in good stead. I think he would ask America's parents to go to a site where they can find the Bill of Rights, the U.S. Constitution and the Declaration of Independence. He'd ask them to print out the documents. He'd say, "Hold that paper in your hand. And pick up one of the little flags we all have now around the house. And say to your child, 'These words are this flag. This flag is these words. Let's read them.'"

He'd like knowing that when the long war is over our kids will have learned something big, something unforgettable that each generation must relearn, and make new again, as it lives on through history.

Epilogue

On a Saturday morning in early February of 2001, Pete Wehner, a speechwriter for the newly inaugurated President George W. Bush, walked into the White House complex with his wife and two young children. He wanted them to see where he worked, to tour the plant and see the unforgettable mansion.

The Wehners' older child, their son, John Paul, age three years and one month, was dressed like children are on a Saturday morning—jeans, a sweatshirt, and on his feet those sneakers that have little lights on the side that blink on and off as you walk. Young John Paul sparkled through the halls, marching along with a plastic toy sword in his hand. When a busy assistant to the president saw him he smiled, bent down and said, "I like your sword. What are you going to do with that?"

"I want to fight bad men!" said John Paul Wehner. And everyone smiled and laughed. But later his father found himself moved by the eagerness and gallantry of his boy's imagination.

The little bodies of children are the repositories of the greatness of a future age. And they must be encouraged, must eat from the tales of those who've gone before, and brandished their swords, and slayed dragons.

Select Bibliography

An Honorable Profession: A Tribute to Robert F. Kennedy. Edited by Pierre Salinger, Edwin Guthman, Frank Mankiewicz and John Seigenthaler. Garden City: Doubleday and Co., 1968.

Anderson, Martin. *Revolution: The Reagan Legacy.* San Diego: Harcourt Brace Jovanovich, 1988.

Benet, Rosemary and Stephen Vincent. *A Book of Americans.* New York: Henry Holt, 1933.

Bush, George Herbert Walker. "The American Presidents: The American Bicentennial Presidential Inaugural Edition." Privately published, January 1989.

Cannon, Lou. *President Reagan: The Role of a Lifetime.* New York: Simon & Schuster, 1991.

———. *Reagan.* New York: Putnam, 1982.

Deaver, Michael K. *Behind the Scenes.* New York: William Morrow, 1987.

Hayman, Ronald. *A Life of Jung.* New York: W. W. Norton, 1999.

Johnson, Paul. *Modern Times: The World from the Twenties to the Eighties.* New York: Harper & Row, 1983.

Kelley, Kitty. *Nancy Reagan: The Unauthorized Biography.* New York: Simon & Schuster, 1991.

Nofziger, Franklin C. *Nofziger.* Washington, D. C.: Regenery Gateway, 1992.

Noonan, Peggy. *What I Saw at the Revolution.* New York: Random House, 1990.

Reagan, Michael. *Michael Reagan on the Outside Looking In.* New York: Zebra Books, 1988.

Reagan, Nancy. *I Love You Ronnie: The Letters of Ronald Reagan to Nancy Reagan.* New York: Random House, 2000.

Reagan, Ronald. *Abortion and the Conscience of the Nation.* Nashville, TN: T. Nelson, 1984.

———. *An American Life.* New York: Simon & Schuster, 1990.

———. *Reagan, in His Own Hand,* edited, with an introduction and commentary by Kiron A. Skinner, Annelise Anderson, Martin Anderson, with a foreword by George P. Shultz. New York: The Free Press, 2001.

———. *Speaking My Mind.* New York: Simon & Schuster, 1989.

———, with Richard G. Hubler. *Where's the Rest of Me?* New York: Karz Publishers, 1981. (This is a reprinted edition of Reagan and Hubler's 1965 book of the same name, published by Elsevier-Dutton Publishing Co., Inc.)

Regan, Donald. *For the Record: From Wall Street to Washington.* New York: Harcourt Brace Jovanovich, 1988.

Robinson, Peter. *It's My Party—A Republican's Messy Love Affair with the GOP.* New York: Warner, 2000.

Schlesinger, Arthur, Jr. *A Life in the Twentieth Century.* Boston: Houghton Mifflin, 2000.

Shultz, George P. *Turmoil and Triumph.* New York: Scribner's, 1993.

Smith, Hannah Whitall. *The Christian's Secret of a Happy Life.* Ulrichsville, OH: Barbour and Company, 1985. (Originally published in 1870.)

Thatcher, Margaret. *The Downing Street Years.* New York: HarperCollins, 1993.

Weinberger, Caspar W. *Seven Criticial Years in the Pentagon.* New York: Warner Books, 1990.

Wilson, Robert A., ed. *Character Above All.* New York: Simon & Schuster, 1995.

Wolfe, Thomas. *The Face of a Nation, Poetical Passages from the Writings of Thomas Wolfe.* Edited by John Hall. New York: Scribner, 1939.

Index